Building and Using
Dynamic Interest Rate Models

Wiley Finance Series

Structured Equity Derivatives: The Definitive Guide to Exotic Options and Structured Notes
Harry Kat

Advanced Modelling in Finance Using Excel and VBA
Mary Jackson and Mike Staunton

Operational Risk: Measurement and Modelling
Jack King

Advanced Credit Risk Analysis: Financial Approaches and Mathematical Models to Assess, Price and Manage Credit Risk
Didier Cossin and Hugues Pirotte

Dictionary of Financial Engineering
John F. Marshall

Pricing Financial Derivatives: The Finite Difference Method
Domingo A. Tavella and Curt Randall

Interest Rate Modelling
Jesssica James and Nick Webber

Handbook of Hybrid Instruments: Convertible Bonds, Preferred Shares, Lyons, ELKS, DECS and Other Mandatory Convertible Notes
Izzy Nelken (ed.)

Options on Foreign Exchange, Revised Edition
David F. DeRosa

The Handbook of Equity Derivatives, Revised Edition
Jack Francis, William Toy and J. Gregg Whittaker

Volatility and Correlation in the Pricing of Equity, FX and Interest-rate Options
Riccardo Rebonato

Risk Management and Analysis vol. 1: Measuring and Modelling Financial Risk
Carol Alexander (ed.)

Risk Management and Analysis vol. 2: New Markets and Products
Carol Alexander (ed.)

Implementing Value at Risk
Philip Best

Credit Derivatives: A Guide to Instruments and Applications
Janet Tavakoli

Implementing Derivatives Models
Les Clewlow and Chris Strickland

Interest-rate Option Models: Understanding, Analysing and Using Models for Exotic Interest-rate Options (second edition)
Ricardo Rebonato

Building and Using Dynamic Interest Rate Models

Ken O. Kortanek
and
Vladimir G. Medvedev

JOHN WILEY & SONS, LTD

Chichester · New York · Weinheim · Brisbane · Singapore · Toronto

Other Wiley Editorial Offices

John Wiley & Sons, Inc., 605 Third Avenue,
New York, NY 10158-0012, USA

WILEY-VCH Verlag GmbH, Pappelallee 3,
D-69469 Weinheim, Germany

John Wiley & Sons Australia, Ltd., 33 Park Road, Milton,
Queensland 4064, Australia

John Wiley & Sons (Asia) Pte, Ltd., 2 Clementi Loop #02-01,
Jin Xing Distripark, Singapore 129809

John Wiley & Sons (Canada), Ltd., 22 Worcester Road,
Rexdale, Ontario M9W 1L1, Canada

Library of Congress Cataloging-in-Publication Data
Kortanek, K. O., 1936–
   Building and using dynamic interest rate models: a dynamical systems approach under
   uncertainty with perturbations / Ken Kortanek and Vladimir Medvedev.
      p. cm. – (Wiley finance series)
   Includes bibliographical references and index.
   ISBN 0-471-49595-6 (alk. paper)
   1. Interest rates – Mathematical models.   I. Medvedev, Vladimir.   II. Title.   III. Series.

   HB539.K67 2001
   332.8'2'015118–dc21   2001039014

British Library Cataloguing in Publication Data

A catalogue record for this book is available from the British Library

ISBN 0 471 49595 6

Typeset in 10/12pt Times from the author's disks by Dobbie Typesetting Limited, Tavistock, Devon
Printed and bound in Great Britain by Biddles Ltd, Guildford, Surrey
This book is printed on acid-free paper responsibly manufactured from sustainable forestry,
in which at least two trees are planted for each one used for paper production.

To Irene, the mascot of this project,

Alexsei and Anastasia

Contents

Preface   xi

Acknowledgements   xix

1   On the conventional and pure multi-period loan structure   **1**
1.1   Pure short-term lending   1
1.2   Pure long-term interest rates   3
    1.2.1   An illustration of a very simple arbitrage   4
    1.2.2   An illustration of a standard definition and day count
        convention   4
    1.2.3   Continuous compounding of an interest rate over a time
        interval   6
1.3   On bonds: face value, coupon rate, premiums, discounts, and yields   7
    1.3.1   Relation of the premium factor to long-term interest rates   9
    1.3.2   Bond yields and their relation to long-term interest rates   10
    1.3.3   Mean average approximations to the yield structure   11
1.4   On spot interest rates, forward interest rates, and the yield to
    maturity   12
    1.4.1   Forward rates as implied by future spot rates (yields to
        maturity)   13
    1.4.2   Instantaneous forward rates   14
1.5   An example in the literature   15
    1.6   Bootstrapping from successive forward rates for a piecewise
    constant forward rate function   16
1.7   Chapter notes   17

2   Differential systems models for asset prices under uncertainty   **19**
2.1   A description of an uncertainty walk for asset prices   19
2.2   Modeling asset prices with input perturbations   23
    2.2.1   Point-impulse perturbations generating discontinuous
        asset prices   23
    2.2.2   Impulse perturbations generating continuous asset prices   24
2.3   Estimating input perturbations and asset price trajectories   25
2.4   On minimax observation problems under uncertainty with
    perturbations   26

2.4.1   Minimax observation problem under uncertainty with
perturbations   27
2.5   Chapter notes   29

3   **Constant maturity, one-factor dynamic models for term structure estimation**   **31**
3.1   A common specification of time intervals and their subintervals   32
3.2   Definitions of parameter spaces and admissible spot rate functions   32
3.3   Modeling bonds having common maturity for yield estimation   33
3.3.1   Observation models and parameter admissible yields   33
3.3.2   Vasicek-type spot rate estimation model using impulse
perturbations   35
3.3.3   Advantages of using perturbations   40
3.3.4   Vasicek-type spot rate estimation using point-impulse
perturbations   46
3.3.5   A Dothan-type model with impulse perturbations   48
3.3.6   A Courtadon-type model with impulse perturbations   53
3.3.7   A nondifferential equation, continuous time model   54
3.3.8   Real-time positional spot rate estimation   55
3.4   Modeling of bonds with differing maturities   57
3.5   A two-dimensional observation model   57
3.6   Chapter notes   61

4   **Constant maturity, bilevel models for term structure estimation**   **63**
4.1   Nature of bilevel perturbations   63
4.2   Bilevel spot rate minimax estimation   64

5   **Numerical experiments with one-factor and bilevel models for extended
periods of observations**   **71**
5.1   Results from the piecewise constant observation model (3.10)   71
5.2   Results from the piecewise linear observation model (3.11)   72
5.3   Some experiments in sensitivities   76

6   **Modeling nonarbitrage and market price of risk in linear differential systems**   **81**
6.1   A nonarbitrage condition for linear dynamical equations models
under uncertainty   81
6.1.1   A sufficient condition for nonarbitrage of constant
maturity yield minimax estimation   84
6.2   Estimating the market price of risk for dynamical systems under
uncertainty   84
6.2.1   A priori estimation of the market price of risk   85
6.2.2   Optimal estimation of the market price of risk   85
6.2.3   Estimating the market price of risk under a fixed observed
current structure   86
6.3   Chapter notes   86

7   **Characteristics of moments in linear dynamical systems under uncertainty
with perturbations**   **89**
7.1   Mean path solutions to dynamical systems (2.17)   89
7.1.1   Numerical experiments on generating spot rate trajectories   90

7.2	Minimax amplitude	90
7.3	Chapter notes	92
8	**Backtesting with Treasury auction data**	**95**
8.1	Data and estimation	95
	8.1.1 Forecasting	95
	8.1.2 Reliability of forecasts	97
	8.1.3 Range of forecasts	97
	8.1.4 Precision of forecasts	97
8.2	A comparison backtest	110
9	**A forward rates-based dynamical system model**	**113**
9.1	Extracting forward rates curves from the term structure of interest rates	113
	9.1.1 The observation model	113
	9.1.2 The optimal observation problem	115
	9.1.3 A linear differential equation under uncertainty model for the forward rate curve	117
	9.1.4 A yield-based optimal observation problem	118
	9.1.5 A price-based optimal observation problem	120
	9.1.6 A bid–ask optimal observation problem	121
	9.1.7 A general optimal observation problem	122
	9.1.8 A tradeoff between smoothness of the estimation and accuracy	122
9.2	Chapter notes	134
10	**A general integro-differential term structure model**	**135**
10.1	A dynamical linear differential equations system for forward rates	135
10.2	Dynamic modeling of the term structure of interest rates	136
10.3	The term structure of interest rates for a fixed maturity	138
	10.3.1 An impulse representation of the spot rate	139
	10.3.2 A piecewise linear representation of the spot rate	140
	10.3.3 A Vasicek-type spot rate model	141
10.4	Chapter notes	141
11	**Applications to pricing futures fairly and trading futures contracts**	**143**
11.1	An equation for the fair future price of Treasury bills	143
11.2	Estimating arbitrage opportunities for a user-selected future time interval	144
	11.2.1 Illustrative use of the estimated forward rates	145
	11.2.2 The estimated nonarbitrage future price interval	145
11.3	An interest rate–futures rate scenario at the close of 8/14/00	145
11.4	An interest rate–futures rate scenario for the data date of 8/17/00	147
11.5	Chapter notes	150
12	**Using term structure estimation in dynamic interest rate models and hedging strategies**	**153**
12.1	A simple term structure having three yields to maturity	153

12.2   On the consistency of interest rate movements with the term
       structure   153
12.3   A linear programming analysis of a hedging opportunity   156
       12.3.1   Summary of data entries   160
12.4   Pricing a simple bond call option using an interest rate tree   160
12.5   Linear programming discounted dual variables as martingale
       probabilities   161
12.6   Chapter notes   163

13   A review of semi-infinite optimization with a focus on finance   165
13.1   Duality of the linear semi-infinite programming problem   165
13.2   On the support problems method (*Belarus*)   167
13.3   Extended support problems method   168
13.4   A simple example   170
13.5   Numerical results on solving nonlinear semi-infinite programming
       problems by support problems method   170
13.6   Chapter notes   172

14   Software documentation of the term structure, constant maturity models   175
14.1   Getting started with the program *TermStructureCAD*   175
14.2   Defining the attributes of the input data   175
14.3   Selecting a model for estimating the term structure   176
14.4   Selecting parameters for the optimal observation problem   176
14.5   Signaling to solve the observation problem   176
14.6   The geometric analysis of solution outputs   184
14.7   Forecasting the yield curve for a selected future period   184
14.8   Forecasting constant maturity rates for a future period and term
       to maturity   184
14.9   The three-dimensional term structure surface rates for a future
       period and maximum time to maturity   197
14.10 Chapter notes   197

15   Software documentation of the forward rate model   199
15.1   Getting started with the program *FRateCAD* and its required
       inputs   199
15.2   Getting started, command buttons: New Project, Open Project,
       Save As Project, and Save Project   199
15.3   Command buttons within the solving-the-estimation-problem
       window   207
       15.3.1   A standard volatility measure   207
15.4   The mathematical programming solution results window   207

References   209

Index   213

Preface

As a real world market acts dynamically under uncertainty, it is natural that the modern theory of mathematical finance is based on the theory of stochastic processes. Stochastic processes theory has a long and distinguished history. It has been extensively explored and published, especially after the appearance of fundamental papers by Wiener [65], Ito [32, 33] and Kalman [35]. By its very structure a stochastic process is a dynamic one.

Perhaps less known to the finance literature is another approach to modeling uncertainty which has its origins in control theory. Mathematical modeling of control problems has a rich history in the optimization of dynamical systems under uncertainty. The fundamental theme of this book is the development and application of a new class of models of this type for the term structure of interest rates.

In this approach unknown uncertainty processes are described as unknown functions taken from a prespecified functional class. Special optimization models are formulated whose inputs are observations of real data. The optimizations deliver estimates of the trajectory of the uncertain dynamical system or its possible trajectory states. Among the earliest publications on nonstochastic uncertainty models of this type are the books of Krasovsky [43], Kurzansky [44] and Chernousko [9], all published in Russian. Their formulations bear the nomenclature of models of *minimax* or *guaranteed* type.

It is by the latter approach to uncertainty that we have modeled fixed income security markets. The underlying dynamical systems equations include arbitrary perturbations influenced by actual market data with unknown, sought-for, parameters being members of an admissible set. The perturbations act as an analog of volatility.

Essentially all significant properties of these dynamical systems models under nonstochastic uncertainty with perturbations are analogs of properties appearing in stochastic differential processes models. The list includes: (a) the type of uncertainty, (b) a model for the spot rate, (c) a norm of uncertainty, (d) nonarbitrage conditions, (e) moments of uncertainty, and (f) treatment of technical phenomena arising from mathematical modeling, such as (i) non-negative spot or forward rates and (ii) construction and computer implementation of one-factor or multiple-factor models.

Specific *observation* modeling of data inputs is intrinsic in our approach. While the dynamical systems approach to uncertainty brings substantial analytical strength through its piecewise continuous modeling structure, one must recognize that input data are necessarily discrete. Data are therefore modeled in a piecewise continuous way without losing the sense or quality of the data. Classes of perturbation functions, such as piecewise constant, piecewise linear and point-impulse functions are introduced into an observation model from due consideration of computational stability and estimation accuracy. Even more general classes of perturbations may be considered.

An Outline of the Book

Chapter 1 is very important for getting started because of its fundamental premise about why the term structure of interest rates is so important: all forward rates are determined from the term structure. The chapter delves immediately into the structure of short period interest rates and long period rates and the relationship between these two different structures. It does not matter whether one uses the elegance and convenience of continuous interest rate compounding or the generally accepted standard discrete rate computations with their various day count conventions.

The chapter also serves as a tutorial for a more algebraic presentation on interest rate calculations of the type familiar to most practitioners. Interest rates are viewed as an economist views them, namely merely as terms of intertemporal exchange. Of course, without the time factor we could be writing about currency rates of exchange. We sometimes refer to τ-period exchanges merely with τ being the length of a period. It is the same as writing *multi-period* exchanges, with more specificity that is convenient when comparing long-term rates to short-term rates. We do address the basic characteristics of bonds, namely the face value, the coupon rate, bond premiums, discounts, and bond yields. Interesting connections abound between bond yields and the structure of long-term interest rates, and we describe some of them. In this sense the material presented is rudimentary interest rate theory, and could be corroborated with any numerical treatment. Finally, as a point of departure from the main continuous models presented in this book, we surge into instantaneous spot rates, instantaneous forward rates and the yield to maturity as modeled by an elementary deterministic differential equation. The treatment motivates a statement about the *unbiased expectations hypothesis* that relates forward rates to expected future spot rates.

In **Chapter 2** the first main model for fixed income securities under nonstochastic uncertainty with perturbations is based on two main components, namely the current time and the time to maturity. In this chapter we present a general dynamical systems model distinguished by using both *functions of uncertainty* and *external input perturbations*, indirectly acting as the volatilities. To get started, we describe what could be termed an *uncertainty walk for asset prices*, which by the choice of words should be, and actually is, an analog of a *random walk*. The uncertainty walk contains a predictable return, such as accruing to a risk-free bond, and an unpredictable effect due to uncertainty and volatility. It is a convenient time to introduce the reader to the *Cauchy formula* that will be a main tool used throughout the book for obtaining closed form solutions, whenever possible, from a linear differential equation. Highlights of this chapter include the formulation of two key observation models used throughout this book: (a) one having point-impulse perturbations generating discontinuous asset prices and (b) one having impulse perturbations generating continuous asset prices. Actually, the first observation model involves *delta functions* which as a class are useful for modeling jump phenomena in asset prices or in yields to maturity. Finally, the first *minimax* optimization problem under uncertainty with perturbations is presented in a form general enough for other specializations in later chapters.

A main goal in **Chapter 3** is the modeling of bonds which have common constant term to maturity. The model is based upon observations of fixed maturity rates obtained at the current time. We also introduce classes of admissible spot rate functions and a definition of parameter spaces, so the reader sees more specifically how the spot rate, which is itself unobservable, is modeled as a specific function class which depends as well on the unknown parameters of perturbation-based uncertainty. Differentiation of the spot rate function is taken with respect to the current time, and the main models are the Vasicek-type spot rate estimation using impulse perturbations and the Vasicek-type model with point-impulse perturbations. Many illustrative figures and interpretations are presented for each of these models under various parameter settings.

Interesting comparisons are made with other models such as the Dothan-type model with impulse perturbations and the Courtadon-type model with impulse perturbations.

Other classes of unknown functions are illustrated, particularly a nondifferentiable one, for governing the law of motion of the dynamic process.

Depending on the degree of differentiability in the underlying dynamical system, including the extreme case of nondifferentiability, we can also obtain a smoothing spline approximation to the yield curve as a special case. But using spline approximations makes it challenging to develop forecasts for the forward rate, for example, at a future time beyond the observation period. This problem arises because there is no underlying 'law of motion' such as a differential equation that holds over time. Some life insurance companies reportedly require the estimation of prices of pure discount bonds with maturities up to 100 years.

All of the models so far in Chapter 3 have unknown perturbations and unknown parameters to be computed at the conclusion of the observation process. But in actual real time trading environments these parameter values are needed adaptively based upon the latest real time observations. The next class of models in Chapter 3 is an adaptive modification of the earlier dynamical systems models whose solutions are now adaptive estimators. As the observation period moves forward, it is sufficient to resolve the model with an advanced start based upon a solution from the previously observed moment of time. Our approach to adaptive and conditional estimation is also described in [39, Section 4.4]. It results in a practical realization of the model's unknown parameters becoming functions of time of rather general types.

Chapter 3 concludes with a section on modeling bonds with differing maturities together with a two-dimensional observation model.

In **Chapter 4** we extend the model of the term structure of interest rates to include jumps in the observed yield. This is accomplished by introducing perturbations on both the spot rate *and* the yield. In this extension the yield (or price) of a bond depends on the underlying differential equations spot rate process and on a *second process* that acts directly on the observed data. An additional 'user control' parameter is introduced to influence the longer term limit properties of the yield. If the parameter is set to zero, then the yield perturbations can be interpreted as *long-run factors* since in this case the perturbations uniformly shift the corresponding yields to maturity. If the parameter is greater than zero, then the yield perturbations affect the corresponding yields for shorter periods of time, and so they can be interpreted as *short-run factors*. Additional motivation for the bilevel model is a graphical comparison on the quality of estimated yields of bonds having different maturities under one-factor and two-factor models.

The chapter presents a basis for selecting the value of the parameter based upon first solving the optimal observation problem. Alternatively, it is possible to employ special optimization problems for its selection, where the objective functions could stem from improving the estimation error and the quality of forecasting results where observed trends in observed data could be of greater influence.

Bilevel model extensions are possible for bonds with differing maturities. While this has not been formally done in Chapter 4, numerical experiments are reported on the extension.

In **Chapter 5** results of many numerical experiments are presented based on the one-factor and bilevel models for extended periods of observations. Results are presented for (a) the piecewise constant observation model and (b) the piecewise linear observation model. In this chapter we examined the sensitivity of our numerical results to (1) choices of perturbations, (2) choices for a 'law of motion' of the spot rate and (3) choices for the modeling of input observations. The results of the sensitivity analyses appear in several figures to assist in making interpretations.

In **Chapter 6** we investigate conditions for nonarbitrage in linear dynamical systems. The approach is analogous to the one usually followed in the stochastic case. We construct a portfolio of bonds with differing maturities and derive a differential condition stating that the return on the portfolio should equal the spot rate, namely the risk-free rate. This analysis and derived condition is not a complete measure of nonarbitrage because our optimization solution depends on actual observations and real data. This leads to distinguishing a *necessary* condition for nonarbitrage from a *sufficient* condition. An interesting feature of the approach is the ability to provide a numerical procedure for estimating the degree to which the nonarbitrage condition is violated. In this chapter a procedure for estimating the related *market price of risk* is also presented. In Chapter 6's Notes we make a brief comparison with the market price of risk in the stochastic case, particularly with respect to the issue of the possible restrictiveness of the sufficient nonarbitrage condition.

Chapter 7 begins with the recognition that in the stochastic processes approach to modeling a risky asset over time, there appear distinguishing characteristics such as *drift* and *volatility*. *Drift* in a stochastic process describes the mean (first-moment) behavior of the stochastic process. In this chapter we address the analogous concepts of 'drift' and 'volatility' that arise in our approach to modeling asset prices. Under the subheading *mean path solutions to dynamical systems*, we require that the *mean function* of the estimate of uncertainty should have the following three properties:

1. the mean function should be a solution to the differential system for the spot rate, and the integral of an optimal solution should approximate the observed yields;
2. the influence or *force* of uncertainty on the mean function estimate should be absent or at least minimal;
3. a mean function should be uniquely determined.

We provide a reference to the literature showing that within the framework of affine stochastic models for the term structure of interest rates with constant parameters, observations of the yield rates process do not in general uniquely determine the parameters of the model. In our approach we obtain a unique estimate of the spot rate by specifying (a) a level of the parameter appearing in the mean reversion limit and (b) a preassigned error of the estimation. We address the question on how the estimated trajectory of the spot rate depends on the choices of these two parameters with some preliminary numerical experiments on generating spot rate trajectories. We also introduce a preliminary model for the purpose of estimating the amplitude of possible values around various characteristics of the estimate of the spot rate model.

Chapter 8 presents our backtesting numerical tabulation over the time period of 1/5/90 to 12/26/97. We focused on observed 3-month Treasury bill auction averages. Within this universal data period we chose a sequence of 375 observation periods of 6 months duration. In this calibration the first 6-month period is 1/5/90–6/29/90. The periods move forward one week at a time, so for example, the second 6-month period is 1/12/90–7/6/90. The approach is flexible in that a user can specify the basic inputs, such as the universal period of time and the subperiods within which observations will be made. Available to the user are the standard performance criteria: (a) maximum absolute value, (b) mean absolute value, (c) relative maximum absolute value, (d) mean absolute percentage error. The user can also perform automatic backtesting while experimenting with trend selection over any universal period for which there are data of the type selected in the estimation procedure.

In **Chapter 9** we develop a dynamical systems approach to extracting forward rates curves from the term structure of interest rates that involves another type of differential equation. It is a manifestation of what we expected since Chapter 1, where we reviewed the importance of the term structure for being able to deliver the forward rate structure. Unlike the earlier constant maturity term models, now differentiation occurs with respect to the *term to maturity* in contrast to the more common choice of differentiation with respect to the *current time*. Our approach is a companion to standard bootstrapping methods or numerical approximation methods, such as smoothing splines and Hermite polynomials applied directly to the yield curve.

In the previous chapters we developed models for estimating the term structure of interest rates for some fixed current moment of time or some fixed terms to maturity. In **Chapter 10** we develop a more general class of differential systems under uncertainty with perturbations in order to model processes having two time variables, namely the current time and the time to maturity. In this extension the basic differential equation is formulated with respect to bond prices. But similar to our previous models we use classes of perturbation functions to model uncertainty, although this time the perturbations are applied to bond prices themselves. The model is very flexible, and any type of observations could be used. Such dynamical systems include the integro-differential equations that bring with them the complexity in obtaining numerical solutions. This is of course a cost for achieving generality in that it does not depend on a specific concrete model for forward rates or spot rates. The integro-differential equations model actually has some analogies to the well-known Heath, Jarrow and Morton model, most easily recognized by the requirement for estimating the perturbation surface, which is itself the analog of the volatility surface. The main goal of this chapter is to construct a general dynamical system of differential equations for the term structure of interest rates, a system having the characteristic that it does not depend on a specific concrete model for forward rates or spot rates.

Chapter 11 is strictly an applications chapter. It begins with an extension of the standard forward rate calculation with respect to two consecutive yields for the period embracing the future period. The standard calculation was already studied and illustrated in Chapter 1 with respect to LIBOR rates and forward rates. We now illustrate how the procedure applies to US Treasury bill rates and futures rates, for example the 90-day SYCOM rates regularly reported in the *Wall Street Journal* and elsewhere. The practical result is an equation for the fair future price of Treasury bills. A user can specify a future period, whether term rates are published or not for the dates chosen. The model provides the estimates of the yields to maturity by chosen user date. Based on these estimates the user can find a range of the forward rate for the future period for which no arbitrage is possible. Based on our estimates we illustrate whether, for example, a bank trading with futures contracts can increase its returns on certain loans. In a later chapter we briefly document a particular implementation of the forward rate model of Chapter 9. A particular software implementation will differ depending on the user. For our particular implementation we illustrate how one can estimate arbitrage opportunities over a selected future time interval. Actually, we went further and conducted a 27 consecutive day experiment beginning with 8/9/00, computing the intervals for which there is no estimated arbitrage.

Chapter 12 presents further applications based on elementary interest rate trees. Such trees must be consistent with the term structure and an illustration is given of how this can be accomplished within a simple three-yields-to-maturity term structure. The illustration focuses on using term structure estimation in dynamic interest rate models for developing hedging strategies among bonds having different maturities. The chapter presents an analysis of this problem by linear programming, and in a simple context introduces martingale measures as dual linear programming variables. It also affords the opportunity to illustrate the pricing of a simple call option on a bond using the interest rate tree.

Chapter 13 is a technical chapter on an optimization topic, *semi-infinite programming*, a class of optimization models that has arisen naturally in the dynamical system modeling we have developed. It is a field that began in 1962 and a field that is still active. Some numerical results of our solution methodology are presented for prototype problems that have appeared in the literature.

We thought it best to place our two software documentation chapters at the end of the book. **Chapter 14** gives a documentation for the term structure constant maturity model of Chapters 3 and 4. Depending on the financial application the user interactively selects (a) the type of input data, (b) the type of underlying dynamical model (one-factor or two-factor), (c) the type of spot rate or forward rate model, (d) the time scale for perturbations (day, week, month), (e) the type of evaluation function to guide the optimizations (minimax, mean least squares, minimum entropy), and (f) parameter settings such as when to stop optimization iterations in order to observe progress and features of various estimates. The book presents results from one kind of implementation termed *YieldCADD*.

We have demonstrated the viability of this approach by computationally testing a procedure for forecasting the spot rate based on observations which are used for improving the estimates of the dynamical system. Here are some details.

Frequent periodic estimates are provided for (a) the yield curve over a user-selected period: 3–6–9 months or from 1 to 30 years, (b) an estimated spot rate trajectory from the *current time* to a selected future time and (c) the surface of the term structure of interest rates.

As input information we may use any of the following generally available series of observations:

1. the Treasury yield curve;
2. Treasury bill rates;
3. Treasury constant maturity rates;
4. prices of Treasury bills, notes, bonds.

Any of these series may be daily, weekly, or monthly in time. Among rich data sources are the FRED series from the St. Louis Federal Reserve Bank.

For estimating the term structure it has been convenient to take just one of the above series as data observations, for example, the 3MO *constant maturity rate* series. But we can also input several yield series simultaneously, say 3MO, 6MO and the 1YR series. Mathematically, we shall denote any of these constant maturity terms by the symbol T.

The parameters appearing in the dynamical systems models are not among the input data. Rather, their estimates are obtained through the solution of an optimal observation problem.

We next briefly describe how the model is implemented, step-by-step.

Step 1   *Initialization.* Choose term to maturity yield input data, for example, constant maturity rates with arbitrary term to maturity T days (say 90 days). Select the length of the observation period in days, say M days.

Step 2   *'Learning' by the system.* An optimal observation problem is solved generating estimates of the unknown coefficients of the dynamical system as well as estimates of computed perturbations from the market. The values of the maximal and the minimal computed perturbations can be compared in a general way with the volatility input for the stochastic processes case. These computed values are also used for specifying bounds for the precision of the forecast. Note that current time is mathematically denoted by t_M, following [39, Remark 4.1, p. 18].

Step 3   *The forecasting procedure.* The point of departure is the fundamental US Treasury yield curve, which we also use for elucidating the mathematical notation $R(t, t+T)$ appearing throughout.

These basic steps can be followed in the single-factor model [39, Section 4] and also in the multi-factor (bilevel) model.

In **Chapter 15** a similar implementation is illustrated with the forward rates model of Chapter 9. It is this implementation that has provided the computational results that were illustrated in the two application chapters, 11 and 12. Basically, the program *FRateCAD* implements the model for estimating the forward rate and yield curve trajectories by observations on the yields to maturity. An example of the input data can already be found in Table 9.2.

In this version of the program the basic problem of Chapter 9 is specified and solved. By a discretization of the constraints of the problem, it is approximated by a discrete quadratic programming problem with linear constraints. Special rules are applied for constructing the underlying sets used in defining the class of impulse perturbations specified in Chapter 9. This chapter also provides an opportunity to compute and illustrate a volatility measure based on the histogram of percentage occurrences of forward rate values.

This book is about building and using term structure models, so in the software implementation chapters we have indicated some practical ways of using the results. We have included many screen copies of an actual computer implementation of several of our models. The purpose is to show that software development is within the reach of any interested reader. Actually, we stand ready to help in this effort if there is interest.

Acknowledgements

We wish to express our gratitude to those who have made it possible for us to present our work at outstanding conferences and thereby to obtain a better understanding of the financial issues and problems we have undertaken to study. We do not mean to imply that any of the people to whom we are indebted endorse the approach we have developed in our research and in this book.

To begin, we wish to thank Professor G. A. Medvedev for his helpful comments on our approach to modeling of fixed interest rate instruments. He is the former chairman of the Department of Actuarial Sciences and Statistics at the Byelorussian State University in Minsk, Belarus, and the father of V. G. Medvedev.

We are indebted to Professor Marco Avellaneda at the Courant Institute of Mathematical Sciences, New York University, for giving us the opportunity to present our approach at the Mathematical Finance Seminar in March 1998. After a lively discussion with him and others at that seminar, our paper appeared in the volume which he edited on the *Collected Papers of the New York University Mathematical Finance Seminar*. During this initial development period we received many helpful and critical comments from another Courant Seminar participant, Dr Alexander Levin, of the Treasury Department at the Dime Bancorp, Inc., New York.

We are indebted to Professor Dr Rainer Tichatschke, Department of Mathematics, Trier University, Germany for his early technical comments that led to improvements in our manuscript. He is the principal investigator of a companion project to ours entitled (in German): *Numerische Lösung von Kontrollproblemen unter Unsicherheit und Störung der Eingangsdaten mit Anwendungen in der Finanzmarktanalyse*, funded by the *Stiftung Rheinland-Pfalz für Innovation*.

We are also indebted to Professor W. T. Ziemba for providing an opportunity to present our approach at the *VII International Conference on Stochastic Programming* at the University of British Columbia, Vancouver, Canada, in August 1998, together with a follow-up presentation in the *Asset & Liability Management Program*. Finally, we wish to express our thanks to the Conference Organizers, Professors David Heath and Steven Shreve, for making possible our participation in Carnegie Mellon's *Quantitative Risk Management in Finance* during August 2000.

We are grateful to Professor G. Olivieri of the Luis "Guido Carli" University, Rome, for making it possible for Maria Sole Staffa to visit Iowa City in January 1999 to investigate the approach with a view towards an application and extension to Italian bond market data in her Ph.D. thesis.

We are indebted to the National Academy of Sciences Program *COBASE: Collaboration in Basic Science and Engineering*, and to Ms Jane Van Voorhis of the International Programs Office at the Henry B. Tippie College of Business, University of Iowa, for making us aware of this program. The *COBASE* grant was used to support a three-week visit of V. G. Medvedev in June 1996 during which the project *Semi-infinite Programming and New Applications in Finance* was begun.

We are very much indebted for the further financial support received for the project from the Donald E. & Felicity A. Sodaro Revocable Trust, California. Their generosity provided salary support for Dr Medvedev during the period 7/4/97–7/2/98.

At the University of Iowa we also acknowledge the Office of Vice President of Research for providing computer equipment during Dr Medvedev's visit, while the Tippie College of Business provided office space for him. We also acknowledge support from the university for an Administrative Leave for K. O. Kortanek during this period. We are also grateful for discussions with Professor Michael Stutzer of the Department of Finance. For a brief period during the Spring term of 1998 he had one of his classes compare the classical naive forecasts for 3 month U.S. Treasury Bill auctions against ours.

Much of the work during the last year was made possible with the support of Mr Domenick Tirabassi, Jr., President of OmniCADD, Inc., Milwaukee who provided V. G. Medvedev with the necessary release time for the project.

Our final personal indebtedness goes to our colleague, Professor Elias S. W. Shiu of the Department of Statistics & Actuarial Science, University of Iowa. Our fine colleague has been an invaluable source of references and information.

1

On the Conventional and Pure Multi-period Loan Structure

1.1 PURE SHORT-TERM LENDING

In intertemporal exchange models an exchange of commodity 1 for commodity 2 represents a loan contract, the seller of 1 being the lender and the seller of 2 being the buyer. The exchange of a commodity at time t for the commodity at time $t+1$ is the temporal equivalent of a one-period loan extended at date t and maturing at date $t+1$. Denote the price of the commodity at time t by p_t, so at time $t+1$ the price is p_{t+1}. The conditions of the exchange are given in Table 1.1.

Basically we 'loan' x today for y tomorrow. Taking $x=1$ to mean that we are willing to exchange one unit of commodity today (time t), we see that the terms of the exchange require that we obtain $y=p_t/(p_{t+1})$ tomorrow (time $t+1$).

A useful way to represent y is to reveal its underlying *short-term interest rate*, namely $y=1+r_{t,1}$, where $r_{t,1}$ denotes the interest rate starting at time t for necessarily one time period. Alternatively, one unit of commodity at time t exchanges for $1+r_{t,1}$ units of the commodity at time $t+1$, with $1+r_{t,1}$ being the price of the commodity at t in terms of the commodity at $t+1$, i.e.

$$r_{t,1} = \frac{p_t}{p_{t+1}} - 1. \tag{1.1}$$

Remark 1.1 *Another important example of exchanges, this time without the time factor entering, are currency exchanges, which we briefly illustrate. Let $p_i=$ the price of commodity i, $i=1, \ldots, n$. We give up one unit of commodity i in exchange for p_i/p_j units of commodity j (Table 1.2). The exchange combines -1 of good i with p_i/p_j of good j for the following accounting balance (Table 1.3):*

$$-p_i + \left(\frac{p_i}{p_j}\right)p_j = 0.$$

Returning to our temporal setting, one is interested in short-term rates over multiple periods and how they combine to give longer term rates. For this presentation we will use a generic symbol, τ, throughout to denote a number of time periods, each having common unit length of any user-chosen scale, say hour, day, week, month or year. We continue to denote 'today' by t, which we will also refer to as the *current time*. But in order to obtain τ short-term interest rates we need $\tau+1$ period prices. Accordingly, the lists of our τ dates and $\tau+1$ prices are:

τ dates	t	$t+1$	$t+2$	...	$t+\tau-1$	
$\tau+1$ prices	p_t	p_{t+1}	p_{t+2}	$\cdots$	$p_{t+\tau-1}$	p_τ.

Table 1.1   An exchange over one period

	Today, t	Tomorrow, $t+1$
Physical exchange	x	y
Price	p_t	p_{t+1}
Terms of exchange	$x p_t = y p_{t+1}$	

Table 1.2   Currency rates of exchange

	p_1	p_2	$\cdots$	p_i	$\cdots$	p_j	$\cdots$	p_n
Row i	p_i/p_1	p_i/p_2	$\cdots$	1	$\cdots$	p_i/p_j	$\cdots$	p_i/p_n
Row j	p_j/p_1	p_j/p_2	$\cdots$	p_j/p_i	$\cdots$	1	$\cdots$	p_j/p_n

Table 1.3   Summary of net revenue from a currency exchange

	Quantity	Revenue
#i	-1	$-p_i$
#j	p_i/p_j	$(p_i/p_j)p_j$

The associated short-term rates are therefore given as follows:

$$1 + r_{t+j,1} = \frac{p_{t+j}}{p_{t+j+1}}, \quad \text{for } j = 0, 1, 2, \ldots, \tau - 1. \tag{1.2}$$

In general, for T periods in a planning horizon there are T prices, $p_1, \ldots, p_T$, and $T - 1$ short-term (one-period) rates $r_{1,1}, \ldots, r_{T-1,1}$. The $T(T-1)/2$ terms of trade between any two dated commodities at t, $t + \tau$ respectively can be expressed in terms of these rates as follows:

$$\frac{p_t}{p_{t+\tau}} = \frac{p_t}{p_{t+1}} \frac{p_{t+1}}{p_{t+2}} \cdots \frac{p_{t+\tau-1}}{p_{t+\tau}} = \prod_{k=t}^{t+\tau-1} (1 + r_{k,1}), \quad \tau = 1, \ldots, T-t; \; t = 1, \ldots, T-1. \tag{1.3}$$

When r is the same for all periods, we have

$$\frac{p_t}{p_{t+\tau}} = (1 + r)^\tau.$$

Formula (1.3) is convenient because other quotients of prices can be evaluated using it. For example

$$\frac{p_i}{p_{j+\tau}} = \frac{p_i}{p_{i+(j-i+\tau)}} = \prod_{k=i}^{j+\tau-1} (1 + r_{k,1}). \tag{1.4}$$

The intertemporal exchange given in (1.3) is defined on periods t and $t + \tau$ directly. It naturally bears the name of a long-term exchange. It generates long-term interest rates, and their connection to the structure of short-term rates is of fundamental importance.

1.2 PURE LONG-TERM INTEREST RATES

If we modified Table 1.1 to accommodate a multi-period exchange, which we also refer to as a τ-period exchange instead of a one-period exchange, then we would require $y = p_t/p_{t+\tau}$ at time $t + \tau$ to give up one commodity unit at time t. As before, there is a more revealing notation for y, and we choose $\mathcal{R}_{t,\tau}$ since it reminds us of the inception date of the exchange and its term or days to maturity. As a practical matter, the price $\mathcal{R}_{t,\tau}$ is referred to as the *pure τ-period long-term rate*, where one commodity unit at time t exchanges for $p_t/p_{t+\tau}$ at time $t + \tau$. The terminology 'long-term' is used here in a relative sense, namely to refer to a situation where there are multiple single time units, whose lengths may, for example, be days, weeks, months or years.

For $\tau = 1$ the pure one-period long-term rate equals the pure short-term rate plus 1, i.e. $\mathcal{R}_{t,1} = 1 + r_{t,1}$. The *pure average τ-period long-term rate*, $r^*_{t,\tau}$, is defined by

$$(1 + r^*_{t,\tau})^\tau = \mathcal{R}_{t,\tau}. \tag{1.5}$$

Hence, using $j = k - t$ in (1.3) yields the following basic relationship:

$$\mathcal{R}_{t,\tau} = \frac{p_t}{p_{t+\tau}} = \prod_{k=t}^{t+\tau-1} (1 + r_{k,1}) = \prod_{j=0}^{\tau-1} (1 + r_{j+t,1}) \tag{1.6}$$

or

$$\mathcal{R}_{t,\tau} = (1 + r_{t,1})(1 + r_{t+1,1})(1 + r_{t+2,1}) \ldots (1 + r_{t+\tau-1,1}).$$

For example, $\mathcal{R}_{1,3} = (1 + r_{1,1})(1 + r_{2,1})(1 + r_{3,1})$. Now using (1.4) we obtain

$$\frac{p_1}{p_{t+\tau}} = \frac{p_1}{p_{1+(t+\tau-1)}} = \mathcal{R}_{1,t+\tau-1}. \tag{1.7}$$

Using (1.7) for both the numerator and denominator in the identity $(p_1/p_{t+\tau})/(p_1/p_t) = p_t/p_{t+\tau}$ yields the following convenient relationship:

$$\mathcal{R}_{t,\tau} = \frac{\mathcal{R}_{1,t+\tau-1}}{\mathcal{R}_{1,t-1}}. \tag{1.8}$$

An application of (1.8) demonstrates that the whole family of one-period rates can be obtained from the structure of the long-term rates defined by (1.6). For example, with $\tau = 1$ we obtain

$$1 + r_{t,1} = \frac{\mathcal{R}_{1,t}}{\mathcal{R}_{1,t-1}}, \quad \text{since } \mathcal{R}_{t,1} = 1 + r_{t,1}. \tag{1.9}$$

If there are markets for long-term loans beginning at date 1 and markets for any other maturity at any other date, then the rates quoted in these markets must satisfy (1.6) and (1.8).

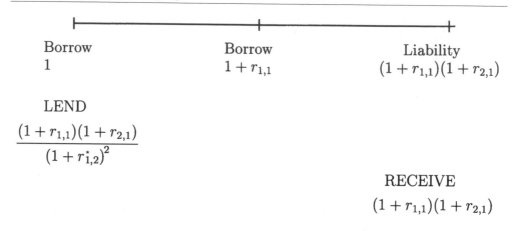

Figure 1.1   Arbitrage when $(1 + r_{1,1})(1 + r_{2,1}) < \mathcal{R}_{1,2}$

1.2.1   An Illustration of a Very Simple Arbitrage

It is illustrative to review the mechanics of a simple arbitrage to independently show that (1.6) must hold.

Figure 1.1 gives the cash flows for the case that, contrary to (1.6), $(1 + r_{1,1})(1 + r_{2,1}) < \mathcal{R}_{1,2}$. By borrowing 1 for one period and lending $(1 + r_{1,1})(1 + r_{2,1})/\mathcal{R}_{1,2}$ for two periods, there is a positive cash flow at the outset. At the outset of the second period we borrow our obligation $(1 + r_{1,1})$ instead of paying the liability. At the end of the second period the proceeds of the two-period loan offset our loan liability $(1 + r_{1,1})(1 + r_{2,1})$. Thus, the initial positive cash flow is maintained as profit.

The second case occurs when we assume $(1 + r_{1,1})(1 + r_{2,1}) > \mathcal{R}_{1,2}$. In this case simply borrow 1 for two periods, leading to a liability of $\mathcal{R}_{1,2}$ at the end of period two. But loan 1 at the beginning of period one, and then loan its receipts $(1 + r_{1,1})$ at the beginning of period two, receiving $(1 + r_{1,1})(1 + r_{2,1})$ at the end of period two. Hence, $(1 + r_{1,1})(1 + r_{2,1}) - \mathcal{R}_{1,2}$ is pure profit. Note that in the first case we receive the profit at the beginning of period one, while in the second case we receive the profit at the end of period two.

1.2.2   An Illustration of a Standard Definition and Day Count Convention

For all applications in this book an instance of time 't' will actually be a date such as 6/26/00. Sometimes the time units themselves will be days. In this setting '$t + 90$' will mean the date 't' plus 90 days. For example, the period $\{6/26/00, 9/26/00\}$ has 92 days. A multi-period, 'τ-period', loan would refer to a loan starting at 6/26/00 with 92 days to maturity. Similarly, for the pair of dates $\{6/26/00, 12/26/00\}$ we would be describing a 'τ-period' loan of 183 days with the same inception date.

Now (1.8) can be rewritten as

$$\mathcal{R}_{1,t-1} \times \mathcal{R}_{t,\tau} = \mathcal{R}_{1,t+\tau-1}. \tag{1.10}$$

However, in this time setting the first subscript '1' has the special meaning of the specific date 6/26/00. Matching days to maturity to symbols in (1.10) we find $t - 1 = 92$ and $t + \tau - 1 = 183$, which implies $t = 93$ and $\tau = 91$. Note that if 6/26/00 is '1', then 9/26/00 itself becomes '93'. Hence, $\mathcal{R}_{93,91}$ becomes $\mathcal{R}_{9/26/00,91}$.

Using actual dates and days to maturity in (1.10) we obtain

$$\mathcal{R}_{6/26/00,92} \times \mathcal{R}_{9/26/00,91} = \mathcal{R}_{6/26/00,183}. \tag{1.11}$$

Let us continue with a numerical illustration.

Suppose at the close of 6/26/00 the LIBOR (London Interbank Offer Rate) is 6.765% for 3 months and 6.92% for 6 months. We follow standard interest rate and currency exchange definitions as they appear in documentation published by the International Swap Dealers Association, Inc.

Connecting the definition of interest rate plus principal with our $\mathcal{R}_{t,\tau}$ notation we obtain the following returns for the respective loan periods:

$$\mathcal{R}_{6/26/00,92} = 1 + 0.0675\left(\frac{92}{360}\right) = 1.0173,$$

$$\mathcal{R}_{6/26/00,183} = 1 + 0.0692\left(\frac{183}{360}\right) = 1.0352. \tag{1.12}$$

The third return is for the future or forward rate period, namely $\mathcal{R}_{9/26/00,91}$, and this rate necessarily is 0.0696 according to (1.11).

It is interesting that the Sep 00 published 3-month Eurodollar futures settled price at the close of 6/26/00 is 93 030. The settled price is necessarily the ask price, and the price implies an annual rate of 6.970% for 3 months. As a rule, this rate should be close to $\mathcal{R}_{9/26/00,91}$ in order to avoid arbitrage opportunities. Here it happens to be exact.

Let us continue our 'numerical' exposition by interpreting the relationship between short-term and long-term rates given in (1.5) in this time context. Under consideration is a multiple day-period loan termed a τ day-period loan starting at day t. We seek the average daily short-term rate, $r_{t,\tau}^*$, such that the expressions of asset value at maturity, day $t + \tau$, are the same whether obtained by the average short-term rate or by the long-term rate itself. Clearly, applying the average short-term rate for τ days yields the total return given in the left-hand side of (1.5), while the right-hand side gives the total return from applying the long-term rate.

If r denotes an annual rate of interest of more or less practical size, then with daily compounding of interest the annual return is $(1 + r/360)^{360}$, and it can be well approximated using the exponential function 'exp'. This is a common function appearing in EXCEL, for example, with $\exp(1) = 2.718281828$ as the beginning of an infinite decimal expansion. The usual mathematical notation for $\exp(r)$ is e^r, and the 'ln' function and 'exp' function are inverses of each other. As a rule, hand calculators have both functions present. It follows that $(1 + r_{t,\tau}^*)^\tau$ can also be well approximated using the exponential function. Here is the detail of the approximation.

With a little manipulation of (1.5), viewing t as a date, τ as the time to maturity in days, and $360 r_{t,\tau}^*$ as a specific annual rate of interest assumed to be of ordinary size, we obtain the following string of equalities:

$$\mathcal{R}_{t,\tau} = (1 + r_{t,\tau}^*)^\tau = \left(\left(1 + \frac{(360\, r_{t,\tau}^*)}{360} \right)^{360} \right)^{\tau/360} = (e^{360\, r_{t,\tau}^*})^{\tau/360} = e^{\tau\, r_{t,\tau}^*}, \qquad (1.13)$$

where the approximation was used to justify the third equality.

Hence

$$r_{t,\tau}^* = \frac{1}{\tau} \ln \mathcal{R}_{t,\tau}. \qquad (1.14)$$

Applying the logarithmic 'ln' function to both sides of (1.10) and substituting with (1.14) yields

$$\ln \mathcal{R}_{1,t-1} + \ln \mathcal{R}_{t,\tau} = \ln \mathcal{R}_{1,t+\tau-1},$$
$$(t-1) r_{1,t-1}^* + \tau r_{t,\tau}^* = (t-1+\tau) r_{1,t+\tau-1}^*. \qquad (1.15)$$

Hence, we immediately obtain the following standard forward rate formula:

$$r_{t,\tau}^* = r_{1,t-1+\tau}^* + \frac{(t-1)}{\tau} [r_{1,t-1+\tau}^* - r_{1,t-1}^*]. \qquad (1.16)$$

An application of (1.16) to the actual data introduced above gives us the data-specific formula for the forward rate $r_{9/26/00,91}^*$:

$$r_{9/26/00,91}^* = r_{6/26/00,183}^* + \frac{92}{91} [r_{6/26/00,183}^* - r_{6/26/00,92}^*]. \qquad (1.17)$$

For the practical purpose of computing forward rates in the day time-regime, (1.16) suffices. For the more general case involving time intervals of arbitrary length we need to invoke the mechanics of continuous interest rate compounding.

1.2.3   Continuous Compounding of an Interest Rate over a Time Interval

Suppose ρ is a rate that applies to some interval of time and that over that interval it is 'compounded continuously'. Continuous time interest rate compounding means (a) that one compounds the given rate over n uniform periods within the given time interval and (b) as n increases indefinitely, the total return converges to a well-defined number. Mathematically

$$\lim_{n \to \infty} \left(1 + \frac{\rho}{n} \right)^n = e^\rho. \qquad (1.18)$$

Let us apply this to the subinterval $[t, T]$, where $T = t + \tau$, over which the pure average τ-period long-term rate $r_{t,\tau}^*$ in (1.5) is constant. Let $R(t, T)$ denote the rate which is continuously compounded over each unit subinterval in $[t, T]$. The continuously compounded rate that returns $1 + r_{t,\tau}^*$ is determined by

$$e^{R(t,T)} = \lim_{n \to \infty} \left(1 + \frac{R(t, T)}{n} \right)^n = 1 + r_{t,\tau}^*.$$

Hence, the relationship between the rate $R(t, T)$ with continuous compounding and the fixed rate $r_{t,\tau}^*$ over an interval $[t, T]$ is

$$R(t, T) = \ln (1 + r_{t,\tau}^*). \tag{1.19}$$

Using (1.5) it now follows that

$$R(t, T) = \frac{1}{\tau} \ln \mathcal{R}_{t,\tau}. \tag{1.20}$$

We can apply continuous compounding over the intervals $[1, t]$, $[t, t + \tau]$ and $[1, t + \tau]$, where now the respective rates $R(1, t)$, $R(t, t + \tau)$ and $R(1, t + \tau)$ are continuously compounded. Repeated application of (1.5) yields

$$(t - 1)R(1, t) = \ln \mathcal{R}_{1,t}, \quad \tau R(t, t + \tau) = \ln \mathcal{R}_{t,\tau}, \quad (t - 1 + \tau)R(1, t + \tau) = \ln \mathcal{R}_{1,t-1+\tau}.$$

With the respective substitutions into (1.15) we obtain the following relationships:

$$(t - 1)R(1, t) + \tau R(t, t + \tau) = (t + \tau - 1)R(1, t + \tau),$$
$$R(t, t + \tau) = R(1, t + \tau) + \frac{t - 1}{\tau}[R(1, t + \tau) - R(1, t)]. \tag{1.21}$$

Under the mathematical idealization of continuous compounding of interest, (1.15) becomes (1.21) directly.

1.3   ON BONDS: FACE VALUE, COUPON RATE, PREMIUMS, DISCOUNTS, AND YIELDS

A unit conventional τ-period loan is a bond with unit face value and coupon rate $r_{1,\tau}$ specified more exactly as follows.

Definition 1.1   *A conventional loan exchanges a unit at time t for a stream of $\tau - 1$ payments of $r_{t,\tau}$ each at time $t + 1$, $t + 2$, . . ., $t + \tau - 1$ and a final payment $1 + r_{t,\tau}$ at time $t + \tau$. The rate $r_{t,\tau}$ is termed the conventional τ-period long-term rate. It is also referred to as the coupon rate of the conventional bond.*

Let us give more detail on this with respect to the exchange rates over the multiple time periods as a convenient way of introducing the present value of a stream of future payments (Table 1.4). The cash payment of 1 at today's price, p_1, must equal the sum of the future coupons at their respective future prices for an exchange to exist. The present value of this stream is simply p_1, and for the exchange to occur it must also be expressed with respect to prices p_2, . . ., $p_{\tau+1}$ in the following manner, where $\tau \geqslant 1$:

$$p_1 = \left(\sum_{j=2}^{\tau+1} p_j \right) r_{1,\tau} + p_{1+\tau}, \tag{1.22}$$

implying

$$r_{1,\tau} = \frac{p_1 - p_{1+\tau}}{\sum_{j=1}^{\tau} p_{j+1}} \quad \text{or} \quad \frac{\sum_{j=1}^{\tau} p_{j+1}}{p_1} = \frac{1}{r_{1,\tau}} \left(1 - \frac{p_{1+\tau}}{p_1} \right).$$

Table 1.4 Temporal terms of exchange for $\tau + 1$ instances of time

Time	t	$t+1$	$\ldots$	$t+\tau-1$	$t+\tau$
For convenience $t = 1$	1	2	$\ldots$	τ	$\tau + 1$
Respective commodity prices	p_1	p_2	$\ldots$	p_τ	$p_{\tau+1}$
Cash payments	-1	$r_{1,\tau}$	$\ldots$	$r_{1,\tau}$	$1 + r_{1,\tau}$

Alternatively

$$1 + r_{1,\tau} = \frac{p_1 - p_{\tau+1} + \sum_{j=1}^{\tau} p_{j+1}}{\sum_{j=1}^{\tau} p_{j+1}}.$$

Hence

$$1 + r_{1,\tau} = \frac{\sum_{j=0}^{\tau-1} p_{j+1}}{\sum_{j=1}^{\tau} p_{j+1}} = \frac{\sum_{i=1}^{\tau} p_i}{\sum_{i=2}^{\tau+1} p_i}. \tag{1.23}$$

To express the conventional τ-period rates in terms of short-term interest rates, first apply (1.6) to obtain

$$\frac{p_i}{p_{1+\tau}} = \frac{p_i}{p_{i+(\tau+1-i)}} = (1 + \mathcal{R}_{i,\tau+1-i}) = \prod_{j=i}^{\tau}(1 + r_{j,1}), \quad \text{for } i \leqslant \tau. \tag{1.24}$$

Now divide both the numerator and denominator of (1.23) by $p_{1+\tau}$ and substitute from (1.24) to obtain

$$1 + r_{1,\tau} = \frac{\sum_{i=1}^{\tau} \dfrac{p_i}{p_{1+\tau}}}{\left(\sum_{i=2}^{\tau} \dfrac{p_i}{p_{1+\tau}} + 1\right)} = \frac{\sum_{i=1}^{\tau} \prod_{j=i}^{\tau}(1 + r_{j,1})}{\sum_{i=2}^{\tau} \prod_{j=i}^{\tau}(1 + r_{j,1}) + 1}. \tag{1.25}$$

For example

$$1 + r_{1,3} = \frac{(1 + r_{1,1})(1 + r_{2,1})(1 + r_{3,1}) + (1 + r_{2,1})(1 + r_{3,1}) + (1 + r_{3,1})}{(1 + r_{2,1})(1 + r_{3,1}) + (1 + r_{3,1}) + 1} \tag{1.26}$$

$$= \frac{\mathcal{R}_{1,3} + \mathcal{R}_{2,2} + \mathcal{R}_{3,1}}{\mathcal{R}_{2,2} + \mathcal{R}_{3,1}}. \tag{1.27}$$

Finally, we illustrate that given $T - 1$ conventional long-term rates, $r_{1,\tau}$, $\tau = 1, \ldots,$ $T - 1$, one can deduce all short-term rates, pure long-term rates and conventional long-term rates *starting at any date t and lasting any number of periods up to $T - 1 - t$*, e.g. a manipulation of (1.26) for $\tau = 2$ gives

$$1 + r_{2,1} = \frac{1 + r_{1,2}}{(1 + r_{1,1} - r_{1,2})}. \tag{1.28}$$

The *term structure of interest rates at time* 1 is simply the set

$$\{\mathcal{R}_{t,\tau} | \tau \geq 0\}. \tag{1.29}$$

In general, a τ-period asset can be described as a claim to the quantity a_j at time $j = 2, \ldots, \tau + 1$. The **market value of the asset** in terms of commodity 1 is

$$X_1 = \sum_{j=1}^{\tau} \frac{p_{1+j} a_{1+j}}{p_1}, \tag{1.30}$$

where

$$a_{1+j} = \begin{cases} a & \text{if } j = 1, \ldots, \tau - 1, \\ a + X_{1+\tau} & \text{if } j = \tau. \end{cases} \tag{1.31}$$

The *standard fixed income securities definitions* include the following.

- The **face value of a bond** $= X_{1+\tau}$, and $c = a/X_{1+\tau}$ is its *coupon rate*.
- A **unit conventional bond** has unit face value and coupon rate $r_{1,\tau}$, according to Definition 1.1.
- A **multi-period annuity** having τ periods is characterized by $X_{1+\tau} = 0$.
- The **current yield** or the **effective coupon rate** is $c = a/X_1$.
- The **premium factor** $(PF) = X_1/X_{1+\tau}$, and $100(PF - 1)$ is the *premium*. When $PF = 1$, the asset is said to sell *at par*.
- The **yield**, ρ, of the asset is defined by

$$\sum_{j=1}^{\tau} a_{1+j}(1 + \rho)^{-j} = X_1, \tag{1.32}$$

which is the market value.

1.3.1 Relation of the Premium Factor to Long-term Interest Rates

Rearranging (1.30) gives

$$p_1 X_1 = a \sum_{j=1}^{\tau} p_{1+j} + p_{\tau+1} X_{\tau+1}.$$

Dividing by $p_1 X_{1+\tau}$ gives

$$PF = \frac{X_1}{X_{1+\tau}} = \frac{a}{X_{1+\tau}} \sum_{j=1}^{\tau} \frac{p_{1+j}}{p_1} + \frac{p_{\tau+1}}{p_1} = c \sum_{j=1}^{\tau} \frac{p_{1+j}}{p_1} + \frac{p_{\tau+1}}{p_1}. \tag{1.33}$$

Substituting for $\Sigma_{j=1}^{\tau} p_{1+j}/p_1$ by (1.22) gives a useful expression of the **premium factor** as a function of c, $r_{1,\tau}$ and $r_{1,\tau}^*$, namely

$$PF(c, r_{1,\tau}, r_{1,\tau}^*) = \frac{c}{r_{1,\tau}}\left(1 - \frac{p_{\tau+1}}{p_1}\right) + \frac{p_{\tau+1}}{p_1} = \frac{c}{r_{1,\tau}}(1 - (1 + r_{1,\tau}^*)^{-\tau}) + (1 + r_{1,\tau}^*)^{-\tau} \tag{1.34}$$

using (1.5) and (1.7) with $t = 1$.

1.3.2 Bond Yields and Their Relation to Long-term Interest Rates

Relation of the Bond Yield to the Conventional Long-term Rate, $r_{1,\tau}$

We obtain an expression of the premium factor, PF, in terms of the bond yield ρ by dividing (1.32) by the face value of the bond $X_{1+\tau}$:

$$PF = \frac{X_1}{X_{1+\tau}} = \frac{a}{X_{1+\tau}} \sum_{j=1}^{\tau} (1 + \rho)^{-j} + (1 + \rho)^{-\tau}. \tag{1.35}$$

But $a/X_{1+\tau} = c$, the coupon rate, and the geometric series substitution in (1.35) gives the following simplification for the premium factor:

$$PF = \frac{c(1 - (1 + \rho)^{-\tau})}{\rho} + (1 + \rho)^{-\tau}, \tag{1.36}$$

justifying the notation $\rho \equiv \rho(c, r_{1,\tau}, r_{1,\tau}^*)$, since the premium factor PF is a function of the three variables as seen from (1.34).

But we wish to express ρ in terms of the τ-period conventional long-term rate, $r_{1,\tau}$. Equating the two expressions for the premium factor, (1.34) and (1.36), yields

$$\frac{c(1 - (1 + \rho)^{-\tau})}{\rho} + (1 + \rho)^{-\tau} = \frac{c}{r_{1,\tau}} (1 - (1 + r_{1,\tau}^*)^{-\tau}) + (1 + r_{1,\tau}^*)^{-\tau}. \tag{1.37}$$

If τ is sufficiently large, then we can ignore the terms in (1.37) having power $-\tau$. Hence, $c/\rho \approx c/r_{1,\tau}$, i.e. $\rho \approx r_{1,\tau}$, namely the bond yield is approximately the conventional long-term rate. The important equality (1.37) is trivially verified if $\rho = r_{1,\tau} = r_{1,\tau}^*$.

But ρ need not equal the conventional long-term rate $r_{1,\tau}$; rather, it is a function of it, the coupon rate and the uniform pure average τ-period long-term rate $r_{t,\tau}^*$. Here is a useful but simple result.

Proposition 1.1 $PF = 1$ *if and only if* $c = r_{1,\tau}$, *in which case* $c = \rho = r_{1,\tau}$.

Proof.   Let $c = r_{1,\tau}$, namely the coupon rate equals the conventional long-term rate. Then the right-hand side of (1.37) is 1, and therefore $c = \rho$ and $PF = 1$, i.e. the bond sells *at par*. Conversely, suppose a τ-period bond sells *at par*, i.e. $PF = 1$. Then using (1.37) we obtain

$$c(1 - (1 + r_{1,\tau}^*)^{-\tau}) = r_{1,\tau}(1 - (1 + r_{1,\tau}^*)^{-\tau}). \tag{1.38}$$

Hence $c = r_{1,\tau}$, which implies $c = \rho$ from the first part of the proof.   □

There are only two cases where ρ equals or well approximates $r_{1,\tau}$.

1. **Bonds at par.** By Proposition 1.1 $c = r_{1,\tau}$. This implies that the right-hand side of (1.37) is 1, and therefore $c = \rho$. Hence, $c = \rho = r_{1,\tau}$ when the bond sells at par.
2. **Bonds not necessarily at par.** Assume $r_{1,\tau} = r_{1,\tau}^*$, namely the conventional and uniform pure τ-rates are equal for τ sufficiently large. Then (1.37) reads

$$\frac{c(1 - (1 + \rho)^{-\tau})}{\rho} + (1 + \rho)^{-\tau} = \frac{c}{r_{1,\tau}} (1 - (1 + r_{1,\tau})^{-\tau}) + (1 + r_{1,\tau})^{-\tau}. \tag{1.39}$$

For 'large' τ it follows from (1.37) that $\rho \approx r_{1,\tau}$, in which case $\rho \approx r_{1,\tau} = r_{1,\tau}^*$. However, in general, the bonds need not be selling at par in this case because even with $\rho \approx r_{1,\tau}$, c may not equal ρ.

1.3.3 Mean Average Approximations to the Yield Structure

Combining (1.5) and (1.6) gives an important relationship between the pure τ-period long-term rate and the τ short-term rates:

$$(1 + r_{t,\tau}^*)^\tau = \prod_{j=0}^{\tau-1} (1 + r_{j+t,1}). \tag{1.40}$$

The classical approach for deriving the set of *forward rates* from the term structure of interest rates for equal length time intervals is as follows.

We first observe that $\ln(1 + x)$ approximates x reasonably well when x is small positive [$\ln 1.1 = 0.0953$, $\ln 1.03 = 0.0295$]. Taking logarithms of (1.40) and using the approximation we see that (1.40) yields

$$r_{t,\tau}^* = \frac{1}{\tau} \sum_{j=0}^{\tau-1} r_{t+j,1}. \tag{1.41}$$

Let us assume that the conventional τ-period long-term rate $r_{t,\tau}$ approximates well the pure τ-period long-term rate $r_{t,\tau}^*$. Also let the dates satisfy

$$t < t + \theta < t + \theta + \tau.$$

Consider the decomposition of the larger period $[t, t + \theta + \tau]$ into the two smaller contiguous intervals $[t, t + \theta]$ and $[t + \theta, t + \theta + \tau]$. Proceeding formally according to (1.41) yields

$$(\tau + \theta) r_{t,\tau+\theta} = \sum_{j=0}^{\tau+\theta-1} r_{t+j,1} = \sum_{j=0}^{\theta-1} r_{t+j,1} + \sum_{j=0}^{\tau-1} r_{t+\theta+j,1} = \theta r_{t,\theta} + \tau r_{t+\theta,\tau}. \tag{1.42}$$

Equation (1.42) gives a simple approximation to the *forward term structure*, i.e.

$$r_{t+\theta,\tau} = r_{t,\theta+\tau} + \frac{\theta}{\tau}(r_{t,\theta+\tau} - r_{t,\theta}). \tag{1.43}$$

Setting $\theta = 1$ gives the implied maturity rates structure at time t for loans beginning the next period:

$$r_{t+1,\tau} = r_{t,1+\tau} + \frac{1}{\tau}(r_{t,1+\tau} - r_{t,1}). \tag{1.44}$$

The next period rate for τ-period loans is the current rate for loans having the same terminal date, adjusted for the effect of dropping the first short rate included in $r_{t,\tau+1}$ but not included in $r_{t+1,\tau}$. These latter two rates are unlikely to differ appreciably from each other when τ is large, since they are averages of quantities which are identical except for $r_{t,1}$, which appears in $r_{t,\tau+1}$ but not in $r_{t+1,\tau}$. Similarly, when τ is large, $r_{t+1,\tau}$ is not much different from $r_{t,\tau}$, since from (1.41)

Table 1.5   Illustrative relations between spot rates and forward rates

Year (n) $n = \theta + 1$	Spot rate for an n-year investment (%/year) $r_{t,\theta+1}$	Forward rate for the nth year $r_{t+\theta,1}$
$\theta = 0$	8.31	8.31
$\theta = 1$	8.73	9.15
	$r_{t+1,1} = r_{t,2} + 1(r_{t,2} - r_{t,1}) = 8.73 + (8.73 - 8.31)$	
$\theta = 2$	9.21	10.17
	$r_{t+2,1} = r_{t,3} + 2(r_{t,3} - r_{t,2}) = 9.21 + 2(9.21 - 8.73)$	
$\theta = 3$	9.79	11.53
	$r_{t+3,1} = r_{t,4} + 3(r_{t,4} - r_{t,3}) = 9.79 + 3(9.79 - 9.21)$	
$\theta = 4$	10.02	10.94
	$r_{t+4,1} = r_{t,5} + 4(r_{t,5} - r_{t,4}) = 10.02 + 4(10.02 - 9.79)$	

$$\tau[r_{t+1,\tau} - r_{t,\tau}] = -r_{t,1} + r_{t+\tau,1},$$

i.e.

$$r_{t+1,\tau} = r_{t,\tau} + \frac{1}{\tau}(r_{t+\tau,1} - r_{t,1}). \tag{1.45}$$

Moreover, by setting $\tau = 1$ in (1.43) we obtain the entire structure of forward short rates, namely

$$r_{t+\theta,1} = r_{t,\theta+1} + \theta(r_{t,\theta+1} - r_{t,\theta}), \quad \theta = 1, \ldots. \tag{1.46}$$

These forward rate relationships emphasize the importance of the term structure of interest rates. All forward rates are determined from the term structure, (1.29).

For a numerical illustration of (1.46) we compute the entries in Table 1.5. Note that

$$5r_{t,5} = \sum_{j=0}^{4} r_{t+j,1}, \tag{1.47}$$

which is (1.41) under the assumption $r_{t,\tau}^{*} = r_{t,\tau}$.

1.4   ON SPOT INTEREST RATES, FORWARD INTEREST RATES, AND THE YIELD TO MATURITY

The term structure of interest rates is the relationship between the yields on default-free discount bonds and their maturities. A default-free discount bond maturing at time T, $T \geqslant 0$, is a security that pays \$1 at time T and nothing at any other time. Let $P(t, T)$ denote the price of the bond at time t, $0 \leqslant t \leqslant T$. By definition, $P(T, T) = 1$.

We can combine all of this in a differential equation (DE) as a way of introducing the spot rate $r(t)$. The DE under perfect certainty for the price of a zero-coupon bond, $P(t, T)$, at current time t returning \$1 at future time $T > t$ is the following:

$$\frac{d}{dt} P(t, T) = r(t) P(t, T), \quad P(T, T) = 1, \tag{1.48}$$

with $r(t)$ termed the spot rate.

Several key constructions stem from the DE (1.48):

- The solution

$$P(t, T) = \exp\left(-\int_t^T r(\tau)\,d\tau\right). \tag{1.49}$$

- The spot rate equals the *instantaneous rate of increase* of the bond price:

$$r(t) = \frac{P_t(t, T)}{P(t, T)}. \tag{1.50}$$

- The yield to maturity prevailing at time t equals the *internal rate of return* at time t of a no-coupon bond having maturity date T:

$$R(t, T) = -\frac{\log P(t, T)}{T - t} = \frac{\int_t^T r(\tau)\,d\tau}{T - t}. \tag{1.51}$$

- The spot rate equals the *instantaneous yield to maturity*:

$$r(t) = \lim_{T \to t} R(t, T), \tag{1.52}$$

from which it follows that

$$r(t) = -\frac{\partial}{\partial T} \log P(t, t). \tag{1.53}$$

- The term structure surface

$$\{(t, T, R(t, T)) \mid T \geqslant t\} \subset \mathbf{R}^3. \tag{1.54}$$

1.4.1 Forward Rates as Implied by Future Spot Rates (Yields to Maturity)

By definition forward rates are the rates implied by future continuous spot rates. Let $T_2 > T_1 > 0$. The relationship between the forward rate for a contract made at the current time t for the future period $[T_1, T_2]$ is defined by

$$P(t, T_2) = P(t, T_1)\,e^{-(T_2 - T_1)f(t, T_1, T_2)} \tag{1.55}$$

or, in terms of the yields to maturity

$$R(t, T_2)(T_2 - t) = R(t, T_1)(T_1 - t) + f(t, T_1, T_2)(T_2 - T_1). \tag{1.56}$$

More generally, we have the following expression for discrete forward rates over the interval $[T_{i-1}, T_i]$, $T_i > T_{i-1} \geqslant t$:

$$f(t, T_{i-1}, T_i) = \frac{R(t, T_i)(T_i - t) - R(t, T_{i-1})(T_{i-1} - t)}{T_i - T_{i-1}}. \tag{1.57}$$

Noting that $f(t, T_0, T_1) = R(t, T_1)$, for $T_0 = t$, we may generalize (1.56) as

$$R(t, T) = \sum_{T_i \geq t} f(t, T_{i-1}, T_i) \frac{(T_i - T_{i-1})}{T - t}, \quad t = T_0 < T_1 < \ldots < T, \qquad (1.58)$$

more clearly demonstrating that the continuous spot rates are weighted averages of the forward rates.

1.4.2   Instantaneous Forward Rates

Let $T_1 = T$ and $T_2 = T + \Delta$, Δ positive. It is no real restriction to assume that the limit $\lim_{\Delta \to 0} f(t, T, T + \Delta)$ exists. We shall denote this limit by $f(t, T)$, referring to it as the 'instantaneous forward rate at future time t'. The phrase 'at future time T' is a convenient way (used throughout this book) of stating that the current time is $t \geq 0$, and $T > t$. The curve $\{(T, f(t, T)) | T \geq t\}$ is termed the 'forward rate curve'. We easily derive the following relationship between the forward rate curve and the yield curve:

$$R(t, T) = \frac{\int_t^T f(t, s)\, ds}{T - t}. \qquad (1.59)$$

Under these circumstances (1.56) then becomes

$$R(t, T + \Delta)(T + \Delta - t) = R(t, T)(T - t) + f(t, T, T + \Delta)\Delta$$

or

$$f(t, T, T + \Delta) = (T - t)\frac{R(t, T + \Delta) - R(t, T)}{\Delta} + R(t, T + \Delta).$$

Taking limits yields the useful formula

$$f(t, T) = (T - t)\frac{\partial R}{\partial T}(t, T) + R(t, T). \qquad (1.60)$$

If the yield curve is increasing, then the forward curve lies above the yield curve, and if the yield curve is decreasing, then the forward curve lies below the yield curve.

Using the forward rate curve we obtain another expression for the discrete forward rates given in (1.57):

$$f(t, T_{i-1}, T_i) = \frac{1}{T_i - T_{i-1}} \int_{T_{i-1}}^{T_i} f(t, s)\, ds. \qquad (1.61)$$

We also observe that the forward rates curve $\{(s, f(t, s)) | s \geq \text{fixed } t\}$ satisfies

$$P(t, T) = \exp\left(-\int_t^T f(t, s)\, ds\right), \quad P(T, T) = 1, \qquad (1.62)$$

from which we derive another form for the forward rate for instantaneous borrowing:

$$f(t, T) = -\frac{\partial}{\partial T} \log P(t, T). \qquad (1.63)$$

Using the instantaneous yield to maturity definition (1.52) together with the particular partial derivative with respect to T, (1.53) gives the following important relationship between the spot rate and the forward rate at time t. We shall return to this relationship when we study general classes of dynamic models for the forward rate in Chapter 10:

$$r(t) = f(t, t), \quad \text{for } t \geqslant 0. \tag{1.64}$$

Finally, differentiating (1.62) above with respect to t yields

$$P_t(t, T) = \left(\exp\left(-\int_t^T f(t, s)\, ds \right) \right)_t' = \exp\left(-\int_t^T f(t, s)\, ds \right)\left(-\int_t^T f(t, s)\, ds \right)_t'$$

$$= P(t, T)\left(f(t, t) - \int_t^T f_t(t, s)\, ds \right) = P(t, T)\left(r(t) - \int_t^T f_t(t, s)\, ds \right). \tag{1.65}$$

Hence, we obtain

$$P_t(t, T) = \left(r(t) - \int_t^T f_t(t, s)\, ds \right) P(t, T). \tag{1.66}$$

The unbiased expectations hypothesis assumes that forward rates $f(t, T)$ and the expectation of future spot rates $E(r_T)$ are equal. In the deterministic theory this hypothesis leads to the following relation between the forward rate $f(t, T)$ and the spot rate:

$$f(t, T) = r(T), \quad \text{for all } T \geqslant t \geqslant 0. \tag{1.67}$$

From (1.67) we obtain that $f_t(t, s) = 0$ in (1.66), and that in turn leads to (1.48). We will start our development from this simple case and then extend it to more general cases in Chapter 4, where the relationship between the forward rate $f(t, T)$ and the spot rate $r(T)$ is more complicated, see (4.8).

Throughout this book we shall assume that the price of a discount bond is determined by the current assessment of the spot rate trajectory over the term of the bond.

Remark 1.2 *It is interesting that in both* (1.60) *and* (1.63) *the differentiation is with respect to the maturity date T. Later on we will develop a differential systems model for the forward rate itself using this type of differentiation.*

1.5 AN EXAMPLE IN THE LITERATURE

We illustrate with an example from the recent book of Paul Wilmott [67, Vol. 2, p. 542], where we have supplied the dates for the notation $R(t, T)$.[1]

All yields are for zero-coupon bonds (Table 1.6). A simple piecewise constant (PWC) yield function extension, $\hat{R}(t, T)$, $t \leqslant T \leqslant T_N$, yields

$$\hat{R}(t, T) = \hat{R}(T_i), \quad \text{for } T_{i-1} < T \leqslant T_i, \ i = \overline{1, N}, \tag{1.68}$$

where $T_0 = t$ and $\hat{R}(t, t) = \hat{R}(T_1)$. See [67, Vol. 2, Figure 38.12, p. 543].

---

[1] *Paul Wilmott on Quantitative Finance, Volumes I & II* by Paul Wilmott, Copyright year 2000; John Wiley & Sons Limited, reproduced with permission.

Table 1.6   Wilmott's piecewise constant yield model over a 10-year horizon

Date	Time to maturity (years)	Observed yield
1/1/00		Current time $t = T_0$
4/1/00	$T_1 - t = 0.25$	$\hat{R}(T_1) = \hat{R}(1/1/00, 4/1/00) = 0.07714$
7/1/00	$T_2 - t = 0.50$	$\hat{R}(T_2) = \hat{R}(1/1/00, 7/1/00) = 0.07915$
1/1/01	$T_3 - t = 1.00$	$\hat{R}(T_3) = \hat{R}(1/1/00, 1/1/01) = 0.08403$
1/1/02	$T_4 - t = 2.00$	$\hat{R}(T_4) = \hat{R}(1/1/00, 1/1/02) = 0.08504$
1/1/03	$T_5 - t = 3.00$	$\hat{R}(T_5) = \hat{R}(1/1/00, 1/1/03) = 0.08402$
1/1/05	$T_6 - t = 5.00$	$\hat{R}(T_6) = \hat{R}(1/1/00, 1/1/05) = 0.08801$
1/1/07	$T_7 - t = 7.00$	$\hat{R}(T_7) = \hat{R}(1/1/00, 1/1/07) = 0.09102$
1/1/10	$T_8 - t = 10.00$	$\hat{R}(T_8) = \hat{R}(1/1/00, 1/1/10) = 0.09200$

1.6   BOOTSTRAPPING FROM SUCCESSIVE FORWARD RATES FOR A PIECEWISE CONSTANT FORWARD RATE FUNCTION

Definition 1.2   *Current time is $t = T_0$ and there are N future times, $T_1, \ldots, T_N$. The PWC extension of the successive discrete forward rates is*

$$f(t, \tau) = \begin{cases} f(t, \tau, T_1) = F_1 & \text{for } T_0 < \tau \leqslant T_1 \\ f(t, \tau, T_2) = F_2 & \text{for } T_1 < \tau \leqslant T_2 \\ \ldots \\ f(t, \tau, T_n) = F_N & \text{for } T_{N-1} < \tau \leqslant T_N \end{cases} \quad \text{for } \tau \in [T_0, T_N). \tag{1.69}$$

The PWC forward function derived from Table 1.6 appears in [67, Vol. 2, Figure 38.13, p. 542]:

$$f(0, \tau) = \begin{cases} F_1 = 0.0771 & \text{for } 0.00 \leqslant \tau \leqslant 0.25 \\ F_2 = 0.0812 & \text{for } 0.25 < \tau \leqslant 0.50 \\ F_3 = 0.0889 & \text{for } 0.50 < \tau \leqslant 1.00 \\ F_4 = 0.0860 & \text{for } 1.00 < \tau \leqslant 2.00 \\ F_5 = 0.0820 & \text{for } 2.00 < \tau \leqslant 3.00 \\ F_6 = 0.0940 & \text{for } 3.00 < \tau \leqslant 5.00 \\ F_7 = 0.0985 & \text{for } 5.00 < \tau \leqslant 7.00 \\ F_8 = 0.0943 & \text{for } 7.00 < \tau \leqslant 10.00 \end{cases} \quad \text{for } \tau \in [0, 10). \tag{1.70}$$

For example

$$F_7 = \frac{7R(1/1/00, 1/1/07) - 5R(1/1/00, 1/1/05)}{7 - 5} = 0.098545.$$

1.7 CHAPTER NOTES

The emphasis on lending as an intertemporal exchange dates back at least to class notes based on courses in economics given by Franco Modigliani at Northwestern University in the early 1960s. Sections 1.1–1.4 are based on notes distributed and taken by K. O. Kortanek in one such class. The material is certainly standard and appears in many books, some of which appear in the reference list. For example, a simple illustration from [16, p. 89] has $PF = 1$, $\tau = 1.5$ years with a 6-month coupon $c = 0.0575/2 = 0.02875$. Also, $c = r_{1,\tau}$, the conventional τ-period loan rate. Then (1.36) becomes

$$1 = 0.02875 \left[\frac{1 - 1.02875^{-3}}{0.02875} \right] + 1.02875^{-3}.$$

In addition, we find the standard, alternate notation for (1.43) appears in [31], where r and r^* are the spot rates respectively for years T and T^*, $T^* > T$, and t is the current time. The forward rate for the future period $[T, T^*]$ is denoted by $\hat{r}$. Formula (1.43) applies with $T = t + \theta$ and $t^* = t + \theta + \tau$, obtaining $\hat{r} = r^* + [(T - t)/(T^* - T)](r^* - r)$. Taking $t = 0$ and rewriting we obtain

$$\hat{r} = r^* + (r^* - r) \frac{T}{T^* - T} \qquad [31, \text{p. } 80].$$

The illustrative example on the relationship between spot rates and forward rates is quite similar to [31, Table 4.1].

Many of the examples in this book, particularly in the later chapters, use specific dates to identify current or future periods. It has been convenient to use Visual Basic's 'Date-Diff' command to compute the number of days between two dates [13]. For example, this command applied to the pair {6/26/00, 6/27/00} yields of course just the number 1. For the pair {6/26/00, 9/26/00} we obtain 92 days.

The most modern approach to interest rate analysis is through continuous compounding. That major approach is also taken in this book, particularly when developing differential systems models. However, there are advantages to considering discrete time interest rates, particularly from a practical point of view. Among the many references to where this approach still applies in practice, we cite [5], [6], [16], [17], [36] and [55].

2
Differential Systems Models
for Asset Prices under Uncertainty

We value the description and review of modeling the behavior of asset prices appearing in Hull [31, Chapter 10] because it provides us with an immediate point of departure for our construction of analogies. Up to now a variable whose value changes in an uncertain way has been modeled as following a stochastic process. Descriptions of stochastic processes involve special classes of functions termed probability distributions, or equivalently the inclusion of random variables in the model, all varying with and dependent on time. How these mathematical structures are connected over different instances of time is an area of evolutionary scholarly research. The classical Brownian motion is a prime example. Special processes are used when one wishes the current value of the asset to be the most relevant predictor of future prices. Such processes are usually described as Markovian, or various generalizations of the 'memoryless' property.

Our modeling approach builds on certain analogies. But instead of specifying various types of input function classes having probabilistic, Markovian or other measure theoretic properties, we require our 'functions of uncertainty', so-to-speak, to be members of broad classes of mathematical functions. Classes of functions are specified 'a priori' and in a real sense are to be 'solved-for'.

Stochastic processes can be classified similarly to probability distributions, namely as (a) discrete, (b) continuous or (c) mixtures of the two. Even though asset price data are always collected at discrete times, no matter how small the intervals of time, we concur with the stochastic processes approach that there are important benefits achievable from modeling discrete data as continuous variable, continuous time formulations. An immediate benefit is one of numerical stability in algorithmic developments.

We have introduced the forward rate curve and the term structure of interest rates in the normal discrete setting in Chapter 1. We now introduce these concepts addressed in continuous-time models.

2.1 A DESCRIPTION OF AN UNCERTAINTY WALK FOR ASSET PRICES

It is often stated that asset prices must move randomly because of the *efficient markets hypothesis*. Generally this hypothesis has two meanings:

1. the past history is fully reflected in the present price, which does not have any additional information;
2. markets respond immediately to any new information about an asset.

Hence, the modeling of asset prices really is concerned with the modeling of new information which affects the price. In this book our response to the two assumptions above is to introduce a class of linear dynamic systems under uncertainty for unanticipated changes in the asset price.

First, we note that the *absolute* change in the asset price is not by itself a useful quantity; a change of \$1 is more significant when the asset price is \$10 than when it is \$500. Therefore, we associate the *investor's return*, which is the change in asset price plus dividends divided by the asset price, a well-established measure of return.

Assume at time t the asset price is S, and consider a small subsequent time interval dt, during which S changes to $S + dS$. The standard way of modeling the return dS/S is to decompose the return into two parts. First there is the *predictable*, deterministic and anticipated return equivalent to a risk-free return in a government bond or certificate of deposit from a bank. This component of return takes the form

$$\mu \, dt,$$

where μ is a measure of the average rate of growth of the asset price. In simple models μ is constant, but it can be a function of S and t.

The second component of dS/S models the uncertain change in the asset price due to unanticipated external effects. We shall assume that upper and lower bounds for uncertain changes in the price are known, denoted respectively as functions of time, t, $w^*(t)$ and $w_*(t)$. Later we will postulate properties for these bounding functions, but now we merely indicate their dependence on time. Therefore, the second component in the return of the asset price reveals its uncertain structure through the following system of inequalities:

$$\frac{w(t)}{S} \, dt, \;\; w_*(t) \leqslant w(t) \leqslant w^*(t),$$

where $w(\cdot)$ will be required to be an integrable function, discontinuous in general.

Combining these two components yields the following differential equation under uncertainty:

$$\frac{dS}{S} = \mu \, dt + \frac{w(t)}{S} \, dt, \;\; w_*(t) \leqslant w(t) \leqslant w^*(t), \tag{2.1}$$

which is the mathematical representation of the recipe we adopt for generating asset prices. Observe that (2.1) is an analog of the classical continuous-time Markov model defined by the following continuous path stochastic process:

$$\frac{dS(t)}{S(t)} = \mu \, dt + \sigma \, dB(t). \tag{2.2}$$

This is the classical model for geometric Brownian motion of stock prices:

$$S(t) = S(0) \exp\{(\mu - 0.5\sigma^2)t + \sigma B(t)\}, \;\; t \geqslant 0, \tag{2.3}$$

where

- $S(0) =$ the nonrandom stock price at time $t = 0$;
- $\mu =$ the mean rate of return of the stock, $E(S(t + dt) - S(t))/S(t) \approx \mu \, dt$;
- $\sigma =$ the constant of volatility, where standard deviation $\mathrm{SD}(S(t + dt) - S(t))/S(t) \approx \sigma \sqrt{t}$;
- $B(t)$ is Brownian motion.

We rewrite (2.1) in a form that enhances the use of the Cauchy formula, a transformation that will be used throughout this book in different linear dynamical system contexts:

$$\frac{dS}{dt} = \mu S + w(t), \quad w_*(t) \leqslant w(t) \leqslant w^*(t). \tag{2.4}$$

Assuming that μ is independent of time, we can represent the value of $S(t)$ as a function of S_0, t_0, μ and w in the following form:

$$S(t) = S_0 e^{\mu(t-t_0)} + \int_{t_0}^{t} e^{\mu(t-\tau)} w(\tau)\, d\tau, \quad t \geqslant t_0; \, w_*(\tau) \leqslant w(\tau) \leqslant w^*(\tau), \, \tau \in [t_0, t], \tag{2.5}$$

where S_0 is the value of the asset at $t = t_0$.

The computationally convenient form of the solution to the differential equation is referred to more generally as the *Cauchy formula*. Later we shall state its mathematical properties, and refer to it by the Cauchy name throughout this book. Applying ordinary calculus differentiation to $S(t)$ yields

$$\frac{dS(t)}{dt} = \mu S_0 e^{\mu(t-t_0)} + \mu \int_{t_0}^{t} e^{\mu(t-\tau)} w(\tau)\, d\tau + w(t), \tag{2.6}$$

readily verifying (2.4) in an elementary way.

Figure 2.1 illustrates these components of a discrete uncertainty walk. Point B corresponds to the deterministic case, while point A corresponds to the maximal asset

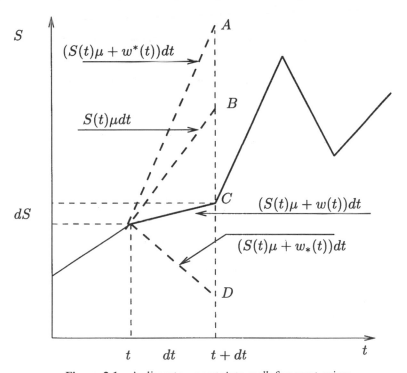

Figure 2.1   A discrete *uncertainty walk* for asset prices

price achieved under current conditions of the market. Next, point D corresponds to the minimal possible asset price, while point C describes the realized current asset price.

The integral in the second term in (2.5) applies to an a priori specified class of integrable functions, $w(\cdot)$, satisfying $w_*(\tau) \leqslant w(\tau) \leqslant w^*(\tau)$, $\tau \in [t_0, t]$, functions which shall generally be termed the *external input perturbations* acting on the asset prices. The first term in (2.5) corresponds to the deterministic return, while the second term models the uncertainty component which is based on the *history of the perturbations* acting on the asset prices up to the current time.

In general, the value $w(t)$ at time t could be generated by a sample from any mixture of discrete and continuous probability distributions. The structure of the second term in (2.5) depends on the class of input perturbations, and these can be chosen to correspond to any probability distribution used for generating uncertainty in the stochastic case. Basically, many general families of functions can be admissible.

Observable data on asset prices are discrete. Figure 2.2 illustrates a set of discrete asset prices $\hat{S}_i$ at day i. For modeling asset price trajectories by means of a differential

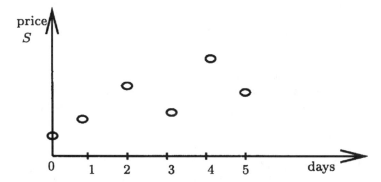

Figure 2.2   A discrete scatter of observed daily prices

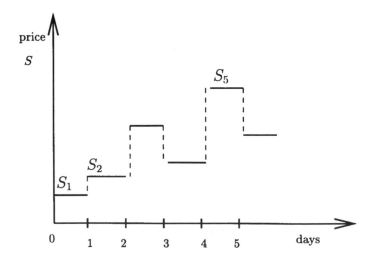

Figure 2.3   Piecewise constant representations of asset prices

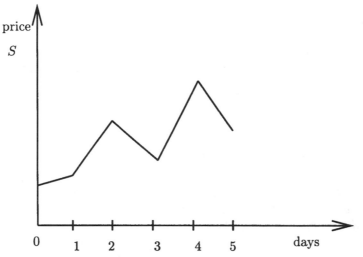

Figure 2.4 Piecewise linear representations of asset prices

equation (2.4), where t varies over a continuum, we need to represent the discrete information as a function of t.

It is clear from (2.5) that the class of input perturbations defines a family of trajectories for the asset price. In the following section we describe the types of observation models we develop in this book. They all depend on the structure of the underlying observed asset prices (Figures 2.3 and 2.4).

2.2 MODELING ASSET PRICES WITH INPUT PERTURBATIONS

In our approach an *observation model* must be constructed incorporating observed discrete data. A class of input perturbations is then chosen to generate an asset price (or yield) trajectory which is a functional form containing certain parameters whose values are determined by solving an *optimal observation problem*. In this book two types of perturbation functions $w(t)$ are employed in (2.4) to determine a price trajectory: (1) the point-impulse type which generates a discontinuous but piecewise continuous price trajectory that exhibits discrete jump behavior and (2) the impulse type which generates a continuous price trajectory. A perturbation-based trajectory based upon an observation model should be compatible with an accurate estimation of the trajectory of real, observed asset prices.

2.2.1 Point-impulse Perturbations Generating Discontinuous Asset Prices

The first *observation model* assumes asset prices are fixed over a specified period of time, such as a day. It is discontinuous and defined as follows:

$$\hat{S}(t) = \hat{S}_i, \ \ t \in [i, i+1[, \ i = \overline{0, n}. \tag{2.7}$$

The initial time '0' has been chosen for convenience; it could have been denoted as t_0 for more generality. Figure 2.3 illustrates the jumps in asset prices at the fixed points, 0, 1, . . ., n. Simply put geometrically, Figure 2.3 is obtained from Figure 2.2 by drawing a constant height line segment for each subinterval of time. We use the jumps to introduce a class of delta functions to obtain specific jump behavior in asset prices, a flexibility that appears to be gaining increasing practical importance. These delta functions are particularly convenient for obtaining these jumps through the second term of (2.5). They are defined as follows.

Definition 2.1   *Point-impulse perturbations: the functional form* $\{w(\tau),\ \tau \in [0,\ n+1]\}$ *employed in* (2.1) *has the following properties:*

1. *w is zero at all points in the closed interval* $[0,\ n+1]$ *except at the integers* $\{0, 1,\ .\ .\ .,\ n\}$. *This is expressed formally as* $w(\tau) = 0,\ \tau \in [0,\ n+1] \setminus \{0,\ .\ .\ .,\ n\}$;
2. *the trajectory* $S(\tau),\ \tau \in [0,\ n+1]$ *of asset prices is described by a modification of the defining differential equation* (2.1):

$$\frac{dS(t)}{dt} = \mu S, \quad \mu \text{ independent of } t \tag{2.8}$$

    on the open intervals $]i,\ i+1[,\ i = \overline{0,\ n}$, *a notation for excluding the endpoints of the interval;*
3. *$S(\tau),\ \tau \in [0,\ n+1]$ has jumps* $w_i \equiv w(i)$ *given by*

$$S(i) = S(i-0) + w_i, \quad w_{i*} \leqslant w_i \leqslant w_i^*, i = \overline{0,\ n} \tag{2.9}$$

    at the points $i = \overline{0,\ n}$.

From (2.8) and (2.9) it follows that the asset price (2.5) can be written in the following generally discontinuous but piecewise continuous form:

$$S(t) = S_0 e^{\mu t} + \sum_{i=0}^{j} w_i e^{\mu(t-i)}, \quad t \in [j, j+1[,\ j = \overline{0,\ n};\ w_{i*} \leqslant w_i \leqslant w_i^*,\ i = \overline{0,\ n}. \tag{2.10}.$$

The properties of this function suggest other classes of admissible functions as the building blocks so-to-speak of the more general dynamical systems models we shall introduce in the next chapter. The admissibility properties are formally presented in a definition in Section 3.2.

2.2.2   Impulse Perturbations Generating Continuous Asset Prices

We now specify our second *observation model* where the asset price is a piecewise linear function of time spanned by the original discrete price data:

$$\hat{S}(t) = S_i + \frac{t - t_i}{t_{i+1} - t_i}(S_{i+1} - S_i), \quad t \in [i,\ i+1],\ i = \overline{0,\ n}. \tag{2.11}$$

Definition 2.2   *Impulse perturbations: the functional form* $\{w(\tau), \tau \in [0, n+1]\}$ *employed in* (2.1) *is the class of piecewise constant functions having the following form:*

$$w(\tau) = w_i, \quad w_{i*} \leqslant w_i \leqslant w_i^*, \tau \in [i,\ i+1[,\ i = \overline{0,\ n}. \tag{2.12}$$

By means of (2.12) we obtain the following specialization of (2.5), where $S(t)$ is continuous:

$$S(t) = S_0 e^{\mu t} + \sum_{i=0}^{j-1} w_i \int_i^{i+1} e^{\mu(t-\tau)} \, d\tau + w_j \int_j^t e^{\mu(t-\tau)} \, d\tau = S_0 e^{\mu t} + \sum_{i=0}^{j-1} \frac{w_i}{\mu} (e^{\mu(t-i)} - e^{\mu(t-(i+1))})$$

$$+ \frac{w_j}{\mu}(e^{\mu(t-j)} - 1), \quad t \in [j, j+1], j = \overline{0, n}; w_{i*} \leqslant w_i \leqslant w_i^*, i = \overline{0, n} \tag{2.13}$$

and where $\Sigma_{i=0}^{j-1} (\cdot) = 0$ if $j < 1$.

For observation model (2.11) under impulse perturbations the trajectory of the asset price is also continuous.

We have described two basic ways of constructing asset price trajectories over a continuum from discrete observations, using respectively point-impulse jump and impulse perturbations. In later chapters we will apply these constructions to US Treasury yield data with constant days-to-maturity, and illustrate graphically the effects of choosing different observation models under different input perturbations.

We next describe how to estimate these input perturbations using 'real' observations.

2.3 ESTIMATING INPUT PERTURBATIONS AND ASSET PRICE TRAJECTORIES

We introduce the underlying features of our approach which uses previous observations of asset prices during a predetermined special period termed the *period of asset price observations*.

Assume that observations $\hat{S}(t)$ are taken over a designated interval $[t_0, T]$, and are modeled by either (2.9) or (2.11) with initial state $S_0 = S(t_0)$. Regardless of what type of perturbation is used in defining the 'Law of Motion' (2.1), the *error of estimation of the asset price* is simply the function:

$$\varepsilon(t, \mu, w(\cdot)) = \hat{S}(t) - S(t) = \hat{S}(t) - S_0 e^{\mu(t-t_0)} - \int_{t_0}^t e^{\mu(t-\tau)} w(\tau) \, d\tau, \quad t \in [t_0, T]. \tag{2.14}$$

One of the most conservative ways to estimate values for the unknown quantity μ and unknown function $w(\cdot)$ is the classical 'minimax' criterion:

$$\varepsilon^* = \min_{\mu, w(\cdot)} \max_{t \in [t_0, T]} \varepsilon(t, \mu, w(\cdot)). \tag{2.15}$$

Let $(\mu^0, w^0(\cdot))$ be a solution of problem (2.15). Then the function

$$S(t) = S_0 e^{\mu^0(t-t_0)} + \int_{t_0}^t e^{\mu^0(t-\tau)} w^0(\tau) \, d\tau, \quad t \in [t_0, T] \tag{2.16}$$

is an estimate of the asset price over the entire observation period. The optimal solution $(\mu^0, w^0(\cdot))$ will be used to predict future values of asset prices beyond the observation period, as well as for updating new bounds for the perturbation functions. The result shall be an automatic updating of asset price trajectories as new information becomes available.

In the chapters to follow we implement a new approach for modeling uncertainty for the purpose of estimating the term structure of interest rates under various models of observation. But now it is time to present our differential equation system and Cauchy solution in a more formal mathematical manner, together with a significant history of the origins of the approach.

2.4 ON MINIMAX OBSERVATION PROBLEMS UNDER UNCERTAINTY WITH PERTURBATIONS

In the early stages of mathematical modeling of control problems involving state variables that can be changed by means of control variables it was generally assumed that exact and complete state measurements could be obtained. It was soon learned that the optimal behavior of a dynamical system under uncertainty cannot be effectively obtained without having an observation system capable of identifying unknown parameters of the underlying dynamical system.

Generally, the problem of estimation occurring in nondeterministic systems has been investigated by means of many stochastic models, beginning with the papers of Wiener [65] and Kalman [35]. Earlier in the 1970s, nonstochastic observation models ('minimax', 'guaranteed') under uncertainty appeared in [9], [43] and [44]. In [21] a new approach for optimization of linear dynamical systems under uncertainty was presented based on the earlier fundamental papers of Gabasov, Kirillova and colleagues [19–21, 42].

This approach to treating uncertainty is in contrast to other *qualitative* approaches, for example, based on stochastic differential equations. In the latter case certain mathematical assumptions are made about the underlying stochastic processes which may be difficult to verify in real situations, for example, in the financial derivatives and assets markets.

Effective computational algorithms are needed for solving problems where estimates of a control mechanism are available based upon sensor observations. There are at least two major extremal problems that must be addressed in order to solve such classes of optimal observation problems. Termed the *program problem*, this model must be solved in order to generate estimates for the underlying linear dynamical system. This problem is solved after all observations are made, and the solution is helpful in understanding the structure of the underlying linear dynamical system. But in practice real-time estimates are needed of the dynamical system, so another type of optimal observation problem arises, termed the *positional problem*. Solving this problem provides estimates of the unknown system parameters in a real-time regime while providing the additional benefit of being able to construct parameter estimates adaptively and continuously as new information from the sensor is received.

During the last 30 years computational methods have been developed that take advantage of the structure of both of these types of problems by employing semi-infinite programming algorithms. Semi-infinite programming optimization models are a next level of extension of ordinary linear programming and have finitely many decision variables appearing in infinitely many constraining inequalities, see [29] and [40]. Algorithmic methods incorporate many properties of the underlying linear control system, such as the classical Cauchy fundamental formula (2.5). The main construction updates the current semi-infinite program optimal solution by taking the previous position as an efficient advanced start. Special rules are based on higher order derivatives and the necessary semi-infinite programming optimality conditions.

Previous uses of ordinary linear programming are extended to more general classes of measurable functions as input disturbances, see [49]–[52].

In this book we will develop more general differential equations modeling than those models that we have presented in our previous sections. These are linear dynamical systems with unknown parameters under nonstochastic uncertainty. A main example of this approach employs actual auction observations from Treasury yield curves, namely observed yields of bonds with either common maturity or differing maturities.

Included in the outputs are the estimated yields to maturity (based on observed yields to maturity), sometimes referred to as the *learning phase* of the process. Observed data are discrete, but stability in the dynamic models is enhanced if we build piecewise continuous extensions of the discrete data. We consider two such extensions: piecewise constant and piecewise linear. We consider *one-factor* dynamical systems where perturbations occur only in the spot rate differential equation and present the results of numerical experiments in tabular and graphical form. We also generate yield estimates from *bilevel* models, where now perturbations are present both for the spot rate and for the piecewise continuous extension of the observed yields.

The basic numerical outputs of the approach are (1) estimated prices of discount bonds, (2) the term structure of interest rates and (3) the predicted future prices of discount bonds. So far we have only worked with US Treasury bond data, but recently in the Ph.D. thesis of Maria Sole Staffa the approach has been applied to the Italian government bond market [61].

We begin by reviewing the basic systems approach from the viewpoint of linear dynamic systems under uncertainty with perturbations.

2.4.1 Minimax Observation Problem under Uncertainty with Perturbations

$$\dot{x} = Ax + Dw(t), \quad x(0) = x_0, \; \forall t, \; t_a \leqslant t \leqslant t_c,$$
$$x_0 \in X_0 = \{x \in \mathbf{R}^n \mid d_* \leqslant x \leqslant d^* \text{ and } g_* \leqslant Gx \leqslant g^*\},$$
$$w(t) \in W(t) = \{w(t) \in \mathbf{R}^l \mid w_* \leqslant w(t) \leqslant w^*\}, \tag{2.17}$$
$$D \in \mathbf{R}^{n \times l}; \; w_*, w^* \in \mathbf{R}^l; \; d_*, d^* \in \mathbf{R}^n; \; g_*, g^* \in \mathbf{R}^m; \; G \in \mathbf{R}^{m \times n}.$$

Associated with (2.17) is the Cauchy fundamental matrix F having the following constructive properties:

$$\dot{F} = AF, \quad F(0) = E, \quad F(t-s) = F(t-p)F(p-s), \quad F(t+s) = F(t)F(s), \quad F^{-1}(t) = F(-t).$$

Throughout this book our common technique will be to construct the form of a solution to system (2.17) by using a more general form of the Cauchy formula presented previously in (2.5), namely

$$x(t) = F(t)x_0 + \int_{t_a}^t F(t)F(-\tau)Dw(\tau) \, d\tau. \tag{2.18}$$

An estimate $\hat{x}(t)$ of the state $x(t)$ of the system (2.17) is obtained from measurements made with a sensor system of the following integral form which is used throughout with varying limits of integration:

$$y(t) = \int_{t_a}^{t} x(\tau)\, d\tau + \epsilon(t), \quad \forall t,\; t_a \leqslant t \leqslant t_b, \text{ where } t_b \leqslant t_c, \tag{2.19}$$

which gives inexact and incomplete information about the current state of system (2.17), where $\epsilon(t)$ is an *unknown* piecewise continuous measurement error function, noting that in general t_a may be a function of t.

Let (2.17), (2.19) represent an observation $y^*(t)$, $t \in T$ with some measurement error $\epsilon^*(t)$, $t \in T$. A measure of the precision of our estimate is the conservative 'minimax' measure of the error, wherein we seek the function $\hat{x}(\cdot)$ according to the following minimax *estimation problem*:

$$\hat{\varepsilon} = \min_{(x,w(\cdot)) \in X_0 \times W(\cdot)} \; \max_{t_a \leqslant t \leqslant t_b} |\varepsilon^*(t)|. \tag{2.20}$$

This problem leads to an **infinite linear program**, see [15] and [29]. First, substitute (2.18) into (2.19) to obtain

$$z^*(t) = y^*(t) - x_0 \int_{t_a}^{t} F(\tau)\, d\tau - \int_{t_a}^{t} F(\tau)\left[\int_{t_a}^{\tau} F(-s)\, Dw(s)\, ds\right] d\tau, \quad \forall t \in [t_a, t_b].$$

The linear structure of (2.20) is seen by rewriting it in the usual equivalent, double inequality form:

$$\min_{(x,w(\cdot)) \in X_0 \times W(\cdot)} \; v \; \text{ subject to}$$

$$y^*(t) \leqslant x \int_{t_a}^{t} F(\tau)\, d\tau - \int_{t_a}^{t} F(\tau)\left[\int_{t_a}^{\tau} F(-s)\, Dw(s)\, ds\right] d\tau + v,$$

$$x \int_{t_a}^{t} F(\tau)\, d\tau - \int_{t_a}^{t} F(\tau)\left[\int_{t_a}^{\tau} F(-s)\, Dw(s)\, ds\right] d\tau - v \leqslant y^*(t), \tag{2.21}$$

$$x \in X_0,\; v \geqslant 0 \text{ and } w(t) \in W(t),\; \forall t \in [t_a, t_b].$$

Our recurring application throughout this book begins with an optimal solution (x^0, w^0, v^0) to (2.21). We obtain an estimate $\hat{x}(\cdot)$ of the state $x(\cdot)$ of the system (2.17) by

$$\hat{x}(t) = x^0 \int_{t_a}^{t} F(\tau)\, d\tau - \int_{t_a}^{t} F(\tau)\left[\int_{t_a}^{\tau} F(-s)\, Dw^0(s)\, ds\right] d\tau, \quad \forall t,\; t_a \leqslant t \leqslant t_c.$$

This estimate gives the minimum of the maximum absolute value v^0 of the measurement error $z(\cdot)$. Problem (2.21) is an infinite linear programming problem. A program algorithm and positional algorithm for (2.20) have been developed by the second author, and we apply these algorithms in our numerical study.

Consistently throughout this book we shall be formulating linear differential equations models under nonstochastic uncertainty with perturbations based on wide classes of fixed income financial modeling that have appeared in the literature for over 25 years.

2.5   CHAPTER NOTES

This chapter proposes a methodology for modeling economic phenomena as deterministic nonlinear dynamical systems. That title could also be very broadly termed *a quantitative description of reality*. Actually, Rebonato referred to this terminology in [56, p. 249]. The quotation from a passage there represents fairly well the motivation of our nonstochastic uncertainty, dynamical systems approach to the study of the term structure.

"In order to price interest-rate-sensitive instruments one needs a much more quantitative description of reality. A second approach to the model has therefore been developed, which I shall call the 'applied' or, using a term borrowed from the physical sciences, the 'phenomenological' approach. In this approach, one presumes to have correctly identified the general structure of the laws governing a given phenomenon (in this case, the dynamics of the yield curve), but one recognises that the detailed knowledge of how its parameters could be arrived at *ab initio* (i.e. from more fundamental quantities, such as the utility function) is still not available. One therefore resorts to fitting free parameters of the model to known observable quantities (for instance the yield curve) in the hope that if the original choice of the model functional form and structure were correct, of obtaining 'empirically' those quantities that cannot be computed directly."

It is fruitful to take a quotation from Paul Wilmott's book [67]. See also Epstein and Wilmott [15].

'What Do I Want From an Interest Rate Model?'

- As few factors as possible, to model any realistic yield curve.
- Easy to price many products quickly.
- Insensitivity of results to hard-to-measure parameters, such as volatilities and correlations.
- Robustness in general.
- Sensible fitting to data.
- Strategy for hedging.

Table 2.1   Comparison of SDE-derived properties with dynamical systems under nonstochastic uncertainty with pertubations

Item	Stochastic	Dynamic
Type of uncertainty	Stochastic process	Unknown function of class of pertubations
Model for spot rate	Stochastic differential equation	DE with nonstochastic uncertainty
Norm of uncertainty	Probabilistic expectation	Minimax L_∞: sum squares L_2
Nonarbitrage condition	Risk-free measure	Constraints in observation problem and nonarbitrage necessary condition
Moments of uncertainty	Drift and volatility	Mean path max/min realized pertubations; minimax amplitude
Other features	Computing non-negative spot and forward rates not always possible	Additional constraints alleviate problem

The basic numerical outputs of the approach are (1) estimated prices of discount bonds, (2) the term structure of interest rates and (3) the predicted future prices of discount bonds or the structure of forward rates. So far we have worked with US Treasury bills, notes and bond data, but recently in the Ph.D. thesis of Maria Sole Staffa of La Sapienza University in Rome, Italy the approach has been investigated with application to the Italian government bond market [61].

It is hoped that the reader of this book will come to an independent judgement as to how close we meet these interesting goals, which allegedly have arisen 'after conversations with many practitioners' [67, p. 660]. We will provide some extra assistance later on.

In summary, our approach to the study of the term structure and eventual pricing of financial derivatives is quantitative, almost in some sense 'data mining', although we employ much more structure than is associated with that term. In a real sense we construct analogous concepts to the stochastic case by proposing a dynamical systems approach under uncertainty with perturbations. Table 2.1 illustrates the analogies.

3

Constant Maturity, One-factor Dynamic Models for Term Structure Estimation

The point of departure for constructing analogous linear dynamical systems models for fixed income instruments is the classical model of Vasicek [63] where the standard Brownian motion Z underlies the stochastic differential equation, and where α, β and σ are parameters, see [2], [8], [22], [37] and [64]:

$$dr = (\alpha + \beta r)\,dt + \sigma\,dZ, \tag{3.1}$$

where r denotes the *spot rate*, usually referred to as the shortest term riskless rate of interest, and the parameters are employed to capture shifts and volatilities of this rate [8]. We associate with (3.1) the following *linear differential equation under uncertainty* which is an instance of our general model (2.17):

$$\dot{r} = \beta r + \alpha + \sigma w(t), \quad r(0) = r_0 \in R_0 = \{r \in R, r_* \leqslant r \leqslant r^*\};$$
$$w_* \leqslant w(t) \leqslant w^*, \ t \in [0, t^*]. \tag{3.2}$$

Here $w(\cdot) = (w(t), t \in [0, t^*])$ is an unknown function for which we seek a solution. We shall term (3.2) the *linear differential systems analog* of the given stochastic system.

For simplicity we assume that the values of $r(t)$, $t \in [0, t^*]$ can be measured with some piecewise continuous error function $\varepsilon(t)$ defined in an observation model as follows:

$$y(t) = r(t) + \varepsilon(t), \tag{3.3}$$

and consider more 'realistic' observation functions in later chapters. Now, compute the estimates of r_0 and $w(\cdot)$ according to minimax estimation based on our earlier presentation (2.20):

$$\hat{\varepsilon} = \min_{x \in R_0, w_* \leqslant w(\cdot) \leqslant w^*} \ \max_{t \in [0, t^*]} |\varepsilon(t)|. \tag{3.4}$$

Following our method, we obtain the following **infinite linear program** [15, 29]:

min v subject to

$$y(t) + \frac{\alpha}{\beta}(1 - e^{\beta t}) \leqslant e^{\beta t} x + \sigma \int_0^t e^{\beta(t-\tau)} w(\tau)\,d\tau + v,$$

$$e^{\beta t} x + \sigma \int_0^t e^{\beta(t-\tau)} w(\tau)\,d\tau - v \leqslant y(t) + \frac{\alpha}{\beta}(1 - e^{\beta t}), \tag{3.5}$$

$$v \geqslant 0, \ r_* \leqslant x \leqslant r^* \text{ and } w_{i*} \leqslant w(t) \leqslant w_i^*, \ \forall t \in [0, t^*].$$

3.1   A COMMON SPECIFICATION OF TIME INTERVALS AND THEIR SUBINTERVALS

Definition 3.1   *Throughout this book T_i shall denote the specific time interval $[t_{i-1}, t_i]$. In addition we shall use the following notation for other intervals for integers $i, j; j \leqslant i$:*

$$T_{i,j} = [t_{i-j}, t_i] \quad \text{and} \quad T^i = [t_0, t_i].$$

For a positive integer N define

$$T^N = \bigcup_{i=1}^{N} T_i = [t_0, t_N] \quad \text{and} \quad \tilde{T}^N = \bigcup_{i=0}^{N} \{t_i\}. \tag{3.6}$$

$T^N \backslash \tilde{T}^N$ *denotes those points in T^N not in $\tilde{T}^N$.*

We approximate the unknown perturbation function $w(\cdot)$ either by point-impulse perturbations (Section 2.2.1) or by impulse perturbations (Section 2.2.2) using the definition of T^N, (3.6). We will return to the specifications later.

Anticipating actual market experience we can obtain the values of a measurement signal once a day. For example, the values of Treasury yield curve rates are updated daily, usually by 5:30 PM Eastern time. So we can assume, for example, that a measurement signal (3.3) is a piecewise-constant function. The actual form of formulation (3.5) will depend upon which class of perturbation functions $w(\cdot)$ we choose, point-impulse (Section 2.2.1) or impulse (Section 2.2.2), as we shall see in later sections.

3.2   DEFINITIONS OF PARAMETER SPACES AND ADMISSIBLE SPOT RATE FUNCTIONS

We have been motivated by the introductory models of Chapter 2 whose solutions suggested the kinds of mathematical properties we should require for admissibility to more general classes of dynamical models. The representation of asset prices according to (2.10) is a case in point.

In order to construct various types of linear dynamical systems corresponding to different models of the term structure of interest rates we specify admissible parameters and spot rate functions next.

Definition 3.2   *Let T^N be chosen according to (3.6). Introduce*

$$\Omega = \{\omega \in \mathbf{R}^{N'}: g_j(\omega) = 0, j = \overline{1, l}; g_j(\omega) \leqslant 0, j = \overline{l+1, m};$$
$$\omega_{i*} \leqslant \omega \leqslant \omega_i^*, i = \overline{1, L}\}, \text{ where } N' \text{ and } N \text{ are integers}, N' \geqslant N. \tag{3.7}$$

We shall term Ω the a priori distribution of unknown parameters. The functions $g_j(\omega)$, $j = \overline{1, m}$ are twice continuously differentiable, with some number of them, l, generating equality constraints and others generating inequality constraints.

In Chapter 1 we defined both discrete and continuous forms of the spot rate. Now we become more specific about what the candidate functions can be for these entities.

Assumption 3.1   ***Spot Rate Representations.*** *Let $\Re(t)$ be a family of functions defined by*

$$\Re(t) = \{h(t, \omega), \omega \in \Omega\}, \ t \in T^N; \tag{3.8}$$

where

1. $h(t, \omega)$ *is twice continuously differentiable for every* $t \in T^N$;
2. $h(t, \omega)$ *is piecewise continuous for every* $\omega \in \Omega$;
3. $h(t, \omega)$ *is twice continuously differentiable inside intervals of continuity for every* $\omega \in \Omega$.

Assume that the behavior of the spot rate $r(\cdot|\omega)$ *(for each fixed* $\omega \in \Omega$*) can be described by the following relations:*

$$r(t|\omega) = h(t, \omega), \ t \in [t_0, t_N], \omega \in \Omega. \tag{3.9}$$

The form of $h(\cdot, \cdot)$ depends on the type of model used for the term structure of interest rates, for example, the type of differential equation governing the spot rate and the class of the perturbations acting on the model. The set Ω describes the unknown parameters of the linear differential systems model (3.2), such as the initial state of the spot rate and the coefficients in the system together with the values of the perturbations acting on the model.

We have been assuming throughout that the price of a discount bond is determined by the current assessment of spot rate trajectory over the term of the bond, for example, see [63, (A.2)].

Assumption 3.2 *The price* $P(t, T)$, $t < T$, *of a discount bond is determined by the assessment at time t of the segment* $\{r(\tau|\omega), t \leqslant \tau \leqslant T\}$ *of the parameterized spot rate curve over the term of the bond.*

Clearly for fixed T, Ω and $h(\cdot, \cdot)$, we can construct a family of trajectories of prices and a family of trajectories of yields of a discount bond from the implied forward rates curve, (1.62).

A basic question addressed throughout this book is how to choose a function $r^0(t) = h(t, \omega^0)$, $t \in T^N$ (3.6), $\omega^0 \in \Omega$, for the purpose of modeling the behavior of a real market. For example, one fruitful answer is to estimate the values of ω^0 by taking observations of Treasury yield curve rates: bills, notes or bonds.

3.3 MODELING BONDS HAVING COMMON MATURITY FOR YIELD ESTIMATION

Assume that we have observed values of the yield to maturity over the interval T^M (3.6), namely $\hat{R}(t, t + T)$, $t \in T^M = [t_0, t_M]$, for some fixed time-to-maturity T during M days.

Since the interval T_i is the ith day of the observation period, the current moment of time is the last day of the observation period, namely t_M.

3.3.1 Observation Models and Parameter Admissible Yields

Definition 3.3 *Let* $R_i^{(T)}$, $i = \overline{0, M}$, *denote the observed Treasury yield (or other data series) with time-to-maturity* T *corresponding to the ith day of observation. By an observation model we mean a specified function constructed from observed data. Two principal functional forms appearing throughout this book are the following.*

Piecewise constant observation model

$$\hat{R}(t, t+T) = R_i^{(T)}, \quad t \in [t_{i-1}, t_i[, \ i = \overline{1, M}. \tag{3.10}$$

Piecewise linear observation model

$$\hat{R}(t, t+T) = R_{i-1}^{(T)} + \frac{t - t_{i-1}}{t_i - t_{i-1}}(R_i^{(T)} - R_{i-1}^{(T)}), \quad t \in T_i, i = \overline{1, M}. \tag{3.11}$$

The models are employed to define the observed yield function.

Depending on which observation model is chosen, we can introduce a measure of error once we define a class of admissible yields. We do both next.

Definition 3.4 *By the Ω-parameter-admissible yield we shall mean the averaged integral*

$$y(t, \omega | T) = \frac{1}{T} \int_t^{t+T} h(\tau, \omega) \, d\tau, \quad t \in T^M, \omega \in \Omega. \tag{3.12}$$

By the interval of definition of the spot rate we shall mean T^N, where $N = M + T$. The estimation error is the difference

$$\varepsilon(t, \omega) = y(t, \omega | T) - \hat{R}(t, t+T), \quad t \in T^M, \omega \in \Omega. \tag{3.13}$$

We compute an estimate ω^0 of unknown parameters ω by minimizing over $\omega \in \Omega$ the maximum absolute value of the function of estimation errors $\varepsilon(t, \omega)$ on the interval T^M. This leads to the following problem:

$$\varepsilon^* = \min_{\omega \in \Omega} \max_{t \in T^M} |\varepsilon(t, \omega)|. \tag{3.14}$$

Problem (3.14) may be written as the following minimax estimation problem (actually, a nonlinear semi-infinite programming problem, see [29]):

min v_T subject to
$$y(t, \omega | T) - v_T \leqslant \hat{R}(t, t+T), \quad \hat{R}(t, t+T) \leqslant y(t, \omega | T) + v_T, \quad t \in T^M; \tag{3.15}$$
$$\omega \in \Omega, v_T \geqslant 0.$$

We shall call problem (3.15) the T-*constant maturity yield minimax estimation problem.* We indicate that we are treating the constant-time-to-maturity case by having T as a subscript when applicable.

Let (ω^0, v_T^0) be an optimal solution to problem (3.15). Then the function

$$r_T(t) = h(t, \omega^0), \quad t \in T^N, N = M + T \tag{3.16}$$

will be *an estimate of the spot rate* over the observation period T^M. Over the future period $T^N \setminus T^M$ (3.16) becomes a forecast of the spot rate, an extra benefit from solving (3.15). (Note that T is not notationally 'tau' τ.)

Additional constraints on the spot rate may be readily adjoined to problem (3.15). For example

$$z_* \leqslant h(t, \omega) \leqslant z^*, \forall t \in T^N, \omega \in \Omega,$$

see (3.8). 'Box' constraints of this type may be used to guarantee non-negativity of the spot rate, i.e. $h(t, \omega) \geqslant 0, \forall t \in T^N, \omega \in \Omega$, see (6.4).

We shall call the function $r_T(\cdot)$ defined by (3.16) the T-*constant maturity-based spot rate minimax estimate*. It follows from (1.62) that the function

$$P(t, s) = \exp\left(- \int_t^s r_T(\tau)\,d\tau \right), \ t \in [t_0, t_M], s \in [t, t_N] \tag{3.17}$$

will be an estimate of the price at time t of a discount bond maturing at time s.

Definition 3.5 *If the function $h(t, \omega^0)$ is defined over the future time $t \in [t_N, t_Q]$, where Q is an operating horizon, that is, an integer satisfying $M + T < Q$, then the forecasted price of a discount bond maturing at time s is given by*

$$\tilde{P}(t, s) = \exp\left(- \int_t^s r_T(\tau)\,d\tau \right), \ \text{for any future time } t \in [t_M, t_Q], \text{ any } s \in [t, t_Q] \tag{3.18}$$

and the forecasted yield is

$$\tilde{R}(t, s) = \frac{1}{s - t} \int_t^s r_T(\tau)\,d\tau, \ t \in [t_M, t_Q], s \in [t, t_Q] \tag{3.19}$$

at time t of a discount bond maturing at time s.

In general we cannot guarantee a global extremum of problem (3.15), but we can analyze the computed solution, for example, by the following procedure. If the optimal solution yields a cost value equal to half the maximal jump of the observed yield to maturity, then the computed solution is globally optimal for problem (3.15).

3.3.2   Vasicek-type Spot Rate Estimation Model Using Impulse Perturbations

We return to the differential equation model (3.2) for a more detailed study of the structure of its solution and how it may be used in practice. Assume that the spot rate is governed by the following linear dynamic system with unknown parameters and nonstochastic uncertainty:

$$\dot{r} = \alpha + \beta r(t) + w(t), \ \beta \neq 0, r(t_0) = r_0; \ t \in T^N. \tag{3.20}$$

Assume that a priori information about the unknown parameters of the linear differential system (3.20) takes the form

$$\alpha_* \leqslant \alpha \leqslant \alpha^*, \ \beta_* \leqslant \beta \leqslant \beta^*, \ r_* \leqslant r_0 \leqslant r^* \tag{3.21}$$

and that the perturbations $w(\cdot)$ are of the *impulse* form as introduced in Definition 2.2, that is

$$w(t) = w_i, \ w_{i*} \leqslant w_i \leqslant w_i^*, \ t \in T_i, i = \overline{1, N}. \tag{3.22}$$

It follows from (3.7) and (3.8) that for model (3.20)–(3.22) we have

$$\omega = (r_0, \alpha, \beta, w_i, i = \overline{1, N}); \ \omega_* = (r_*, \alpha_*, \beta_*, w_{i*}, i = \overline{1, N});$$
$$\omega^* = (r^*, \alpha^*, \beta^*, w_i^*, i = \overline{1, N});$$
$$\Omega = \{\omega \in \mathbf{R}^{N+3}: \omega_* \leqslant \omega \leqslant \omega^*\}. \tag{3.23}$$

Note that the unknown parameters determining the perturbations are included in the 'list' ω.

By means of the Cauchy formula (2.5), (2.6), the solution of the differential equation (3.20) has the form

$$
r(t|\omega) = e^{\beta t} r_0 + \frac{\alpha}{\beta}(e^{\beta t} - 1) + \sum_{j=1}^{i-1} w_j \frac{e^{\beta t}}{\beta}(e^{-\beta t_{j-1}} - e^{-\beta t_j}) + w_i \frac{1}{\beta}(e^{\beta(t - t_{i-1})} - 1),
$$
$$
t \in T_i, \; i = \overline{1, N}. \tag{3.24}
$$

In this way we have specified a member of the family Ω, see Assumption 3.1, namely

$$
h(t, \omega) = r(t|\omega), \quad t \in T^N, \omega \in \Omega. \tag{3.25}
$$

We derive an explicit form of problem (3.15), by first specifying the special function $y(t, \omega | T)$, $t \in T_i$, $i = \overline{1, M}$ (3.12). We proceed as follows, recalling that T is the time-to-maturity:

$$
\begin{aligned}
y(t, \omega | T) &= \frac{1}{T} \int_t^{t+T} h(\tau, \omega) \, d\tau = \frac{1}{T} \Bigg[r_0 \int_t^{t+T} e^{\beta \tau} \, d\tau + \frac{\alpha}{\beta} \int_t^{t+T} (e^{\beta \tau} - 1) \, d\tau \\
&\quad + \int_T^{t_i} \left(\sum_{k=1}^{i-1} w_k \frac{e^{\beta \tau}}{\beta}(e^{-\beta t_{k-1}} - e^{-\beta t_k}) + w_i \frac{e^{\beta(\tau - t_{i-1})} - 1}{\beta} \right) d\tau \\
&\quad + \sum_{j=i+1}^{i+T-1} \int_{t_{j-1}}^{t_j} \left(\sum_{k=1}^{j-1} w_k \frac{e^{\beta \tau}}{\beta}(e^{-\beta t_{k-1}} - e^{-\beta t_k}) + w_j \frac{e^{\beta(\tau - t_{j-1})} - 1}{\beta} \right) d\tau \\
&\quad + \int_{t_{i+T-1}}^{t+T} \left(\sum_{k=1}^{i+T-1} w_k \frac{e^{\beta \tau}}{\beta}(e^{-\beta t_{k-1}} - e^{-\beta t_k}) + w_{i+T} \frac{e^{\beta(\tau - t_{i+T-1})} - 1}{\beta} \right) d\tau \Bigg] \\
&= \frac{1}{T} \Bigg[\frac{e^{\beta(t+T)} - e^{\beta t}}{\beta} r_0 + \left(\frac{e^{\beta(t+T)} - e^{\beta t}}{\beta^2} - \frac{T}{\beta} \right) \alpha + \sum_{k=1}^{i-1} \frac{e^{-\beta t_{k-1}} - e^{-\beta t_k}}{\beta} w_k \int_t^{t+T} e^{\beta \tau} \, d\tau \\
&\quad + \left(\frac{1}{\beta} \int_t^{t_i} (e^{\beta(\tau - t_{i-1})} - 1) \, d\tau + \frac{e^{-\beta t_{i-1}} - e^{-\beta t_i}}{\beta} \int_{t_i}^{t+T} e^{\beta \tau} \, d\tau \right) w_i \\
&\quad + \sum_{k=i+1}^{i+T-1} \left(\frac{1}{\beta} \int_{t_{k-1}}^{t_k} (e^{\beta(\tau - t_{k-1})} - 1) \, d\tau + \frac{e^{-\beta t_{k-1}} - e^{-\beta t_k}}{\beta} \int_{t_k}^{t+T} e^{\beta \tau} \, d\tau \right) w_k \\
&\quad + \frac{1}{\beta} \int_{t_{i+T-1}}^{t+T} (e^{\beta(\tau - t_{i+T-1})} - 1) w_{i+T} \, d\tau \Bigg] \\
&= \frac{e^{\beta(t+T)} - e^{\beta t}}{T\beta} r_0 + \left(\frac{e^{\beta(t+T)} - e^{\beta t}}{T\beta^2} - \frac{1}{\beta} \right) \alpha \\
&\quad + \sum_{k=1}^{i-1} \frac{e^{\beta(t - t_{k-1} + T)} - e^{\beta(t - t_k + T)} + e^{\beta(t - t_k)} - e^{\beta(t - t_{k-1})}}{T\beta^2} w_k \\
&\quad + \left(\frac{e^{\beta(t - t_{i-1} + T)} - e^{\beta(t - t_i + T)} - e^{\beta(t - t_{i-1})} + 1}{T\beta^2} - \frac{t_i - t}{T\beta} \right) w_i \\
&\quad + \sum_{k=i+1}^{i+T-1} \left(\frac{e^{\beta(t - t_{k-1} + T)} - e^{\beta(t - t_k + T)}}{T\beta^2} - \frac{t_k - t_{k-1}}{T\beta} \right) w_k \\
&\quad + \left(\frac{e^{\beta(t - t_{i+T-1} + T)} - 1}{T\beta^2} - \frac{t - t_{i+T-1} + T}{T\beta} \right) w_{i+T}, \quad t \in T_i. \tag{3.26}
\end{aligned}
$$

Let

$$a_k^i(\beta, t \mid T) = \begin{cases} \dfrac{e^{\beta(t-t_{k-1}+T)} - e^{\beta(t-t_k+T)} + e^{\beta(t-t_k)} - e^{\beta(t-t_{k-1})}}{T\beta^2} & \text{if } k < i, \\[3mm] \dfrac{e^{\beta(t-t_{k-1}+T)} - e^{\beta(t-t_k+T)} - e^{\beta(t-t_{k-1})} + 1}{T\beta^2} - \dfrac{t_k - t}{T\beta} & \text{if } k = i, \\[3mm] \dfrac{e^{\beta(t-t_{k-1}+T)} - e^{\beta(t-t_k+T)}}{T\beta^2} - \dfrac{t_k - t_{k-1}}{T\beta} & \text{if } i < k < i+T, \\[3mm] \dfrac{e^{\beta(t-t_{k-1}+T)} - 1}{T\beta^2} - \dfrac{t - t_{k-1} + T}{T\beta} & \text{if } k = i+T. \end{cases} \tag{3.27}$$

From (3.15)–(3.27) we obtain the following optimization problem, which we term the *constant maturity-based, impulse perturbation spot rate estimation problem*:

min v_T subject to

$$\frac{e^{\beta(t+T)} - e^{\beta t}}{T\beta} r_0 + \left(\frac{e^{\beta(t+T)} - e^{\beta t}}{T\beta^2} - \frac{1}{\beta} \right) \alpha + \sum_{k=1}^{i+T} a_k^i(\beta, t \mid T) w_k - v_T \leqslant \hat{R}(t, t+T),$$

$$\hat{R}(t, t+T) \leqslant \frac{e^{\beta(t+T)} - e^{\beta t}}{T\beta} r_0 + \left(\frac{e^{\beta(t+T)} - e^{\beta t}}{T\beta^2} - \frac{1}{\beta} \right) \alpha + \sum_{k=1}^{i+T} a_k^i(\beta, t \mid T) w_k + v_T,$$

$$t \in T_i, \ i = \overline{1, M}; \tag{3.28}$$

$$\alpha_* \leqslant \alpha \leqslant \alpha^*, \ \beta_* \leqslant \beta \leqslant \beta^*, \ r_* \leqslant r_0 \leqslant r^*, \ v \geqslant 0;$$

$$w_* \leqslant w_i \leqslant w^*, \ i = \overline{1, N}.$$

Let (ω^0, v_T^0) be an optimal solution to problem (3.28). It follows that the function

$$r_T(t) = r(t \mid \omega^0), \ t \in T^M$$

will be the associated problem (3.28)-based spot rate forecast. From (3.24) it follows that for some $Q > N$ we have

$$r_T(t) = e^{\beta^0 t} r_0^0 + \frac{\alpha^0}{\beta^0}(e^{\beta^0 t} - 1) + \sum_{j=1}^{N} w_j^0 \frac{e^{\beta^0 t}}{\beta^0}(e^{-\beta^0 t_{j-1}} - e^{-\beta^0 t_j}),$$

$$t \in T_i, \ i = \overline{N+1, Q}.$$

Hence we obtain a forecast of prices and a forecast of yields by means of (3.18), (3.19) for any points t and s, $t \in [0, t_Q]$ and $s \in [t, t_P]$. As a rule, in the theory of the term structure of interest rates the price of a bond has the following form:

$$P(t, s) = \exp\{A(t, s) + r(t) B(t, s)\}, \ t \leqslant s, \tag{3.29}$$

with $A(0, 0) = 0$ and $B(0, 0) = 0$.

Theorem 3.1 *Vasicek-type Model with Impulse Perturbations. From (1.62) and (3.24) we obtain the following forms of $A(t, s)$ and $B(t, s)$:*

$$B(t, s) = \frac{1 - e^{\beta(s-t)}}{\beta}, \quad A(t, s) = \frac{\alpha}{\beta}[(s - t) + B(t, s)]$$

$$+ \left(\frac{e^{\beta s}}{\beta}(e^{\beta t_i} - e^{-\beta t}) + t_i - t \right)\frac{w_i}{\beta} - \sum_{k=i+1}^{j-1}\left(\frac{e^{\beta s}}{\beta}(e^{-\beta t_{k-1}} - e^{-\beta t_k}) - (t_k - t_{k-1}) \right)\frac{w_k}{\beta}$$

$$- \frac{w_i}{\beta}\left(\frac{e^{\beta(s-t_{j-1})} - 1}{\beta} - (s - t_{j-1}) \right), \quad t \in T_l, s \in T_j \text{ and } i \leqslant j.$$

Proof.

Case 1 $t \in T_i, s \in T_j, i \leqslant j$.

$$P(t, s) = \exp\left\{ -\int_t^s r(\tau)\, d\tau \right\} = \exp\left\{ -\frac{e^{\beta s} - e^{\beta t}}{\beta}r_0 - \frac{\alpha}{\beta}\left(\frac{e^{\beta s} - e^{\beta t}}{\beta} - (s - t) \right) \right.$$

$$- \sum_{k=1}^{i-1}\frac{e^{\beta(s-t_{k-1})} - e^{\beta(s-t_k)} + e^{\beta(t-t_k)} - e^{\beta(t-t_{k-1})}}{\beta^2}w_k$$

$$- \left(\frac{e^{\beta(s-t_{i-1})} - e^{\beta(s-t_i)} - e^{\beta(t-t_{i-1})} + 1}{\beta^2} - \frac{t_i - t}{\beta} \right)w_k$$

$$- \sum_{k=i+1}^{j-1}\left(\frac{e^{\beta(s-t_{k-1})} - e^{\beta(s-t_k)}}{\beta^2} - \frac{t_k - t_{k-1}}{\beta} \right)w_k - \left(\frac{e^{\beta(s-t_{j-1})} - 1}{\beta^2} - \frac{s - t_{j-1}}{\beta} \right)w_i \Bigg\}$$

$$= \exp\left\{ \frac{1 - e^{\beta(s-t)}}{\beta}\left(e^{\beta t}r_0 + \frac{\alpha}{\beta}(e^{\beta t} - 1) + \frac{e^{\beta t}}{\beta}\sum_{k=1}^{i-1}(e^{-\beta t_{k-1}} - e^{-\beta t_k})w_k + w_i\frac{e^{\beta(t-t_{i-1})} - 1}{\beta} \right) \right.$$

$$+ \frac{e^{\beta(s-t_i)} - e^{\beta(s-t)}}{\beta^2}w_i + \frac{t_i - t}{\beta}w_i - \sum_{k=i+1}^{j-1}\left(\frac{e^{\beta(s-t_{k-1})} - e^{\beta(s-t_k)}}{\beta^2} - \frac{t_k - t_{k-1}}{\beta} \right)w_k$$

$$- \left(\frac{e^{\beta(s-t_{j-1})} - 1}{\beta^2} - \frac{s - t_{j-1}}{\beta} \right)w_j + \frac{\alpha}{\beta}(s - t) \Bigg\}$$

$$= \exp\left\{ \frac{1 - e^{\beta(s-t)}}{\beta}r(t) + \frac{\alpha}{\beta}(s - t) + \frac{\alpha}{\beta}\frac{1 - e^{\beta(s-t)}}{\beta} + \left(\frac{e^{\beta s}}{\beta^2}(e^{\beta t_i} - e^{-\beta t}) + \frac{t_i - t}{\beta} \right)w_i \right.$$

$$- \sum_{k=i+1}^{j-1}\left(\frac{e^{\beta s}}{\beta}\left(\frac{e^{-\beta t_{k-1}} - e^{-\beta t_k}}{\beta} \right) - (t_k - t_{k-1}) \right)\frac{w_k}{\beta} - \left(\frac{e^{\beta(s-t_{j-1})} - 1}{\beta} - (s - t_{j-1}) \right)\frac{w_j}{\beta} \Bigg\}.$$

Denote

$$B(t, s) = \frac{1 - e^{\beta(s-t)}}{\beta}, \quad A(t, s) = \frac{\alpha}{\beta}(s - t + B(t, s))$$

$$+ \left(\frac{e^{\beta s}}{\beta}(e^{\beta t_i} - e^{-\beta t}) + t_i - t \right)\frac{w_i}{\beta} - \sum_{k=i+1}^{j-1}\left(\frac{e^{\beta s}}{\beta}(e^{-\beta t_{k-1}} - e^{-\beta t_k}) - (t_k - t_{k-1}) \right)\frac{w_k}{\beta}$$

$$- \left(\frac{e^{\beta(s-t_{j-1})} - 1}{\beta} - (s - t_{j-1}) \right)\frac{w_j}{\beta}.$$

Hence it follows that (3.29) holds.

Case 2 $t \in T_i$, $s \in T_j$, $i = j \leqslant N$.

$$P(t, s) = \exp\left\{-\int_t^s r(\tau)\,d\tau\right\} = \exp\left\{-\frac{e^{\beta s} - e^{\beta t}}{\beta}r_0 - \frac{\alpha}{\beta}\left(\frac{e^{\beta s} - e^{\beta t}}{\beta} - (s - t)\right)\right.$$

$$-\sum_{k=1}^{i-1}\frac{e^{\beta(s-t_{k-1})} - e^{\beta(s-t_k)} + e^{\beta(t-t_k)} - e^{\beta(t-t_{k-1})}}{\beta^2}w_k$$

$$\left.-\left(\frac{-e^{\beta(t-t_{i-1})} + e^{\beta(s-t_{i-1})}}{\beta^2} - \frac{s-t}{\beta}\right)w_i\right\}$$

$$= \exp\left\{\frac{1 - e^{\beta(s-t)}}{\beta}\left(e^{\beta t}r_0 + \frac{\alpha}{\beta}(e^{\beta t} - 1) + \frac{1}{\beta}\sum_{k=1}^{i-1}(e^{\beta(t-t_{k-1})} - e^{\beta(t-t_k)})w_k + \frac{w_i}{\beta}(e^{\beta(t-t_{i-1})} - 1)\right)\right.$$

$$\left.+ \frac{\alpha}{\beta}(s - t) + \frac{\alpha}{\beta}\frac{1 - e^{\beta(s-t)}}{\beta} + \frac{s-t}{\beta}w_i + \frac{w_i}{\beta}\frac{1 - e^{\beta(s-t)}}{\beta}\right\}$$

$$= \exp\left\{\frac{1 - e^{\beta(s-t)}}{\beta}r(t) + \left(\frac{1 - e^{\beta(s-t)}}{\beta} + s - t\right)\left(\frac{\alpha}{\beta} + \frac{w_i}{\beta}\right)\right\}.$$

Set $B(t, s) = (1 - e^{\beta(s-t)})/\beta$, implying that $A(t, s) - (B(t, s) \mid s - t)((\alpha/\beta) + (w_i/\beta))$.

Case 3 $t \in T_i$, $s \in T_j$, $i > N$.

$$P(t, s) = \exp\left\{-\int_t^s r(\tau)\,d\tau\right\} = -\frac{e^{\beta s} - e^{\beta t}}{\beta}r_0 - \frac{\alpha}{\beta}\left(\frac{e^{\beta s} - e^{\beta t}}{\beta} - (s - t)\right)$$

$$-\sum_{k=1}^{N}\frac{e^{\beta(s-t_{k-1})} - e^{\beta(s-t_k)} - e^{\beta(t-t_k)} - e^{\beta(t-t_{k-1})}}{\beta^2}w_k$$

$$= \exp\left\{\frac{1 - e^{\beta(s-t)}}{\beta}\left(e^{\beta t}r_0 + \frac{\alpha}{\beta}(e^{\beta t} - 1) + \sum_{k=1}^{N}(e^{\beta(t-t_{k-1})} - e^{\beta(t-t_k)})w_k\right)\right.$$

$$\left.+ \frac{\alpha}{\beta}(s - t) + \frac{\alpha}{\beta}\frac{1 - e^{\beta(s-t)}}{\beta}\right\} = \exp\left\{\frac{1 - e^{\beta(s-t)}}{\beta}r(t) + \frac{\alpha}{\beta}\left(\frac{1 - e^{\beta(s-t)}}{\beta} + s - t\right)\right\}.$$

Let $B(t, s) = (1 - e^{\beta(s-t)})/\beta$; then $A(t, s) = (\alpha/\beta)(s - t + B(t, s))$.   □

Numerical Results with Impulse Perturbations

In Table 3.1 we use the following legend. We shall use this legend in reporting all of our numerical results.

- ITER — number of iterations for solving support problems.
- NFUN — number of times the objective and the constraint functions are evaluated during solving support problems.
- NGRAD — number of times the gradients of the objective and the constraint functions are evaluated during the support problems.
- NQP — number of QP subproblems solved during the support problems.
- ACCSP — stopping tolerance for solving the support problems.
- NSP — number of support problems solved.

Table 3.1 Vasicek-type model with impulse perturbations under (3.28) and (3.10)

NPROB	4.1	4.2	4.3	4.4	4.5
β_0	-0.1	-0.5	-1.0	-1.5	-5.0
r_0^0	0.4672776	0.130256	0.136899	0.132424	0.163735
α^0	1.193621	2.401215	4.190845	4.453236	9.8241185
β^0	-0.2326357	-0.474331	-0.832853	-0.885401	-1.960342
$-\alpha^0/\beta^0$	5.130859	5.062310	5.031914	5.029626	5.011431
v_T^0	0.045	0.045	0.045	0.045	0.045
ITER	30	36	29	30	37
NFUN	30	38	29	30	37
NQP	30	36	29	30	37
NGRAD	30	36	29	30	37
ACCSP	10^{-5}	10^{-5}	10^{-7}	10^{-7}	10^{-7}
NSP	3	2	2	2	2
NCONSP	174	125	125	125	125
CPU (s)	376.8	415.43	325.78	370.04	385.05

- NCONFP—maximum number of constraints in the generated support problems.
- CPU—elapsed CPU using a PC PENTIUM 120, coding in BORLAND PASCAL 6.0.
- NPROB—number of the problem.

Example 3.1 *For testing our approach we considered the observed values of Treasury yield rates from 1MAR96 to 31MAR96 for a time-to-maturity of 3 months. We choose (3.10) for the observation model. In this example $M = 31$, $T = 91$, $N = 122$. The following initial point used in (3.15), (3.28) was selected:*

$$\alpha_0 = 0, \quad \beta_0 \text{ as given by problem}, \quad r_0 = 0, \quad v_T^0 = 0; \quad w_k = 0, \, k = \overline{1, N}.$$

The numerical results for five different initial points are given in Table 3.1.

We observe that the problem (3.56) has optimal solutions.

Figures 3.1–3.4 all refer to problem NPROB4.1. Figure 3.1 illustrates the computed estimate $y(\cdot | \cdot)$ of the yield, the observed yield $R(\cdot, \cdot)$ and the computed estimate of the spot rate $r(\cdot)$. Figure 3.2 illustrates the trust region for the estimated yield function. Figure 3.3 illustrates the forecast for the spot rate. Finally, Figure 3.4 illustrates the estimation error for the computed yield function.

3.3.3 Advantages of Using Perturbations

From a numerical point of view the main advantage of introducing perturbations is the reduction of estimation error. We have already seen the trust region for the Vasicek-type model which incorporates impulse perturbations, see Figure 3.2.

Assume that the spot rate follows the following linear dynamical system having no perturbation variables [3, 5, 58]:

$$\dot{r} = \alpha(\gamma - r), \quad r(t_0) = r_0; \quad t \in T^N. \tag{3.30}$$

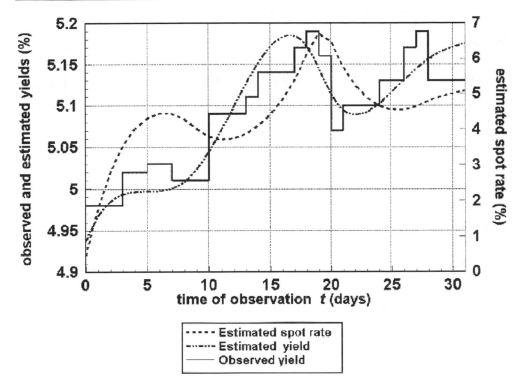

Figure 3.1   Impulse-based estimates: 1MAR–31MAR96 NPROB4.1

A priori information about unknown parameters employed in (3.30) shall take the following form:

$$\omega = (r_0, \alpha, \gamma); \quad \omega_* = (r_*, \alpha_*, \gamma_*); \quad \omega^* = (r^*, \alpha^*, \gamma^*); \quad \Omega = \{\omega \in \mathbf{R}^3 : \omega_* \leqslant \omega \leqslant \omega^*\}.$$

Using the Cauchy formula, the solution of the differential equation (3.30) is

$$r(t\,|\,\omega) = \gamma + (r_0 - \gamma)e^{-\alpha(t-t_0)}, \quad t \in T_i, \quad i = \overline{1, N}. \tag{3.31}$$

Define the function $h(\cdot, \cdot)$ by (3.25) and derive the function $y(t, \omega\,|\,T)$, $t \in T_i$, $i = \overline{1, M}$ according to (3.31) and (3.12). It follows that

$$y(t, \omega\,|\,T) = \frac{1}{T}\int_t^{t+T} h(\tau, \omega)\,d\tau = \frac{1}{T}\int_t^{t+T} (\gamma + (r_0 - \gamma)e^{-\alpha(\tau-t_0)})\,d\tau$$

$$= \gamma + \frac{r_0 - \gamma}{\alpha T}(e^{-\alpha(t-t_0)} - e^{-\alpha(t+T-t_0)}). \tag{3.32}$$

By substituting (3.32) into (3.15) we obtain the following optimization problem for estimating the unknown parameters ω of (3.30):

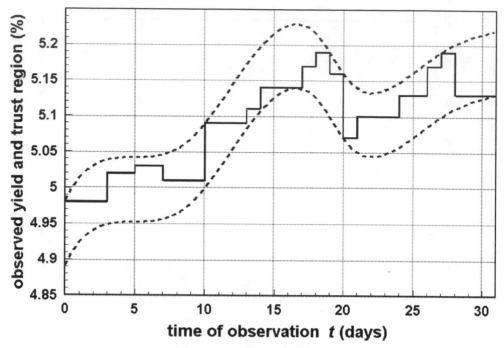

Figure 3.2   Impulse-based trust region: 1MAR–31MAR96 NPROB4.1

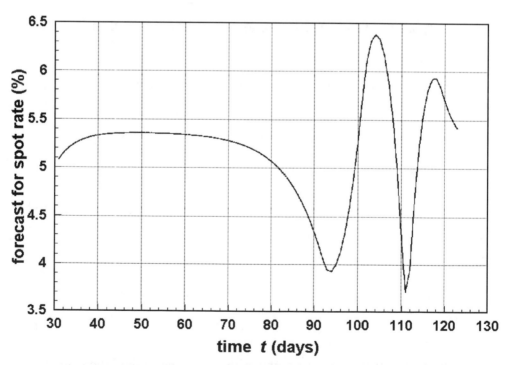

Figure 3.3   Impulse-based spot rate forecast: 1MAR–31MAR96 NPROB4.1

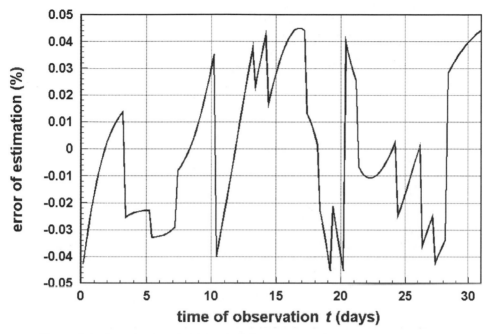

Figure 3.4   Impulse-based yield estimation error: 1MAR–31MAR96 NPROB4.1

$\min\ v_T$ subject to

$$\gamma + \frac{r_0 - \gamma}{\alpha T}(e^{-\alpha(t-t_0)} - e^{-\alpha(t+T-t_0)}) - v_T \leqslant \hat{R}(t,\ t+T),$$

$$\hat{R}(t,\ t+T) \leqslant \gamma + \frac{r_0 - \gamma}{\alpha T}(e^{-\alpha(t-t_0)} - e^{-\alpha(t+T-t_0)}) + v_T,\quad t \in T^M;$$

$$\alpha_* \leqslant \alpha \leqslant \alpha^*,\quad \gamma_* \leqslant \gamma \leqslant \gamma^*,\quad r_* \leqslant r_0 \leqslant r^*,\quad v_T \geqslant 0. \tag{3.33}$$

Example 3.2   *We consider the observed Treasury yield rates for maturity term 3 months from 1OCT95 to 31DEC95. We select the piecewise constant observation model (3.10) for modeling the discrete values of the observed yield. Several starting points α_0, r_0, γ_0 are taken. The numerical results for different initial points are given in Table 3.2.*

Figure 3.5 illustrates the computed estimates $y(\cdot|\cdot)$ of the yield and the observed yield $R(\cdot,\ \cdot)$ for NPROB = 1, 2. Figure 3.6 illustrates the computed estimates of the spot rate $r(\cdot)$ for NPROB = 1, 2, 3.

In Example 3.2, we see that the estimate of γ is equal to 5.285 in all cases. The maximum value of observed Treasury yield rate is equal to 5.59, and the minimum value is equal to 4.98. So, the estimate of γ is equal to the median value of the observed Treasury yield rate and the error of estimation is equal to half the difference between the maximum value of the observed Treasury yield rate and the minimum value of the observed Treasury yield rate on the *whole interval of observation*

Table 3.2 Deterministic model (3.30) under (3.10) with optimization (3.33): 1OCT–31DEC95

NPROB	1	2	3
α_0	1	5	10
γ_0	1	5	10
r_0	1	5	10
r_0^0	1	5	10
α^0	1	5	10
γ^0	5.285	5.285	5.285
$v_{\mathcal{T}}^0$	0.305	0.305	0.305
ITER	4	2	2
NFUN	4	2	2
NQP	4	2	2
NGRAD	4	2	2
ACCSP	10^{-5}	10^{-5}	10^{-5}
NCONSP	2024	2024	2024
CPU (s)	< 1	< 1	< 1

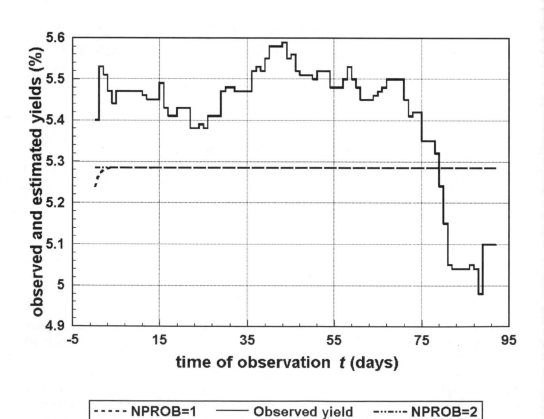

Figure 3.5   Deterministic model yield estimates: 1OCT–31DEC95 NPROB1, 2

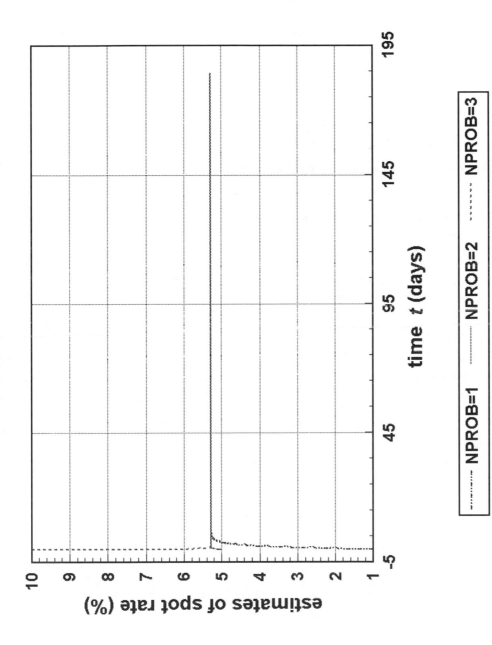

Figure 3.6 Deterministic model spot rate estimates: 1OCT–31DEC95 NPROB1–3

$((5.59 - 4.98)/2 = 0.305)$. This is the essence of Figure 3.5. But when perturbations are introduced as in the two Vasicek-type models (3.28) and (3.39), the error of estimation equals *half the maximum jump in the observed Treasury yield rate* (0.065 for these data). This reduction in the computed error of the estimation is dramatically illustrated in Figure 3.2.

In a later section in Chapter 4 we describe a *bilevel* model which takes into account the jumps occurring in the observed Treasury yield rates.

3.3.4 Vasicek-type Spot Rate Estimation Using Point-impulse Perturbations

Assume that the spot rate follows the differential systems model (3.20), (3.21). Recall the definition of $\tilde{T}^N$ in (3.6). According to Definition 2.1 point-impulse perturbations $\{w(t), t \in T^N\}$ acting on (3.20) and (3.21) are specified by the following.

1. Over the interval T^N, w is zero except at possible jump points $\tilde{T}^N$, formally

$$w(t) = 0, \quad t \in T^N \setminus \tilde{T}^N. \tag{3.34}$$

2. The trajectory $r(t)$, $t \in T^N$ of the system (3.20), (3.21) is described by the following differential equation:

$$\dot{r} = \alpha + \beta r(t) \tag{3.35}$$

on the intervals $]t_{i-1}, t_i[$, $i = \overline{1, N}$.

3. The trajectory $r(t)$, $t \in T^N$ has jumps

$$r(t_i + 0) = r(t_i - 0) + w(t_i), \quad w_{i*} \leqslant w_i \equiv w(t_i) \leqslant w_i^* \tag{3.36}$$

at the points $t_i \in \tilde{T}^N$, $\gamma \leqslant 0$.

By means of the Cauchy formula (2.5), (2.6), the solution of the differential equation (3.20) with point-impulse perturbations defined by (3.34)–(3.36) has the form

$$r(t|\omega) = e^{\beta t} r_0 + \frac{\alpha}{\beta}(e^{\beta t} - 1) + \sum_{j=1}^{i} e^{\beta(t-t_{j-1})} w_j, \quad t \in T_i, i = \overline{1, N}, \tag{3.37}$$

where $w_i = w(t_{i-1})$, $t_{i-1} \in \tilde{T}$, $i = \overline{1, N}$. Define the yield function

$$y(t, \omega|T), \quad t \in T_i, i = \overline{1, M}$$

by (3.12) and (3.25). From (3.37) it follows that

$$
\begin{aligned}
T\, y(t, \omega|T) &= \int_t^{t+T} h(\tau, \omega)\, d\tau = \left(r_0 \int_t^{t+T} e^{\beta\tau}\, d\tau + \frac{\alpha}{\beta} \int_t^{t+T} (e^{\beta\tau} - 1)\, d\tau \right.\\
&\quad + \sum_{k=1}^{i} \int_t^{t+T} w_k e^{\beta(\tau - t_{k-1})}\, d\tau + \sum_{k=i+1}^{i+T} \int_{t_{k-1}}^{t+T} w_k e^{\beta(\tau - t_{k-1})}\, d\tau \Bigg)\\
&= \left(\frac{e^{\beta(t+T)} - e^{\beta t}}{\beta} r_0 + \left(\frac{e^{\beta(t+T)} - e^{\beta t}}{\beta^2} - \frac{T}{\beta} \right)\alpha \right)\\
&\quad + \sum_{k=1}^{i} \frac{e^{\beta(t-t_{k-1}+T)} - e^{\beta(t-t_{k-1})}}{\beta} w_k + \sum_{k=i+1}^{i+T} \frac{e^{\beta(t-t_{k-1}+T)} - 1}{\beta} w_k.
\end{aligned}
$$

Let

$$
a_k^i(\beta, t \mid T) = \begin{cases} \dfrac{e^{\beta(t-t_{k-1}+T)} - e^{\beta(t-t_{k-1})}}{\beta T} & \text{if } k \leqslant i, \\[3mm] \dfrac{e^{\beta(t-t_{k-1}+T)} - 1}{\beta T} & \text{if } i < k \leqslant i + T. \end{cases} \tag{3.38}
$$

Hence the T-constant maturity-based, point-impulse perturbation spot rate minimax estimation problem is formulated as follows:

min v_T subject to

$$
\frac{e^{\beta(t+T)} - e^{\beta t}}{T\beta} r_0 + \left(\frac{e^{\beta(t+T)} - e^{\beta t}}{T\beta^2} - \frac{1}{\beta} \right)\alpha + \sum_{k=1}^{i+T} a_k^i(\beta, t \mid T) w_k - v_T \leqslant \hat{R}(t, t+T),
$$

$$
\hat{R}(t, t+T) \leqslant \frac{e^{\beta(t+T)} - e^{\beta t}}{T\beta} r_0 + \left(\frac{e^{\beta(t+T)} - e^{\beta t}}{T\beta^2} - \frac{1}{\beta} \right)\alpha + \sum_{k=1}^{i+T} a_k^i(\beta, t \mid T) w_k + v_T,
$$

$$
t \in T_i, \, i = \overline{1, M}; \tag{3.39}
$$

$$
\alpha_* \leqslant \alpha \leqslant \alpha^*, \, \beta_* \leqslant \beta \leqslant \beta^*, \, r_* \leqslant r_0 \leqslant r^*, \, v_T \geqslant 0;
$$

$$
w_* \leqslant w_i \leqslant w^*, \, i = \overline{1, N}.
$$

Theorem 3.2 *Vasicek-type Model with Point-impulse Perturbations. The functions $A(t, s)$ and $B(t, s)$ appearing in (3.29) have the following form:*

$$
B(t, s) = \frac{1 - e^{\beta(s-t)}}{\beta}, \quad A(t, s) = \frac{\alpha}{\beta}(s - t + B(t, s)) + \frac{1}{\beta} \sum_{k=i+1}^{j} (1 - e^{\beta(s-t_{k-1})}) w_k
$$

for $t \in T_i$, $s \in T_j$, $i \leqslant j$.

Proof. Let $t \in T_i$, $s \in T_j$, $i \leqslant j$. Then

$$
P(t, s) = \exp\left\{ -\int_t^s r(\tau)\, d\tau \right\} = \exp\left\{ -\frac{e^{\beta s} - e^{\beta t}}{\beta} r_0 \right.
$$

$$
\left. -\alpha \left(\frac{e^{\beta s} - e^{\beta t}}{\beta^2} - \frac{s-t}{\beta} \right) - \sum_{k=1}^{i} \frac{e^{\beta(s-t_{k-1})} - e^{\beta(t-t_{k-1})}}{\beta} w_k - \sum_{k=i+1}^{j} \frac{e^{\beta(s-t_{k-1})} - 1}{\beta} w_k \right\}
$$

$$
= \exp\left\{ \frac{1 - e^{\beta(s-t)}}{\beta} \left(e^{\beta t} r_0 + \frac{\alpha}{\beta}(e^{\beta t} - 1) + \sum_{k=1}^{i} e^{\beta(t-t_{k-1})} \right) + \frac{1}{\beta} \sum_{k=i+1}^{j} (1 - e^{\beta(s-t_{k-1})}) w_k \right.
$$

$$
\left. + \frac{\alpha}{\beta} \frac{1 - e^{\beta(s-t)}}{\beta} + \frac{\alpha}{\beta}(s-t) \right\} = \exp\left\{ \frac{1 - e^{\beta(s-t)}}{\beta} r(t) + \frac{\alpha}{\beta}\left(\frac{1 - e^{\beta(s-t)}}{\beta} + (s-t) \right) \right.
$$

$$
\left. + \frac{1}{\beta} \sum_{k=i+1}^{j} (1 - e^{\beta(s-t_{k-1})}) w_k \right\}.
$$

Denote

$$
B(t, s) = \frac{1 - e^{\beta(s-t)}}{\beta}, \quad A(t, s) = \frac{\alpha}{\beta}(s - t + B(t, s)) + \frac{1}{\beta} \sum_{k=i+1}^{j} (1 - e^{\beta(s-t_{k-1})}) w_k.
$$

As a consequence, we also obtain formula (3.29). $\qquad \square$

Table 3.3 Vasicek-type model with point-impulse perturbations under piecewise constant observation model (3.10) and (3.39)

NPROB	5.1	5.2	5.3	5.4
β_0	-0.1	-0.5	-1.0	-1.5
r_0^0	0.550814	0.0991620	0.113943	0.113943
α^0	1.343350	2.4453550	4.196010	4.196010
β^0	-0.261763	-0.4832893	-0.834356	-0.834356
$-\alpha^0/\beta^0$	5.131932	5.059816	5.029040	5.029040
v_T^0	0.045	0.045	0.045	0.045
ITER	19	28	25	25
NFUN	19	28	25	25
NQP	19	28	25	25
NGRAD	19	28	25	25
ACCSP	10^{-5}	10^{-5}	10^{-5}	10^{-5}
NSP	2	2	2	2
NCONSP	125	125	125	125
CPU (s)	204.8	282.27	254.68	253.71

Example 3.3 *Consider again the data from Example 3.1. The following initial point:*

$$\alpha_0 = 0, \quad \beta_0 \text{ as given}, \quad r_0 = 0, \quad v_0^T = 0; \quad w_k = 0, \quad k = \overline{1, N}$$

was chosen for problem (3.39). The numerical results for four different initial points are given in Table 3.3.

It can be shown that problem (3.39) has optimal solutions. Figures 3.7–3.9 refer to NPROB5.1. Figure 3.7 illustrates the computed estimate $y(\cdot|\cdot)$ of the yield, the observed yield $R(\cdot, \cdot)$ and the computed estimate of the spot rate $r(\cdot)$ for NPROB5.1. Figure 3.8 illustrates the computed estimates of the spot rate $r(\cdot)$ for different initial points β_0. Figure 3.9 gives the computed estimate $y(\cdot|\cdot)$ of the yield curve for different initial points β_0.

Table 3.3 and Figures 3.8 and 3.9 show that the spot rate estimation problem (3.28) coupled with the piecewise constant observation model (3.10) does not in general have a unique solution. However, additional criteria could be used for identifying one solution from all the alternate optima, for example, choosing the estimate of the spot rate that minimizes a preselected norm. We will discuss this approach later, in Chapter 7.

We now show how our model applies to other laws of motion. Actually our approach contains spline approximations as a special case as we shall soon see in (3.50).

3.3.5   A Dothan-type Model with Impulse Perturbations

Assume that the spot rate follows another linear dynamic system of *Dothan type* with unknown parameters and nonstochastic uncertainty:

$$\dot{r} = rw(t), \quad r(t_0) = r_0; \quad t \in T^N. \tag{3.40}$$

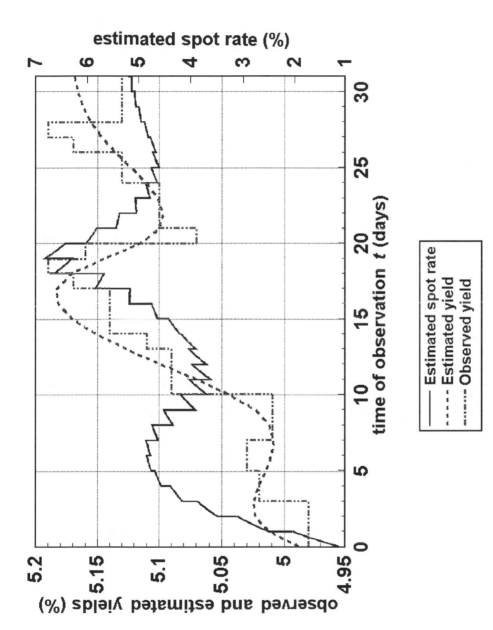

Figure 3.7   Point-impulse estimates: 1MAR–31MAR96 PROB5.1

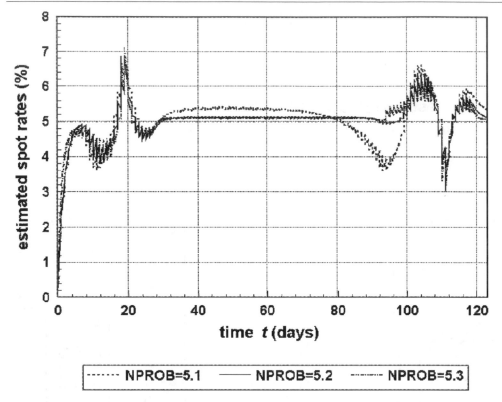

Figure 3.8   Point-impulse spot rate estimates for different starting points: 1MAR–31MAR96

Assume that a priori information about unknown parameters of the linear dynamical system (3.40) has the form (3.21) while the perturbations $w(\cdot)$ are of impulse type (3.22). It follows from (3.7) and (3.8) that for the model (3.40), (3.22) we have

$$\omega = (r_0, w_i, i = \overline{1, N}); \quad \omega_* = (r_*, w_{i*}, i = \overline{1, N}); \quad \omega^* = (r^*, w_i^*, i = \overline{1, N});$$

$$\Omega = \{\omega \in \mathbf{R}^{N+1} : \omega_* \leqslant \omega \leqslant \omega^*\}.$$

By means of the Cauchy formula the solution of the differential equation (3.40) has the form

$$r(t \mid \omega) = r_0 \exp\left(\sum_{k=1}^{i-1} w_k(t_k - t_{k-1}) + w_i(t - t_{i-1})\right), \quad t \in T_i, \ i = \overline{1, N}. \tag{3.41}$$

The function $h(\cdot, \cdot)$ is specified by (3.25) via (3.41) (analogous to the procedure (3.24), (3.25) for the analog of the Vasicek model), and $p(t, \omega \mid T)$ is specified next by formula (3.12), namely

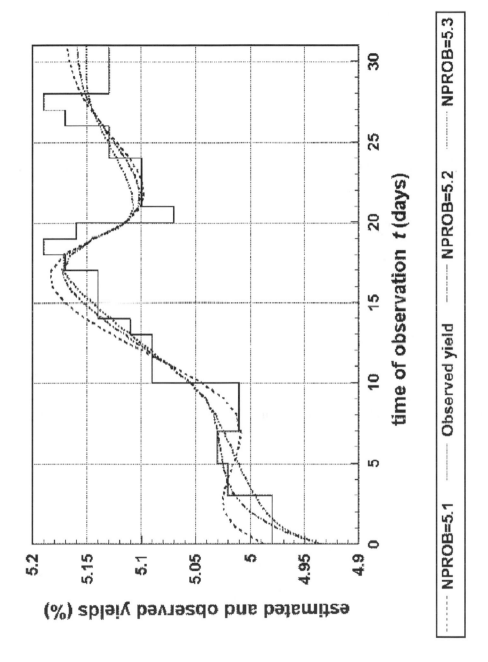

Figure 3.9 Point-impulse yield estimates for different starting points: 1MAR–31MAR96

$$p(t, \omega \mid \mathcal{T}) = \frac{1}{\mathcal{T}} \int_t^{t+\mathcal{T}} h(\tau, \omega)\, d\tau$$

$$= \frac{1}{\mathcal{T}} \left(\int_t^{t_i} h(\tau, \omega)\, d\tau + \sum_{k=i+1}^{i+\mathcal{T}-1} \int_{t_{k-1}}^{t_k} h(\tau, \omega)\, d\tau + \int_{t_{i+\mathcal{T}-1}}^{t+\mathcal{T}} h(\tau, \omega)\, d\tau \right)$$

$$= \frac{r_0}{\mathcal{T}} \left(\exp\left(\sum_{k=1}^{i-1} w_k(t_k - t_{k-1}) \right) \int_t^{t_i} \exp\left(w_i(\tau - t_{i-1}) \right) d\tau \right.$$

$$+ \sum_{k=i+1}^{i+\mathcal{T}-1} \exp\left(\sum_{j=1}^{k-1} w_k(t_j - t_{j-1}) \right) \int_{t_{k-1}}^{t_k} \exp\left(w_k(\tau - t_{k-1}) \right) d\tau$$

$$\left. + \exp\left(\sum_{k=1}^{i+\mathcal{T}-1} w_k(t_k - t_{k-1}) \right) \int_{t_{i+\mathcal{T}-1}}^{t+\mathcal{T}} \exp\left(w_{i+\mathcal{T}-1}(\tau - t_{i+\mathcal{T}-1}) \right) d\tau \right)$$

$$= \frac{r_0}{\mathcal{T}} \left(\exp\left(\sum_{k=1}^{i-1} w_k(t_k - t_{k-1}) \right) \frac{e^{w_i(t_i - t_{i-1})} - e^{w_i(t - t_{i-1})}}{w_i} \right.$$

$$+ \sum_{k=i+1}^{i+\mathcal{T}-1} \exp\left(\sum_{j=1}^{k-1} w_k(t_j - t_{j-1}) \right) \frac{e^{w_k(t_k - t_{k-1})} - 1}{w_k}$$

$$\left. + \exp\left(\sum_{k=1}^{i+\mathcal{T}-1} w_k(t_k - t_{k-1}) \right) \frac{e^{w_{i+\mathcal{T}-1}(t + \mathcal{T} - t_{i+\mathcal{T}-1})} - 1}{w_{i+\mathcal{T}}} \right); \quad t \in T_i, \, i = \overline{1, N}.$$

$$(3.42)$$

By substituting (3.42) into (3.15) we obtain a nonlinear semi-infinite programming problem for estimating the spot rate $r_{\mathcal{T}}(\cdot)$. However, some additional constraints are needed in order to guarantee that $w_i \neq 0$, $i = \overline{1, N}$. The functions $A(t, s)$, $B(t, s)$ for the bond pricing formula (3.29) have the following special form.

Theorem 3.3   *Dothan Model with Impulse Perturbations*

$$B(t, s) = \frac{1}{w_i} - \frac{1}{w_j} \exp\left(\sum_{k=i}^{j+1} w_k(t_k - t_{k-1}) + w_j(s - t_{j-1}) - w_i(t - t_{i-1}) \right),$$

$$A(t, s) = -\frac{r_0}{w_i} \exp\left(\sum_{k=1}^{i} w_k(t_k - t_{k-1}) \right)$$

$$- r_0 \sum_{k=i+1}^{j-1} \frac{\exp\left(\sum_{l=1}^{k} w_l(t_l - t_{l-1}) \right) - \exp\left(\sum_{l=1}^{k-1} w_l(t_l - t_{l-1}) \right)}{w_k}$$

$$+ \frac{r_0}{w_j} \exp\left(\sum_{k=1}^{j-1} w_k(t_k - t_{k-1}) \right).$$

Proof. Let $t \in T_i$, $s \in T_j$, $i \leq j$. Then

$$P(t, s) = \exp\left\{-\int_t^s r(\tau)\, d\tau\right\} = \exp\left\{-r_0\left(\exp\left(\sum_{k=1}^{i-1} w_k(t_k - t_{k-1})\right)\frac{e^{w_i(t_i - t_{i-1})} - e^{w_i(t - t_{i-1})}}{w_k}\right.\right.$$

$$+ \sum_{k=i+1}^{j-1} \exp\left(\sum_{l=1}^{k-1} w_l(t_l - t_{l-1})\right)\frac{e^{w_k(t_k - t_{k-1})} - 1}{w_k}$$

$$\left.\left.+ \exp\left(\sum_{k=1}^{j-1} w_k(t_k - t_{k-1})\right)\frac{e^{w_j(s - t_{j-1})} - 1}{w_j}\right)\right\}$$

$$= \exp\left\{\frac{r_0}{w_i}\exp\left(\sum_{k=1}^{i-1} w_k(t_k - t_{k-1}) + w_i(t - t_{i-1})\right)\right.$$

$$- \frac{r_0}{w_j}\exp\left(\sum_{k=1}^{j-1} w_k(t_k - t_{k-1}) + w_j(s - t_{i-1}) + w_i(t - t_{k-1}) - w_i(t - t_{k-1})\right)$$

$$- \frac{r_0}{w_i}\exp\left(\sum_{k=1}^{i} w_k(t_k - t_{k-1})\right)$$

$$- r_0 \sum_{k=i+1}^{j-1} \frac{\exp\left(\sum_{l=1}^{k} w_l(t_l - t_{l-1})\right) - \exp\left(\sum_{l=1}^{k-1} w_l(t_l - t_{l-1})\right)}{w_k}$$

$$\left.+ \frac{r_0}{w_j}\exp\left(\sum_{k=1}^{j-1} w_k(t_k - t_{k-1})\right)\right\}$$

$$= \exp\left\{-r(t)\left(-\frac{1}{w_i} + \frac{1}{w_j}\exp\left(\sum_{k=i}^{j+1} w_k(t_k - t_{k-1}) + w_j(s - t_{j-1}) - w_i(t - t_{i-1})\right)\right)\right.$$

$$\left.+ A(t, s)\right\}$$

$$= \exp\{A(t, s) + r(t)B(t, s)\},$$

which is (3.29), where

$$B(t, s) = \frac{1}{w_i} - \frac{1}{w_j}\exp\left(\sum_{k=i}^{j+1} w_k(t_k - t_{k-1}) + w_j(s - t_{j-1}) - w_i(t - t_{i-1})\right),$$

$$A(t, s) = -\frac{r_0}{w_i}\exp\left(\sum_{k=1}^{i} w_k(t_k - t_{k-1})\right)$$

$$-r_0\sum_{k=i+1}^{j-1}\frac{\exp\left(\sum_{l=1}^{k} w_l(t_l - t_{l-1})\right) - \exp\left(\sum_{l=1}^{k-1} w_l(t_l - t_{l-1})\right)}{w_k} + \frac{r_0}{w_j}\exp\left(\sum_{k=1}^{j-1} w_k(t_k - t_{k-1})\right).$$

$\square$

3.3.6   A Courtadon-type Model with Impulse Perturbations

Assume that the spot rate follows a linear dynamic system of *Courtadon type* with unknown parameters and nonstochastic uncertainty:

$$\dot{r} = \alpha + \beta r + w(t)r, \quad r(t_0) = r_0; \quad t \in T^N. \tag{3.43}$$

In addition, we assume that the a priori information about unknown parameters of the linear dynamical system (3.40) has the form (3.21) and the perturbations $w(\cdot)$ are still of impulse form, (3.22). Then ω and Ω are defined by (3.23). Using the Cauchy formula again the solution of the differential equation (3.43) has the form?tpb=-6pt>

$$r(t|\omega) = -\frac{\alpha}{\beta + w_i} + \left(\frac{\alpha}{\beta + w_i} + r(t_{i-1})\right) e^{(\beta + w_i)(t - t_{i-1})}, \quad t \in T_i, i = \overline{1, N} \tag{3.44}$$

or

$$r(t|\omega) = -\frac{\alpha}{\beta + w_i} + \gamma_i(\omega) e^{(\beta + w_i)(t - t_{i-1})}, \quad t \in T_i, i = \overline{1, N}, \tag{3.45}$$

where

$$\gamma_1(\omega) = \frac{\alpha}{\beta + w_1} + r_0, \quad \gamma_2(\omega) = \frac{\alpha}{\beta + w_2} - \frac{\alpha}{\beta + w_1} + \left(\frac{\alpha}{\beta + w_1} + r_0\right) e^{(\beta + w_1)(t_1 - t_0)},$$

$$\gamma_i(\omega) = \left(\frac{\alpha}{\beta + w_i} - \frac{\alpha}{\beta + w_{i-1}}\right) + \left(\frac{\alpha}{\beta + w_1} + r_0\right) \exp\left(\sum_{k=1}^{i-1}(\beta + w_k)(t_k - t_{k-1})\right)$$

$$+ \sum_{k=2}^{i-1}\left(\frac{\alpha}{\beta + w_k} - \frac{\alpha}{\beta + w_{k-1}}\right) \exp\left(\sum_{j=k}^{i-1}(\beta + w_j)(t_j - t_{j-1})\right), \quad i = \overline{3, N}.$$

Define the function $h(\cdot, \cdot)$ by (3.25), and find the special function $p(t, \omega|T)$, $t \in T_i$, $i = \overline{1, M}$, (3.12). From (3.45), (3.12) it follows that

$$p(t, \omega|T) = \frac{1}{T}\int_t^{t+T} h(\tau, \omega)\,d\tau$$

$$= \frac{1}{T}\left(\int_t^{t_i} h(\tau, \omega)\,d\tau + \sum_{k=i+1}^{i+T-1}\int_{t_{k-1}}^{t_k} h(\tau, \omega)\,d\tau + \int_{t_{i+T-1}}^{t+T} h(\tau, \omega)\,d\tau\right)$$

$$= \frac{1}{T}\left(-\frac{\alpha}{\beta + w_i}(t_i - t) + \frac{\gamma_i(\omega)}{\beta + w_i}(e^{(\beta + w_i)(t_i - t_{i-1})} - e^{(\beta + w_i)(t - t_{i-1})})\right.$$

$$+ \sum_{k=i+1}^{i+T-1}\left(-\frac{\alpha}{\beta + w_k}(t_k - t_{k-1}) + \frac{\gamma_k(\omega)}{\beta + w_k}(e^{(\beta + w_k)(t_k - t_{k-1})} - 1)\right)$$

$$\left. -\frac{\alpha}{\beta + w_{i+T}}(t + T - t_{i+T-1}) + \frac{\gamma_{i+T}(\omega)}{w_{i+T} + \beta}(e^{(\beta + w_{i+T})(t+T - t_{i+T-1})} - 1)\right). \tag{3.46}$$

By substituting (3.46) into (3.15) we obtain the nonlinear semi-infinite programming problem for estimating the spot rate $r_T(\cdot)$. However, some additional constraints are needed to guarantee that $\beta + w_i \neq 0$, $i = \overline{1, N}$.

3.3.7 A Nondifferential Equation, Continuous Time Model

The models from previous sections were constructed by means of linear differential equations with uncertainty. In this section we consider another way of modeling the problem of estimating spot rates.

Assume that the spot rate $r(\cdot)$ belongs to the class of impulse functions of the form

$$r(t) = r_i, \ r_{i*} \leqslant r_i \leqslant r_i^*; \ t \in T_i, \ i = \overline{1, N}. \tag{3.47}$$

In this case we obtain

$$\omega = (r_i, \ i = \overline{1, N}); \quad \omega_* = (r_{i*}, \ i = \overline{1, N}); \quad \omega^* = (r_i^*, \ i = \overline{1, N});$$

$$\Omega = \{\omega \in \mathbf{R}^N: \ \omega_* \leqslant \omega \leqslant \omega^*\}, \tag{3.48}$$

with corresponding yield

$$p(t, \omega \,|\, T) = \frac{1}{T}\left((t_i - t)\omega_i + \sum_{k=i+1}^{i+T-1}(t_k - t_{k-1})\omega_k + (t + T - t_{i+T-1})\omega_{i+T}\right), \tag{3.49}$$

$$t \in T_i, \ i = \overline{1, M}, \ \omega \in \Omega.$$

Denote

$$a_{(i)}(t \,|\, T) = \left(a_{(i),k}(t) = \begin{cases} 0 & \text{if } \ k < i, \\[2mm] \dfrac{t_i - t}{T} & \text{if } \ k = i, \\[3mm] \dfrac{t_k - t_{k-1}}{T} & \text{if } \ i < k \leqslant i + T - 1, \\[3mm] \dfrac{t + T - t_{i+T-1}}{T} & \text{if } \ k = i + T, \\[3mm] 0 & \text{if } \ i + T < k \leqslant N, \end{cases}\right), \ t \in T_i, \ i = \overline{1, M}. \tag{3.50}$$

Hence the *T-programmed problem of spot riskless rate estimation* is

min v_T subject to

$$\langle a_{(i)}(t), \omega \rangle - v_T \leqslant \hat{R}(t, t+T), \ \hat{R}(t, t+T) \leqslant \langle a_{(i)}(t), \omega \rangle + v_T, \ t \in T_i, \ i = \overline{1, M}; \tag{3.51}$$

$$\omega \in \Omega, \ v \geqslant 0.$$

Problem (3.51) is a linear semi-infinite programming problem.

3.3.8   Real-time Positional Spot Rate Estimation

In the previous models the estimates ω^0 of unknown parameters ω were calculated at the conclusion of the observation process. In actual on-line operations real-time estimates are needed. These are calculated based on current observations of $\hat{R}(t, t+T)$.

Assume that we have observed the values of the yield to maturity function $\hat{R}(t, t+T)$ for some fixed time-to-maturity T during τ days. By a *position of the observed system* we shall mean the following subset of the time domain:

$$\{\tau; \ \hat{R}(t, t+T), \ t \in T^\tau\},$$

where $T^\tau = \bigcup_{i=1}^\tau T_i$. Let $N(\tau) = \tau + T$. Introduce

$$\omega(\tau) = (\omega_i(\tau),\ i = \overline{1,\ N(\tau)});\quad \omega_*(\tau) = (\omega_{i*},\ i = \overline{1,\ N(\tau)});$$

$$\omega^*(\tau) = (\omega_i^*,\ i = \overline{1,\ N(\tau)});\quad \Omega(\tau) = \{\omega(\tau) \in \mathbf{R}^{N(\tau)}\colon \omega_*(\tau) \leqslant \omega(\tau) \leqslant \omega^*(\tau)\}. \tag{3.52}$$

The following optimization problem is an extension of (3.15):

$$\min v_T(\tau)\ \text{subject to}$$

$$y(t,\ \omega(\tau)\,|\,T) - v_T(\tau) \leqslant \hat{R}(t,\ t + T),$$

$$\hat{R}(t,\ t + T) \leqslant y(t,\ \omega(\tau)\,|\,T) + v_T(\tau),\quad t \in [t_0,\ t_\tau]; \tag{3.53}$$

$$\omega(\tau) \in \Omega(\tau);\ v_T(\tau) \geqslant 0.$$

We shall call problem (3.53) the τ-*positional spot rate estimation problem*. It is helpful to compare this problem with the earlier problems (3.15) and (3.56). Assume that $(\omega^0(\tau),\ v_T^0(\tau))$ is an optimal solution of problem (3.53). We shall continue to use $\mathcal{P}$ as the operating horizon according to Definition 3.3.

Problem (3.53) has the same formal structure as problem (3.15) except for the appearance of time τ and $t \in [t_0,\ t_\tau]$ instead of $t \in T^M$. Furthermore, the set $\Omega(\tau)$ contains vectors $\omega(\tau)$ whose components are the same as ω in (3.23) except they now depend on τ. We are particularly interested in how $\alpha(\tau)$ and $\beta(\tau)$ vary as τ varies.

Definition 3.6 By an **adaptive spot rate estimator** we shall mean a system for which it is possible to calculate the estimates $w^0(\tau)$ for each $\tau \in [0,\ \mathcal{P}]$, in real time.

The basic mathematical principles for constructing adaptive estimators in this setting originally appeared in [21]. We describe the main idea for synthesizing the estimator.

Suppose we have observed a signal on the interval $[0,\ \tau]$ and have found a solution $(\omega^0(\tau),\ v_T^0(\tau))$ of (3.53). When we obtain the new observation of the data at time $\bar{\tau} = \tau + h$, where $h > 0$ small enough, then it is clear that the solution $(\omega^0(\bar{\tau}),\ v_T^0(\bar{\tau}))$ of problem (3.53) at moment $\bar{\tau}$ will not differ much from $(\omega^0(\tau),\ v_T^0(\tau))$ (at moment τ). Hence, it is not necessary to solve (3.53) at $\bar{\tau}$ again. It is sufficient to resolve (3.53) with the advanced start $(\omega^0(\tau),\ v_T^0(\tau))$, namely the optimal solution of problem (3.53) at the previous position. Special procedures for solving this problem with advanced starts are given in [51].

We can also construct the τ-positional spot rate estimation problem for bonds of differing maturities following the modeling in (3.55). In a modification of problem (3.53) the number of constraints would be increased during the observation process.

Assume that for estimating the spot rate adaptively only $\tau - S$ of the last observations of $\hat{R}(t,\ t + T)$ are used. This input data specification leads to the following optimization problem:

$$\min v_T(\tau)\ \text{subject to}$$

$$y(t,\ \omega(\tau)\,|\,T) - v_T(\tau) \leqslant \hat{R}(t,\ t + T),$$

$$\hat{R}(t,\ t + T) \leqslant y(t,\ \omega(\tau)\,|\,T) + v_T(\tau),\quad \text{for all } t \in T_{\tau,S} \tag{3.54}$$

$$\omega(\tau) \in \Omega(\tau);\ v_T(\tau) \geqslant 0,$$

where $T_{\tau,S} = [t_{\tau-S},\ t_\tau] = \bigcup_{i=\tau-S+1}^{\tau} T_i$.

Assume that $(\omega^0(\tau), v_T^0(\tau))$ is the optimal solution of problem (3.54).

Definition 3.7   *A system for which estimates $\omega^0(\tau)$ can be computed from (3.54) for each $\tau \in [S, Q]$ (our operating horizon, see Definition 3.3) in real time shall be termed an adaptive spot rate estimator with fixed observation period.*

We performed numerical experiments to see how $\alpha(\tau)$ and $\beta(\tau)$ vary in models (3.53) and (3.54) with τ. Figures 3.10 and 3.11 show the computed functions graphically as τ varies in half-day increments from 31MAR95 to 31DEC95. We chose $\tau - S = 3$ months for the estimator in (3.54). Figures 3.12 and 3.13 present the number of iterations required for resolving problems (3.53), (3.54) in each time position τ.

3.4   MODELING OF BONDS WITH DIFFERING MATURITIES

Assume that we can observe the values of yields to maturity $\hat{R}(t, t + T(j)), j = \overline{1, L}$, for different times-to-maturity $T(j)$.

It follows from (1.50) that when the spot rate is independent of t, then (3.12) is extended in this case to

$$R(t, t + T(j)) = \frac{1}{T(j)} \int_t^{t+T(j)} h(\tau, \omega)\, d\tau, \ j = \overline{1, L}. \tag{3.55}$$

From (3.15) we obtain the following nonlinear optimization problem:

$$\min \sum_{j=1}^{L} v_j \ \text{subject to}$$

$$y(t, \omega | T(j)) - v_j \leqslant \hat{R}(t, t + T(j)), \ \hat{R}(t, t + T(j)) \leqslant y(t, \omega | T(j)) + v_j, \tag{3.56}$$

$$t \in T^M; \omega \in \Omega; v_j \geqslant 0, j = \overline{1, L}.$$

We shall call problem (3.56) the *multiple constant-maturity yield minimax estimation problem*.

Let (ω^0, v^0), $v^0 = (v_1^0, \ldots, v_L^0)$ be the solution of problem (3.56), and recall the definition of T^N in (3.6). It follows that the function

$$r(t) = h(t, \omega^0), \ t \in T^N, N = M + \max_{j=\overline{1,L}} T(j) \tag{3.57}$$

will be an estimate of the spot riskless rate. We shall call the function $r(\cdot)$ defined by (3.57) the *multiple maturity-based spot rate estimate*. Analogous to theoretical developments we are able to compute one spot rate based on observations on bond yields for differing maturities.

3.5   A TWO-DIMENSIONAL OBSERVATION MODEL

In this chapter we have developed models for bonds having common maturities (as one observed curve, see (3.15)) and for observations of yields having different maturities (as a family of observed curves, see (3.56)). Based on observed yield curves, we can assume that there are two independent arguments of time, namely *current* time t and *maturity*

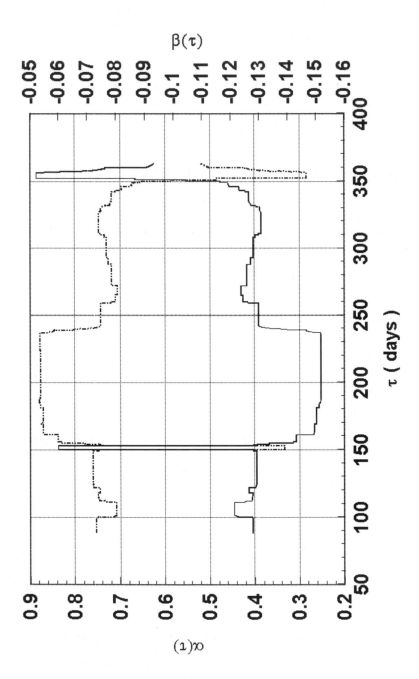

Figure 3.10 Computed functions $\alpha(\cdot)$, $\beta(\cdot)$ resolving (3.53): 31MAR–31DEC95

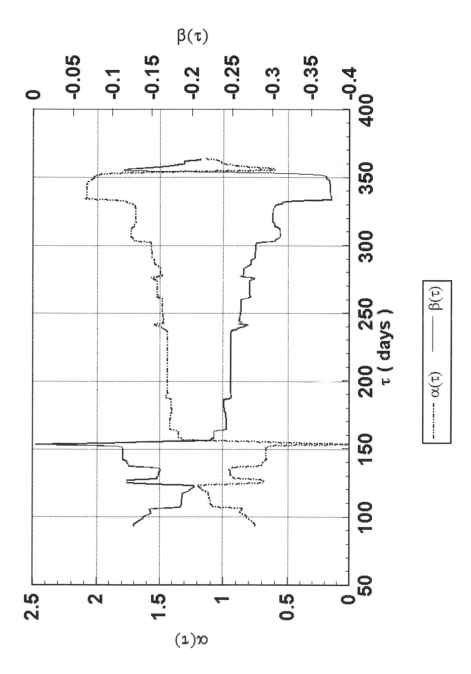

Figure 3.11 Computed functions $\alpha(\cdot)$, $\beta(\cdot)$ resolving (3.54): 31MAR–31DEC95

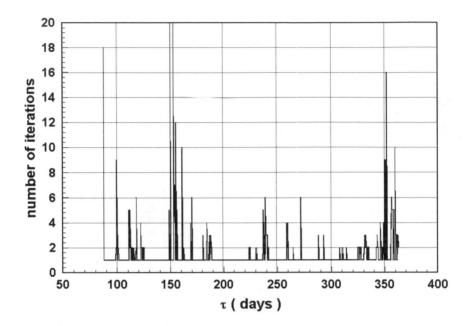

Figure 3.12   Number of iterations resolving problems (3.53): 31MAR–31DEC95

time T. Then we construct an observation surface-model by interpolating the values of the observed yield curves according to the argument T, for example, as follows.

Definition 3.8   *Let*

$$\tilde{T}_j(t) = [t + T(j-1),\, t + T(j)],\ j = \overline{1, L}\ \ and\ \ \tilde{T}^L(t) = \bigcup_{j=1}^{L} \tilde{T}_j,\ \ T(0) = 0.$$

Then the observation surface interpolation is the following:

$$\hat{R}(t, \tau) = R_{i-1,j-1} + \frac{t - t_{i-1}}{t_i - t_{i-1}}(R_{i,j-1} - R_{i-1,j-1}) + \frac{\tau - t - T(j-1)}{T(j) - T(j-1)}(R_{i-1,j} - R_{i-1,j-1})$$

$$+ \frac{(t - t_{i-1})(\tau - t - T(j-1))}{(t_i - t_{i-1})(T(j) - T(j-1))}(R_{i,j} - R_{i,j-1} - R_{i-1,j} + R_{i-1,j-1}),\ \ t \in T_i,\ i = \overline{1, M},$$

$$\tau \geqslant t;\ \ \tau \in \tilde{T}_j,\ j = \overline{1, L}. \tag{3.58}$$

For this case the form of the Ω-based yield is

$$y(t, \tau, \omega) = \frac{1}{\tau - t} \int_t^\tau h(s, \omega)\, ds,\ \ \omega \in \Omega,\ t \in T^N,\ \tau \in \tilde{T}^L(t).$$

Hence, we obtain the following problem, which is a nonlinear semi-infinite programming problem with a two-dimensional infinite index set for t, T:

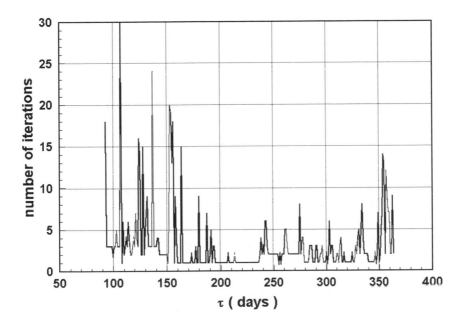

Figure 3.13 Number of iterations resolving problems (3.54): 31MAR–31DEC95

$$\min \sum_{j=1}^{L} v_j \text{ subject to}$$

$$y(t, \omega \mid \mathcal{T}(j)) - v_j \leqslant \hat{R}(t, t + \mathcal{T}(j)), \quad \hat{R}(t, t + \mathcal{T}(j)) \leqslant y(t, \tau, \omega \mid \mathcal{T}(j)) + v_j, \tag{3.59}$$

$$t \in T^M; \quad \tau \in \tilde{T}_j(t); \quad \omega \in \Omega; \quad v_j \geqslant 0, j = \overline{1, L}.$$

3.6 CHAPTER NOTES

The Samuelson Prize-winning book *The Econometrics of Financial Markets* by John Campbell, Andrew Lo and Craig MacKinlay has an interesting and fruitful critique on modeling economic phenomena by nonlinear deterministic dynamical systems [7, p. 475].

It is fruitful and constructive to frame a possible response to this critique based on the theoretical paper underlying this book, namely the authors' paper [39].

'There are two serious problems in modeling economic phenomena as deterministic nonlinear dynamical systems. First, unlike the theory that is available in many natural sciences, economic theory is generally not specific about functional forms. Thus, economists rarely have theoretical reasons for expecting to find one form of nonlinearity rather than another.' [7, p. 475]

Response. In [39] no specific functional forms are assumed, only their general mathematical properties, see Assumption 4.1 therein. The form of the spot rate function, for example, depends on the type of model used for the term structure of interest rates.

'Second, economists are rarely able to construct controlled experiments, and this makes it almost impossible to deduce the parameters of a deterministic dynamical system governing economic phenomena, even if such a system exists and is low-dimensional.' [7, p. 475]

Response. Parameters of [39] lie in an a priori set of unknown parameters. They are obtained by means of an extremal principle applied to real data available during a pre-specified observation period. Parameters appear in specific ways depending on the form of the economic governing function chosen, for example, a 'programmed problem of spot riskless rate estimation'.

'The possibility that a relatively simple set of nonlinear deterministic equations can generate the kind of complexities we see in financial markets is tantalizing, but it is of little interest if we cannot recover these equations with any degree of precision.' [7, p. 475]

Response. Based on many computer runs with real T-bill data, the accuracy of the obtained estimates to the observable yields is sufficient, but we cannot guarantee any given required accuracy.

'Moreover, the impact of statistical sampling errors on a system with sensitive dependence to initial conditions makes dynamical systems theory even less practical. Of course, given the rapid pace at which this field is advancing, these reservations may be much less serious in a few years.' [7, p. 475]

Response. For some models of dynamical systems we cannot guarantee a global extremum, but we can analyze any computer solution, see Note 2 in Section 6 of [39]. Model sensitivity issues are also discussed in Note 3. A characterization of the estimation error appears in Note 7. The response to the uniqueness issue and the dependence upon the starting point is discussed in Note 1. Regarding computational feasibility, [39, Introduction] describes how in very recent years optimization algorithms have been able to take advantage of the special structure of many of these financial models.

The [39] model admits serial correlations because perturbations are implicitly connected, although they are specified as sought-for variables associated with intervals of time. This topic is currently being investigated.

4
Constant Maturity, Bilevel Models for Term Structure Estimation

4.1 NATURE OF BILEVEL PERTURBATIONS

In our previous models for the term structure of interest rates we constructed continuous estimates of observed yield $\hat{R}(t, t+T)$, $t \in T^M$. These forms arose through integrations. For this special case of the model (3.10) the value of the trust region for the yield cannot be less than the maximum value in the jumps of the observed yield (see, for example, Figure 3.2). By *trust region* we mean the tube having minimal width that covers the observed yield curve.

In this chapter we reformulate the model of the term structure of interest rates to now include additionally jumps in the observed yield. This is done by introducing perturbations on *both* the spot rate *and* the yield.

In this case Assumption 3.2 does not hold because now the yield (price) of the bond depends not only on the spot rate process but, in addition, on the *second process* that acts directly on the observed data.

Assume that the spot rate follows the Vasicek model (3.20), (3.21) either under (a) impulse perturbations (3.22), (3.23) or (b) the point-impulse perturbations (3.34)–(3.36). The *bilevel model* introduces perturbations on the structural form of the yield $R(t, t+T)$, $t \in T^M$. The admissible class of these particular perturbations $\{\bar{w}(t), t \in T^M\}$ is of the point-impulse perturbation type, defined as follows, recalling (3.6) and (3.34).

1. The $\bar{w}$ perturbations are zero outside possible jump points, namely

$$\bar{w}(t) = 0, \quad t \in T^M \backslash \tilde{T}^M. \tag{4.1}$$

2. The trajectory $R(t, t+T)$ of the yield prevailing at time $t \in T^M$ is described by equations (3.9), (3.12) (suppressing the ω notation in R) as

$$R(t, t+T) = \frac{1}{T} \int_t^{t+T} r(\tau | \omega) \, d\tau \tag{4.2}$$

on the intervals $]t_{i-1}, t_i[$, $i = \overline{1, M}$.
3. The trajectory $R(t, t+T)$ has jumps defined by

$$R(t_i + 0, t_i + 0 + T) = R(t_i - 0, t_i - 0 + T) + Te^{\gamma(t-t_i)}\bar{w}(t_i), \quad \bar{w}_* \leqslant w(t_i) \leqslant \bar{w}^* \tag{4.3}$$

at the points $t = t_i \in \tilde{T}^M$. Introduce additional *bilevel perturbations* into the structural equation for the yield function from the standard model as follows. Denote $\bar{w}_i = \bar{w}(t_i)$, $t_i \in \tilde{T}^M$. Then from (3.19), (3.12) and (4.1)–(4.3) it follows that

$$R(t, t + T) = \frac{1}{T} \int_t^{t+T} r(\tau \,|\, \omega) \, d\tau + T \sum_{k=1}^{i-1} e^{\gamma(t-t_k)} \bar{w}_k, \quad t \in T_i, \, i = \overline{1, M}. \qquad (4.4)$$

4.2   BILEVEL SPOT RATE MINIMAX ESTIMATION

Building upon the constructions introduced in the previous section we construct the T-constant maturity-based bilevel spot rate minimax estimation problem as follows:

min v_T subject to

$$\frac{e^{\beta(t+T)} - e^{\beta t}}{T\beta} r_0 + \left(\frac{e^{\beta(t+T)} - e^{\beta t}}{T\beta^2} - \frac{1}{\beta} \right) \alpha + \sum_{k=1}^{i+T} a_k^i(\beta, t \,|\, T) w_k + T \sum_{k=1}^{i-1} e^{\gamma(t-t_k)} \bar{w}_k - v_T$$

$$\leqslant \hat{R}(t, t + T),$$

$$\hat{R}(t, t + T) \leqslant \frac{e^{\beta(t+T)} - e^{\beta t}}{T\beta} r_0 + \left(\frac{e^{\beta(t+T)} - e^{\beta t}}{T\beta^2} - \frac{1}{\beta} \right) \alpha + \sum_{k=1}^{i+T} a_k^i(\beta, t \,|\, T) w_k \qquad (4.5)$$

$$+ T \sum_{k=1}^{i-1} e^{\gamma(t-t_k)} \bar{w}_k + v_T,$$

$$t \in T_i, \, \bar{w}_* \leqslant \bar{w}_i \leqslant \bar{w}^*, \, i = \overline{1, M},$$

$$\alpha_* \leqslant \alpha \leqslant \alpha^*, \, \beta_* \leqslant \beta \leqslant \beta^*, \, r_* \leqslant r_0 \leqslant r^*, \, v_T \geqslant 0; \, w_* \leqslant w_i \leqslant w^*, \, i = \overline{1, N};$$

where $a_k^i(\beta, t \,|\, T), \, k = \overline{1, i + T}, \, i = \overline{1, M}$ is defined by (3.27) or (3.38) depending on the type of perturbation for the spot rate we use.

The parameter γ influences the longer term limit of the yield. If $\gamma = 0$, then the yield perturbations can be interpreted as 'long-run factors' since in this case, the perturbations uniformly shift the corresponding yields to maturity. If $\gamma \neq 0$, then the yield perturbations affect the corresponding yields for shorter periods of time and so can be interpreted as 'short-run factors'.

It is possible to introduce into (4.3) actually *two* forms of the perturbations, namely simultaneously long-run factors and short-run factors.

The recommended value of γ should be obtained from solving the optimal observation problem. Alternatively, it is possible to employ special optimization problems for the selection of γ, where objective functions could stem from improving the estimation error and the quality of forecasting where observed trends in observed data could be of influence.

Clearly (4.5) and (3.56) can be combined to obtain a bilevel model extension for bonds with differing maturities. While we have not formally done this, we have done experiments on the extension and some of them are detailed in Tables 4.1 and 4.2.

From (4.4) we have for $T \geqslant t$, where $t + T = T$

$$R(t, T) = \frac{1}{T - t} \int_t^T r(\tau) \, d\tau + (T - t) \sum_{k=1}^{i-1} e^{\gamma(t-t_k)} \bar{w}_k, \quad t \in T_i, \, i = \overline{1, M}. \qquad (4.6)$$

From the deterministic asset price, spot rate equation (1.49), it follows that

$$-\log P(t, T) = \int_t^T r(\tau) \, d\tau + (T - t)^2 \sum_{k=1}^{i-1} e^{\gamma(t-t_k)} \bar{w}_k, \quad t \in T_i, \, i = \overline{1, M}. \qquad (4.7)$$

Table 4.1 Bilevel perturbations under piecewise constant observation model (3.10) with optimization (4.5) NPROB1–3

NPROB	1	2	3
β_0	-0.1	-0.5	-1.0
r_0^0	3.1792402	2.9672991	3.3461018
α^0	4.7066660	3.4655109	4.4081008
β^0	-0.9216965	-0.6798958	-0.8657656
$-\alpha^0/\beta^0$	5.106524	5.097120	5.091563
v_T^0	10^{-8}	10^{-8}	10^{-8}
ITER	238	220	229
NFUN	238	220	229
NQP	238	220	229
NGRAD	238	220	229
NCONSP	372	372	372
ACCSP	10^{-7}	10^{-7}	10^{-7}
CPU (s)	14 700	13 810	14 004

Table 4.2 Bilevel perturbations model under (3.10) with optimization (4.5) and different accuracy same starting point

NPROB	4	5	6	7
r_0^0	0.5714122	1.5869700	3.1792462	3.1792444
α^0	2.6360272	5.0857674	4.7066660	4.7066660
β^0	-0.518674	-1.0	-0.9216965	-0.9216965
$-\alpha^0/\beta^0$	5.082242	5.085767	5.106524	5.106524
v_T^0	0.0286725	0.0043419	0.0000125	0.00000001
ITER	33	87	221	238
NFUN	33	87	221	238
NQP	33	87	221	238
NGRAD	33	87	221	238
ACCSP	10^{-4}	10^{-5}	10^{-6}	10^{-7}
CPU (s)	758.52	4035	12 600	14 700

By the definition of the instantaneous forward rate (1.63), it follows that

$$f(t, T) = r(T) + 2(T - t) \sum_{k=1}^{i-1} e^{\gamma(t - t_k)} \bar{w}_k, \quad t \in T_i, \, i = \overline{1, M}. \tag{4.8}$$

Note that the linear function $T - t$ could be replaced with a sufficiently regular function $s(t, T)$ satisfying $s(t, t) = 0$.

In general (4.8) does not guarantee a non-negative forward rate for some future time because the forward rate depends on the values of the perturbations appearing in (4.8). However, it is straightforward to include additional constraints to problem (4.5) in order to guarantee non-negativity, namely $f(t_M, s) \geqslant 0$, $s \in [t_M, t_{M+T}]$.

In modern stochastic theory it is known that the expected path of the short rate should lie above the forward rate curve, see for example [4], [45] and [46]. This follows

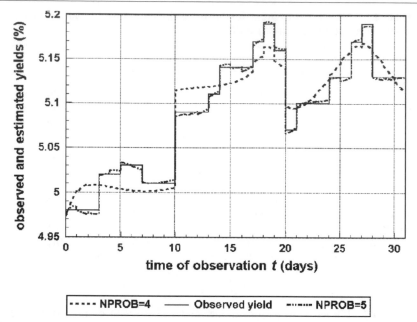

Figure 4.1   Estimated yield function, bilevel model: 1MAR–31MAR96 NPROB4, 5

from Jensen's inequality[1] applied to the expectation of the exponential function of the stochastic spot rate function. In our approach we use another norm (in contrast to *expectation*) for uncertainty, so this property is not a feature of our model. It is sufficient to adjoin constraints such as $r(s) \geqslant f(t_M, s)$, $s \in [t_M, t_{M+T}]$ to problem (4.5).

Example 4.1   *We use the observed yield data from Example 3.1. Assume that the spot rate follows the linear differential equations system* (3.20)–(3.22). *We set* $\gamma = 0$ *in all numerical experiments.*

We solve problem (4.5) *on a grid with* 186 *points with the following initial point:*

$$\alpha_0 = 0, \ \beta_0, \ r_0 = 0, \ v_0^T = 0; \ w_k = 0, k = \overline{1, N}; \ \bar{w}_k = 0, k = \overline{1, M},$$

where the choice of β *is given in Table 4.1.*

The numerical results for different initial points are given in Table 4.1.

The numerical results for different stopping tolerances, denoted by ACCSP, for solving the support problem and fixed initial point

$$\alpha_0 = 0, \ \beta_0 = -0.1, \ r_0 = 0, \ v_0^T = 0; \ w_k = 0, k = \overline{1, N}; \ \bar{w}_k = 0, k = \overline{1, M}$$

are given in Table 4.2.

Figure 4.1 illustrates the computed yield estimates $y(\cdot | \cdot)$ together with the observed yield $R(\cdot, \cdot)$ for **NPROB** = 4, 5. Figure 4.2 illustrates the error of the estimated yield

---

[1]If g is a concave function and X is a random variable, then $E\{g(X)\} \leqslant g(E\{X\})$.

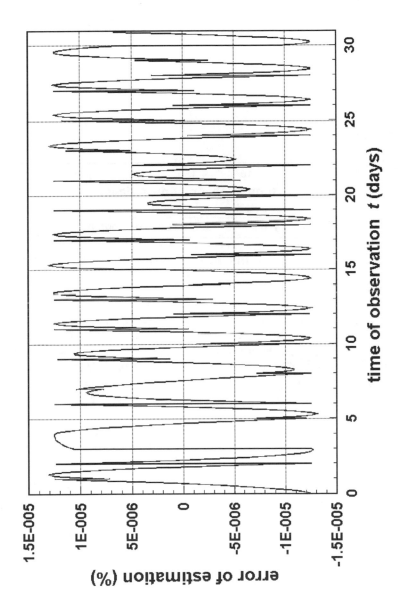

Figure 4.2   Estimation error of the yield function: 1MAR–31MAR96 NPROB6

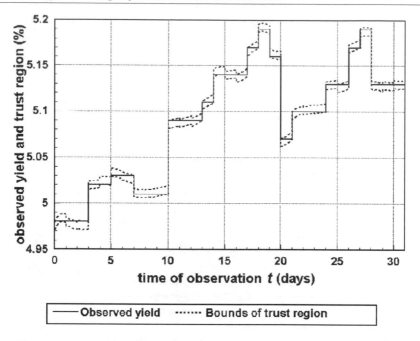

Figure 4.3   Estimated yield trust region, bilevel model: 1MAR–31MAR96

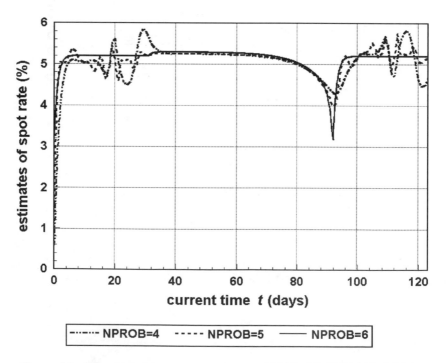

Figure 4.4   Bilevel model spot rate estimates: 1MAR–31MAR96 NPROB4–6

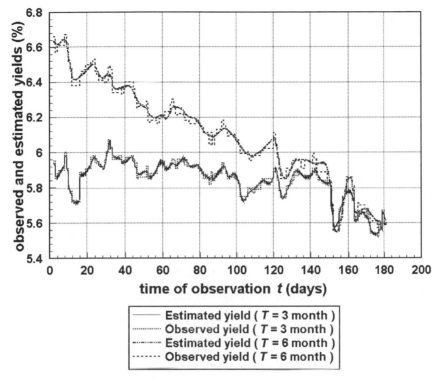

Figure 4.5   Estimated and observed yields, bilevel model, differing maturities: 3JAN–30JUN95

for NPROB = 6. Figure 4.3 illustrates the trust region for the yield for NPROB = 5. Figure 4.4 illustrates the computed estimates of the spot rate $r(\cdot)$ for NPROB = 4, 5, 6.

Figure 4.3 shows that when we introduce bilevel perturbations into the model, then with increasing accuracy of the approximation, the role of the yield perturbations is increased, and trajectories of the estimated spot rate become more 'smooth'. The interpretation is that the behavior of the spot rate reflects more of an average property, while the main role of the perturbations on the yield function (also to be estimated) is to provide a higher accuracy in the final yield estimation. The task is to find a balance between the accuracy of estimation and the influence of the spot rate on the observed yield to maturity. We conclude this chapter by commenting on the nature of the spot rate estimation error relative to the following three yield curve models:

1. the deterministic model (3.30);
2. a one-factor model such as (3.20);
3. the bilevel perturbation model (4.4) employed in the optimization problem (4.5).

   We draw the following conclusions.

   (1) From the deterministic model we see that the error of the estimation is equal to *half the difference between the maximum value of the observed yield and the minimum value of the observed yield for the entire interval of observation.*

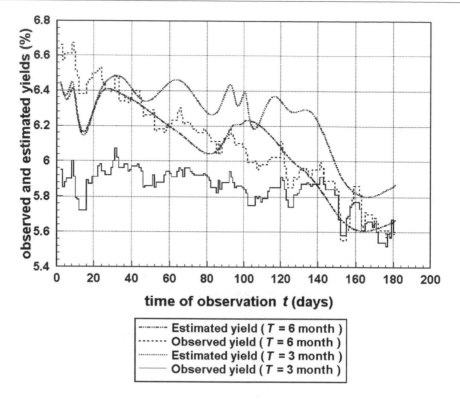

Figure 4.6 Estimated and observed yields for (3.56), differing maturities and spot rate model (3.24); observed surface (3.58): 3JAN–30JUN95

(2) Using the one-factor model under nonstochastic uncertainty yields an error of the estimation which equals *half of the maximum jump of the observed yield.*

(3) Using the bilevel perturbation model yields an error of estimation that does not depend on the structure of the observed yields, but depends on the stopping criterion used for solving problem (4.5). This conclusion is based in part on Figure 4.5, where two estimates are given respectively for two levels of required accuracy.

Figure 4.5 shows the estimated yields and observed yields for the extended bilevel model with differing maturities, combining problem (3.56) with (3.39), and spot rate model (3.24). The observation period is the same as above (3JAN–30JUN95), and the observations are yields to maturity of 3 months and 6 months.

Figure 4.6 gives the estimated yields and observed yields for model (3.56) (bonds with differing maturities) and the one-factor model (3.24) for the spot rate. The observations are on yields to maturity terms of 3 months and 6 months during the observation period 3JAN–30JUN95.

From these figures it is clearly seen that the one-factor model is not effective when the observation describes several terms to maturity. More than one factor is necessary to adequately model multiple maturities more accurately.

5

Numerical Experiments with One-factor and Bilevel Models for Extended Periods of Observations

In this chapter we group numerical estimation results for various time horizon and spot rate models according to the type of observation model: piecewise constant (3.10) or piecewise linear (3.11). The choice of input parameters is

$$w_* = \beta_* = -10, \ w^* = r^* = \alpha^* = 10, \ \alpha_* = r_* = 0,$$

$$\beta^* = -10^{-5}; \ r_0 = 5, \ \alpha_0 = 0.0, \ \beta_0 = -0.1.$$

We have used the *support problems method* for some of the optimizations, see Section 13.1. A common stopping tolerance for the support problems is ACCSP $= 10^{-5}$ for all examples. We solve a finite discretization of the nonlinear semi-infinite programming problem on a grid having step size 0.5. In some cases we choose step size 0.1, especially for the case where the period of observation is only 3 months.

5.1 RESULTS FROM THE PIECEWISE CONSTANT OBSERVATION MODEL (3.10)

Tables 5.1–5.5 give the results of numerical experiments for different periods of observation of Treasury yield rates for maturity term 3 months and different models of the spot rate. The common additional legend for all the tables in this chapter is:

- TT denotes the period of observation;
- NCONSP denotes the number of constraints in the finite nonlinear programming problem obtained from the given nonlinear semi-infinite programming problem;
- NVAR denotes the number of variables in the corresponding nonlinear programming problem;
- MAX denotes the maximum value of the observed Treasury yield rate;
- MIN denotes the minimum value of the observed Treasury yield rate.

Figure 5.1 gives the spot rate estimates for different models of the spot rate from the yield to maturity from 3JAN95 to 31DEC95. Figure 5.2 gives the yield to maturity and the estimates of the yield to maturity for different models of the spot rate from observations of the yield to maturity over the period 3JAN95 to 31DEC95.

Figure 5.3 gives spot rate estimates for successively shorter periods of observation of the yield to maturity from the analog of the Vasicek model with impulse perturbations. Figure 5.4 gives an estimate of the term structure surface of interest rates computed from the analog of the Vasicek model with piecewise constant perturbations for observations of yield to maturity from 1OCT95 to 31DEC95.

Table 5.1   Vasicek-type model with impulse perturbations over 3, 6, 9, 12MO ending DEC95

TT	1OCT–31DEC95	1JUL–31DEC95	1APR–31DEC95	3JAN–31DEC95
r_0^0	4.882779	5.028930	5.204785	4.997817
α^0	0.300465	0.413059	0.255036	0.222343
β^0	−0.055194	−0.076130	−0.045490	−0.039272
$-\alpha^0/\beta^0$	5.443798	5.425706	5.606419	5.661616
v_T^0	0.065	0.075	0.075	0.085
MAX	5.59	5.68	5.94	6.07
MIN	4.98	4.98	4.98	4.98
NCONSP	1104	1104	1650	2178
NVAR	188	280	371	459
ITER	21	18	44	45
NFUN	21	18	45	46
NQP	21	18	44	45
NGRAD	21	18	44	45
CPU (h:m:s)	0:03:21	0:06:27	0:41:31	1:25:13

Table 5.2   Vasicek-type model with impulse perturbations over 3, 6, 9, 12MO starting JAN95

TT	3JAN–31MAR95	3JAN–30JUN95	3JAN–30SEP95	3JAN—31DEC95
r_0^0	4.898917	4.976673	5.035318	4.997817
α^0	0.748241	0.701506	0.637142	0.222343
β^0	−0.126938	−0.120722	−0.112358	−0.039272
$-\alpha^0/\beta^0$	5.894539	5.816921	5.670642	5.661616
v_T^0	0.085	0.085	0.085	0.085
MAX	5.59	5.68	5.94	6.07
MIN	4.98	4.98	4.98	4.98
NCONSP	528	1074	1626	2178
NVAR	182	275	367	459
ITER	18	35	38	45
NFUN	18	35	38	46
NQP	18	35	38	45
NGRAD	18	35	38	45
CPU (h:m:s)	0:01:54	0:14:08	0:33:30	1:25:13

5.2 RESULTS FROM THE PIECEWISE LINEAR OBSERVATION MODEL (3.11)

Table 5.6 presents the results of numerical experiments for the piecewise linear model (3.11) of observation and different models of spot rates by observation yield to maturity from 1OCT95 to 31DEC95. Here NPROB = 1 corresponds to the analog of the Vasicek model with impulse perturbations and NPROB = 2 corresponds to the analog of the Vasicek model with point impulse perturbations. NPROB = 3 corresponds to the analog of the Dothan model.

Table 5.3 Vasicek-type model with point-impulse perturbations with four horizons of Table 5.1

TT	1OCT–31DEC95	1JUL–31DEC95	1APR–31DEC95	3JAN–31DEC95
r_0^0	4.909963	5.031434	5.204212	5.025502
α^0	0.304368	0.413545	0.247247	0.206829
β^0	−0.056144	−0.076373	−0.044135	−0.036717
$-\alpha^0/\beta^0$	5.421203	5.414806	5.602062	5.633058
v_T^0	0.065	0.075	0.075	0.085
MAX	5.59	5.68	5.94	6.07
MIN	4.98	4.98	4.98	4.98
NCONSP	1104	1104	1650	2178
NVAR	188	280	371	459
ITER	20	17	38	42
NFUN	20	17	39	43
NQP	20	17	38	42
NGRAD	20	17	38	42
CPU (h:m:s)	0:02:43	0:06:04	0:32:07	1:27:47

Table 5.4 Dothan-type model with four horizons of Table 5.1

TT	1OCT–31DEC95	1JUL–31DEC95	1APR–31DEC95	3JAN–31DEC95
r_0^0	5.001765	5.002267	5.003071	5.003747
v_T^0	0.065	0.075	0.075	0.085
NCONSP	1104	1104	1650	2178
NVAR	188	280	371	459
ITER	8	9	15	13
NFUN	10	12	21	15
NQP	8	9	15	13
NGRAD	8	9	15	13
CPU (h:m:s)	0:02:47	0:05:28	0:19:46	2:14:45

Table 5.5 Impulse model (3.47) with four horizons of Table 5.1

TT	1OCT–31DEC95	1JUL–31DEC95	1APR–31DEC95	3JAN–31DEC95
v_T^0	0.065	0.075	0.075	0.085
NCONSP	1104	1104	1650	2178
NVAR	185	277	368	456
ITER	30	41	71	76
NFUN	30	41	71	76
NQP	30	41	71	76
NGRAD	30	41	71	76
CPU (h:m:s)	0:02:59	0:07:25	0:35:35	1:50:34

Table 5.6   Piecewise linear model of observations with spot rate models of the analogs of the Vasicek and Dothan models

NPROB	1	2	3
r_0^0	3.550961	3.938536	4.979456
α^0	0.651080	0.615566	
β^0	−0.120340	−0.113778	
$-\alpha^0/\beta^0$	5.4103373	5.4102374	
v_T^0	0.018687	0.003889	0.017648
ITER	127	182	53
NFUN	133	194	94
NQP	127	182	53
NGRAD	127	182	53
CPU (h:m:s)	0:18:26	0:51:28	0:16:01

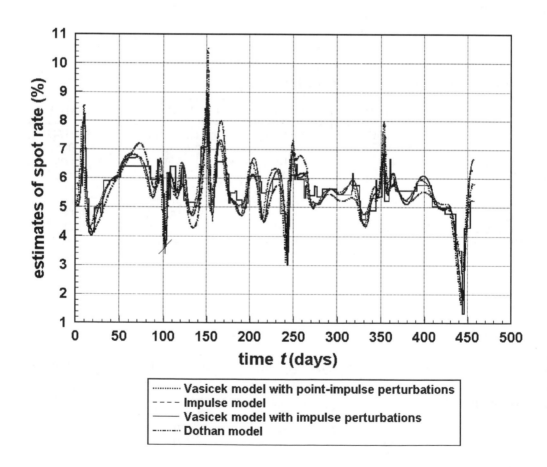

Figure 5.1   Spot rate model estimates, piecewise constant observation model: 3JAN–31DEC95

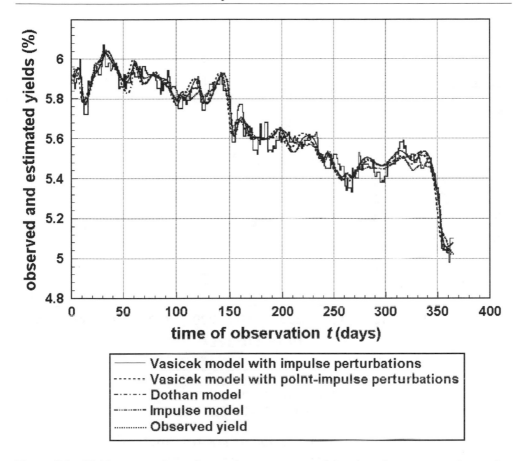

Figure 5.2 Yield to maturity estimates by spot rate models, piecewise constant observation model: 3JAN–31DEC95

Figure 5.5 gives the observed yield to maturity and the estimates of yield to maturity for different models of spot rate and the piecewise linear observation model (3.11). Figure 5.7 gives the estimates of the spot rate for both the piecewise constant (3.10) and the piecewise linear (3.11) observation models from the analog of the Vasicek model with impulse perturbations.

Figure 5.6 presents the forecasted yield curve and estimated yield curves for different periods of observation with current time 1APR95 obtained from the analog of the Vasicek model with impulse perturbations.

Finally, a comparison was made between both models of observations. Figure 5.7 illustrates estimates of the spot rate for piecewise constant and piecewise linear observation models, where the spot rate model is the analog of the Vasicek model with impulse perturbations.

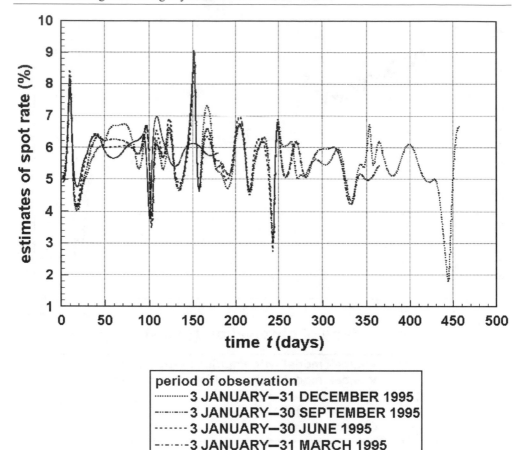

Figure 5.3   Spot rate estimates, different observation periods, impulse perturbations: 3JAN–31DEC95

5.3   SOME EXPERIMENTS IN SENSITIVITIES

We examined the sensitivity of our numerical results to (a) choices of perturbations, (b) choices for a 'law of motion' of the spot rate and (c) choices for the modeling of input observations. The results of the sensitivity analysis appear in several figures and are described as follows

Models (3.28) and (3.39) are sensitive to rapid changes in the observed yield. For example, in Figure 3.1 the value of the observed yield to maturity decreases from 5.16 to 5.08 at time 20. As is well known, the spot rate is the instantaneous rate of increase of the bond price. If the yield to maturity decreases rapidly, then the price of the bond increases rapidly. Hence, the spot rate should be rapidly increasing at this particular moment too. In Figure 3.8 we see that at time 20 the trajectory of the spot has a very high peak, see also Figures 5.1 and 5.2. On the other hand, the spot rate represents the instantaneous yield to maturity (see (1.52)), so if the bond price increases rapidly, then the instantaneous yield to maturity should increase sharply too. Moreover, the

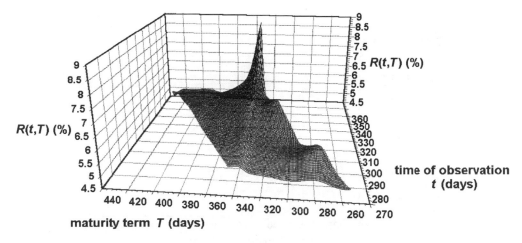

Figure 5.4 Estimated term structure surface, impulse perturbations: 1OCT–31DEC95

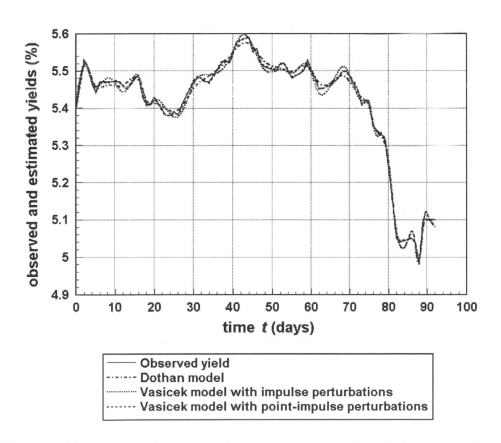

Figure 5.5 Observed and estimated yields for various spot rate models with the piecewise linear observation model (3.11), observation period: 1OCT–31DEC95

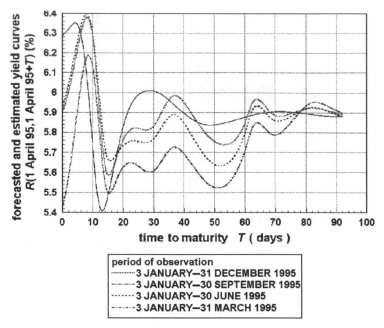

Figure 5.6 Estimated yields and forecasted yields for various observation periods, current time 1APR95 with impulse perturbations

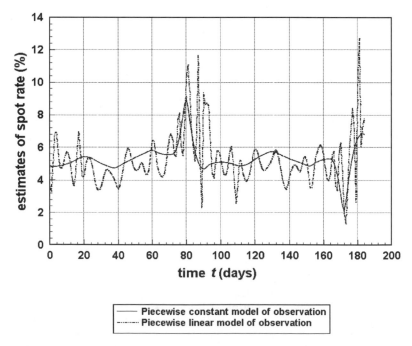

Figure 5.7 Spot rate estimates for the piecewise constant (3.10) and the piecewise linear observation models (3.11), with Vasicek-type impulse perturbations, observation period: 1OCT–31DEC95

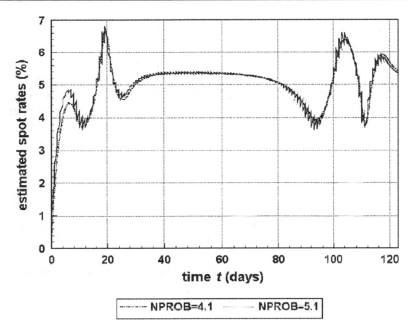

Figure 5.8 Comparison of spot rate estimates, impulse vs. point-impulse: 1MAR–31MAR96

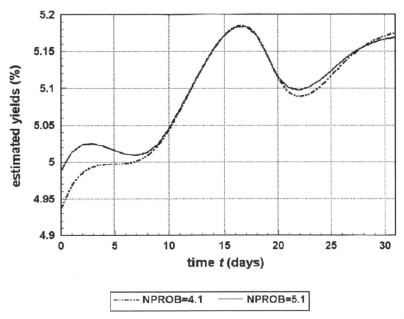

Figure 5.9 Comparison of yield estimates, impulse vs. point-impulse: 1MAR–31MAR96

instantaneous yield to maturity should decrease sharply at the moment of time equalling the current time plus the term of maturity. We do observe the 'bottom valley' of the spot rate at time 20 days + 3MO, namely day 111.

Figure 5.8 illustrates the computed estimates of the spot rate $r(\cdot)$ from NPROB4.1 and NPROB5.1. Figure 5.9 illustrates the computed estimate $y(\cdot|\cdot)$ of the yield from NPROB4.1 and NPROB5.1. Therefore, Figures 5.8 and 5.9 show a comparison between the two types of perturbations tested within one particular model of the spot rate, namely the impulse and point-impulse perturbations respectively. The figures show that the spot rates for both cases are almost identical. It supports the hypothesis that the solution is not very sensitive to the type of perturbation used. Moreover, from Figures 5.1 and 5.2 we can see the solution is not very sensitive to the type of model for generating the spot rate (e.g. differential equation or seeking some unknown function as in nondifferential equations models), given the piecewise constant observation model (3.10). On the other hand, from Figure 5.7 we see that the trajectories of the estimated spot rate differ for different models of observation of the yield to maturity. We can conclude that when using a one-factor model for the spot rate such as (3.28) or (3.39), the task of most significance is how to model the observed data values of the yield to maturity, and not so much (i) which 'law of motion model' is selected for the spot rate or (ii) what type of perturbation is chosen.

6

Modeling Nonarbitrage and Market Price of Risk in Linear Differential Systems

6.1 A NONARBITRAGE CONDITION
FOR LINEAR DYNAMICAL EQUATIONS MODELS
UNDER UNCERTAINTY

Analogous to the stochastic case, we construct a portfolio with two bonds with differing maturities, T_1 and T_2, selling one unit of the T_1 maturity and buying Δ of the T_2 maturity. The value of the portfolio is

$$\Pi(t) = P(t, T_1) - \Delta P(t, T_2). \tag{6.1}$$

Analogously, we differentiate $\Pi(t)$ with respect to time t, recognizing that all of our parameters are independent of time. Hence we obtain

$$\frac{d\Pi(t)}{dt} = \Pi(t)h(t, \omega). \tag{6.2}$$

But (6.2) states that the return on the portfolio equals the risk-free rate, the spot rate [66, p. 271]. But this required condition is not our complete measure of nonarbitrage because our approach depends on actual observations and real data. Let us be more precise.

If at time T_1 \$1 is invested in the risk-free market (what the observations of actual data show) and grows to \$M$ at time T_2, then \$M$ must be compared with what the estimated spot rate returns over this period, where we assume $h(s, \omega) \geqslant 0$ for all ω, i.e.

$$\exp\left(\int_{T_1}^{T_2} h(s, \omega) \, ds \right).$$

If $M > \exp(\int_{T_1}^{T_2} h(s, \omega) ds)$, we borrow \$1 at T_1 at the spot rate and invest it in the risk-free market during the period $[T_1, T_2]$. At T_1 we make a profit of $M - \exp(\int_{T_1}^{T_2} h(s, \omega) ds)$. If $M < \exp(\int_{T_1}^{T_2} h(s, \omega) ds)$, we borrow \$1 in the risk-free market (supported by observed data) and invest it at the spot rate over the period $[T_1, T_2]$. We make a profit of $\exp(\int_{T_1}^{T_2} h(s, \omega) ds) - M$.

We summarize the equilibrium of an investor who at time t^* issues an amount W_1 of bonds having maturity T_1 and simultaneously buys an amount W_2 of a bond maturing at time T_2. Without an arbitrage opportunity the following equation must hold:

$$W_1 \exp\left(-\int_{t^*}^{T_1} h(\tau, \omega) \, d\tau \right) = W_2 \exp\left(-\int_{t^*}^{T_2} h(\tau, \omega) \, d\tau \right). \tag{6.3}$$

Assume

$$h(\tau, \omega) \geqslant 0, \quad \text{for all } \tau \in \bar{T}, \omega \in \Omega. \tag{6.4}$$

We may suppose without loss of generality from (6.3) and (6.4) that $T_1 < T_2$. Rewrite (6.3) in the form

$$W_1 \left(\exp \left(-\int_{t^*}^{T_1} h(\tau, \omega) \, d\tau \right) - \frac{W_2}{W_1} \exp \left(-\int_{t^*}^{T_2} h(\tau, \omega) \, d\tau \right) \right)$$

$$= W_1 \exp \left(-\int_{t^*}^{T_1} h(\tau, \omega) \, d\tau \right) \left(1 - \frac{W_2}{W_1} \exp \left(-\int_{T_1}^{T_2} h(\tau, \omega) d\tau \right) \right) = 0.$$

Since $W_1 \neq 0$ and $\exp(-\int_{t^*}^{T_1} h(\tau, \omega) \, d\tau) \neq 0$, it follows from the last equation that

$$\exp \left(-\int_{T_1}^{T_2} h(\tau, \omega) \, d\tau \right) = \frac{W_1}{W_2}$$

or

$$-\int_{T_1}^{T_2} h(\tau, \omega) \, d\tau = \log \frac{W_1}{W_2}.$$

Let $W = W(T_1, T_2) = |\log(W_1/W_2)|$. Since $W_1 < W_2$ we have $\log(W_1/W_2) < 0$, and hence we obtain

$$\int_{T_1}^{T_2} h(\tau, \omega) \, d\tau = W.$$

Since the above equation is valid for any $T_1 < T_2$ and $W > 0$, it follows that we can state the following *nonarbitrage necessary condition*.

Nonarbitrage Necessary Condition.   *Let the function $h(\cdot, \cdot)$ satisfy (3.7), (3.8), and (6.4). For any arbitrary T_1, T_2 and W satisfying $T_1 < T_2$, $W > 0$, there exists $\hat{\omega} = \hat{\omega}(T_1, T_2) \in \Omega$ such that the following statement is true:*

$$\int_{T_1}^{T_2} h(\tau, \hat{\omega}) \, d\tau = W. \tag{6.5}$$

Hence, we can guarantee the existence of nonarbitrage if we include the non-negativity of the spot rate and the *nonarbitrage necessary condition* in Definition 3.2 and Assumption 3.2.

At first it may seem that condition (6.5) significantly complicates the application of model (3.7), (3.8), (6.4), (6.5) for estimating the spot rate. But now we show that this assertion is not true. Our primary model type is the analog of the model with impulse perturbations, (3.28), where the abstract form of the solution is given in (3.24). Assume that $\hat{w}_i = w_i = 0$, $i = \overline{1, N}$, i.e. all perturbations are set to zero. From (3.24) we obtain

$$h(t, \omega | \hat{w}) = e^{\beta t} r_0 + \frac{\alpha}{\beta} (e^{\beta t} - 1).$$

From (6.5), given arbitrary T_1, T_2, $T_1 < T_2$ and $W > 0$ it follows that

$$\int_{T_1}^{T_2} h(\tau, \omega \mid \hat{w} = 0)\, d\tau = \int_{T_1}^{T_2} (e^{\beta\tau} r_0 + \frac{\alpha}{\beta}(e^{\beta\tau} - 1))\, d\tau = r_0 \frac{e^{\beta T_2} - e^{\beta T_1}}{\beta}$$

$$+ \alpha \frac{e^{\beta T_2} - e^{\beta T_1}}{\beta^2} - \frac{\alpha}{\beta}(T_2 - T_1) = W.$$

Choose $\beta = \hat{\beta} < 0$. It follows that

$$r_0 = \left| \frac{\hat{\beta}}{e^{\hat{\beta} T_2} - e^{\hat{\beta} T_1}} \right| \left(W - \alpha \frac{T_2 - T_1}{|\hat{\beta}|} + \alpha \left| \frac{e^{\hat{\beta} T_2} - e^{\hat{\beta} T_1}}{\beta^{*2}} \right| \right)$$

$$= \bar{W} + \alpha \left(\frac{1}{|\hat{\beta}|} - \frac{T_2 - T_1}{|e^{\hat{\beta} T_2} - e^{\hat{\beta} T_1}|} \right),$$

where

$$\bar{W} = W \frac{|\hat{\beta}|}{|e^{\hat{\beta} T_2} - e^{\hat{\beta} T_1}|} > 0.$$

Choose $\alpha = \hat{\alpha} \geqslant 0$ so that

$$\bar{W} + \hat{\alpha} \left(\frac{1}{|\hat{\beta}|} - \frac{T_2 - T_1}{|e^{\hat{\beta} T_2} - e^{\hat{\beta} T_1}|} \right) \geqslant 0, \tag{6.6}$$

which always holds because $\bar{W} > 0$. Hence, for any arbitrary $W > 0$, T_1, T_2, $T_1 < T_2$, we can choose $\hat{\alpha} \geqslant 0$ such that $\hat{r}_0 \geqslant 0$.

The nonarbitrage necessary condition therefore holds if, for example, we define the admissible set of parameters Ω of Definition 3.2 as follows:

1. $r_0 \geqslant 0$, i.e. $r_* = 0$, $r^* = +\infty$;
2. $\alpha \geqslant 0$, i.e. $\alpha_* = 0$, $\alpha^* = +\infty$; $\beta < 0$, e.g. $\beta_* = -\infty$, $\beta^* = -\epsilon$, where $\epsilon > 0$ is sufficiently small;
3. $w_{*i} < 0$, $w_i^* > 0$, $i = \overline{1, N}$.

Conditions 1–3 are usually used for describing the unknown parameters. Indeed, constraint 1 serves to guarantee the non-negativity of the initial spot rate, constraint 2 guarantees the mean-reversion property for the spot rate, where we use the following definition:

Definition 6.1 *We say that the spot rate has mean reversion if $\lim_{t\to\infty} r(t)$ exists and is finite.*

The models developed in this book are *mean-reverting*. For example, for the analog of the Vasicek model we have

$$\lim_{t\to\infty} r(t) = -\frac{\alpha}{\beta}.$$

For the Dothan model we obtain

$$r(t) = r_0 \exp \left(\sum_{i=1}^{N} w_i(t_i - t_{i-1}) \right), \quad \text{for all } t > t_N.$$

Finally constraint 3 permits positive or negative perturbations on the spot rate.

In order to satisfy the nonarbitrage necessary condition (6.5) only two parameters in the linear dynamical system model are needed: α and β. This has some meaning. Indeed, the perturbations realized in an actual market have influence only on the value of W. Note that the choice of the values of r_0, α and β serves the purpose of calibrating the nonarbitrage condition (6.5). Moreover, as (6.6) is valid for any initial time t_0, the parameter β plays the role of the *speed* of discounting of the bond, and parameter α is a *step size* selection for fitting the non-negativity condition of the spot rate.

6.1.1 A Sufficient Condition for Nonarbitrage of Constant Maturity Yield Minimax Estimation

Let the function $h(\cdot, \cdot)$ satisfy (3.7), (3.8) and (6.4). For all arbitrary T_1, T_2, $W = W(T_1, T_2)$ there exists $\hat{\omega}$, independent of time, such that (6.5) holds.

Of course this condition is a strong one. There is also an issue about the existence of $\hat{\omega}$. However, we recommend the following procedure for discovering existence of arbitrage.

Step 1   Employ the nonarbitrage necessary condition. Construct the set Ω for a particular model of the spot rate leading to the addition of constraints with parameter vector ω in an optimal observation problem, whose generic form appeared in (2.17).

Step 2   Solve the associated optimal observation problem obtaining the objective function value ϵ.

Step 3   Use ϵ as a measure of the *violation* of the nonarbitrage sufficient condition. Hence, in general in our model arbitrage exists, but in this case we can quantitatively measure the amount of the violation of nonarbitrage.

Equation (6.5) is conditioned by the data. Solving problem (3.28) with the additional conditions adjoined for an optimum gives a sufficient condition for nonarbitrage, namely delivering an optimal ω^* having $v_T = 0$. When conditions 1–3 above are adjoined to the model, then given any $W > 0$ an admissible ω exists for nonarbitrage, but the resulting estimation error may be unacceptable. On the other hand, if the program (3.28) value v_T were zero, then

$$\int_t^{t+T} h(\tau, w)\, dw = T\, \hat{R}(t, t+T) \quad \text{for every } t \text{ in the observation period } T^M. \quad (6.7)$$

We replace the range of W in (6.5) by the range implied by our observations, namely (6.7), thereby having another range than the original (6.5). In this sense our general arbitrage condition (6.5) is conditioned by the data.

6.2   ESTIMATING THE MARKET PRICE OF RISK FOR DYNAMICAL SYSTEMS UNDER UNCERTAINTY

The *market price of risk* is a well-known concept in stochastic differential equations models of the spot riskless rate. In this section we introduce the concept of *market price of risk* from the point of view of what gain or loss could occur in the future from present buying and selling of assets. Of course, we develop this concept from our dynamical systems approach under nonstochastic uncertainty with perturbations.

Consider an investor who at time $\hat{t}$ issues an amount W_1 of a bond with maturity T_1 and simultaneously buys an amount W_2 of a bond maturing at time T_2. The basic problem is to determine the profit or loss of this operation at time $s > \hat{t}$ in a market functioning under uncertainty. Following our approach, we assume that the set Ω of the a priori distribution of unknown parameters (3.7) and the family of functions $h(t, \omega)$ in Assumption 3.2 are defined. Introduce

$$z(\omega, s) = W_1 \exp\left\{-\int_s^{T_1} h(\tau, \omega)\, d\tau\right\} - W_2 \exp\left\{-\int_s^{T_2} h(\tau, \omega)\, d\tau\right\}, \quad \omega \in \Omega. \qquad (6.8)$$

By the nonarbitrage property, we have $z(\omega, \hat{t}) = 0$.

Definition 6.2 *The function $z(\omega, s)$ defined in (6.8) is termed the linear dynamical system market price of risk.*

Of course the linear dynamical system market price of risk also depends on W_1, W_2, T_1, T_2, but we assume that these values are given.

6.2.1   A Priori Estimation of the Market Price of Risk

We seek an upper bound $z^*(s)$ and a lower bound $z_*(s)$ of $z(\cdot, \cdot)$. An immediate approach is to solve the following two nonlinear problems:

$$z^*(s) = z^*_{\mathrm{AP}}(s) := \max_{\omega \in \Omega} z(\omega, s), \quad z_*(s) = z_{*\mathrm{AP}}(s) = \min_{\omega \in \Omega} z(\omega, s). \qquad (6.9)$$

Note that estimates (6.9) are obtained only from a priori information about the unknown parameters, and therefore we shall term them the *a priori bounds on the market price of risk*. More precise estimates can be obtained by using observations of the yield curve. For simplicity, consider model (3.15).

Assume observations have been made by the piecewise constant observation model (3.10) or by the piecewise linear observation model (3.11) for some given time-to-maturity T during M days. Clearly, not all members ω of Ω can generate observed values of the yield. Hence, a subset $\hat{\Omega}$ of Ω exists consisting of members ω that can generate points on the yield curve. It shall be termed the *a posteriori distribution of unknown parameters ω*. We next describe how to obtain extremal values $z^*(s)$, $z_*(s)$ on certain subsets of $\hat{\Omega}$ itself.

6.2.2   Optimal Estimation of the Market Price of Risk

Let (ω^0, v_T^0) be a solution of problem (3.15). We shall estimate the z-extremal values on the subset of $\hat{\Omega}$ of members which can guarantee an optimal estimation error v_T^0 of the observed yield. For this purpose, define

$$\Omega_{\mathrm{OPT}} = \{\omega \in \hat{\Omega} \mid |y(t, \omega \mid T) - \hat{R}(t, t+T)| \leqslant v_T^0, \forall t \in T^M\}.$$

We term the set Ω_{OPT} the *optimal a posteriori distribution of unknown parameters* ω. Analogous to (6.9) we obtain the following optimization problems:

$$z^*(s) = z^*_{\text{OPT}}(s) := \max_{\omega \in \Omega_{\text{OPT}}} z(\omega, s), \;\; z_*(s) = z_{*\text{OPT}}(s) = \min_{\omega \in \Omega_{\text{OPT}}} z(\omega, s). \tag{6.10}$$

The values $z^*_{\text{OPT}}(s)$ and $z_{*\text{OPT}}(s)$ are termed the *optimal observation bounds for the market price of risk*.

6.2.3   Estimating the Market Price of Risk under a Fixed Observed Current Structure

Let (ω^0, v^0_T) be a solution of problem (3.15). Denote $\bar{k} = k - \mathcal{T}$. The goal here is to fix estimates of unknown parameters corresponding to the current moment of time. Define a subset of $\hat{\Omega}$ as follows:

$$\Omega_{\text{FIX}} = \{\omega \in \hat{\Omega} \,|\, \omega_i = \omega^0_i, \, i = \overline{1, \bar{k}}\}.$$

Analogous to (6.9) and (6.10) we obtain the optimization problems

$$z^*(s) = z^*_{\text{FIX}}(s) := \max_{\omega \in \Omega_{\text{FIX}}} z(\omega, s), \;\; z_*(s) = z_{*\text{FIX}}(s) = \min_{\omega \in \Omega_{\text{FIX}}} z(\omega, s). \tag{6.11}$$

In all cases the functions $z^*(s)$ and $z_*(s)$ can be generated by the adaptive estimators (3.53) or (3.54) applied to problems (6.9)–(6.11). However, problems (6.9)–(6.11) are nonlinear and nonconvex so that global optimization methods must be used to compute bounds for the market price of risk.

6.3   CHAPTER NOTES

In this chapter we have described necessary and sufficient conditions for nonarbitrage. In general, distinguishing a 'necessary' condition from a 'sufficient' condition often arises in optimization theory and mathematics. In our context each condition has a different meaning and financial interpretation. The necessary condition is used for checking the optimal observation model for the existence of arbitrage. If the necessary condition were not to hold for some optimization model constructed from the parameter set Ω, see Definition 3.1, and functional form chosen for the spot rate, see Assumption 3.1, then the optimization model has arbitrage a priori. This means that the parameter set or functional class should be adjusted to satisfy the necessary condition.

The sufficient condition is used for determining the level of arbitrage associated with the computed solution to the optimal observation problem. This level is actually bounded by the scope of the observed data that underlie the optimization problem. Ideally, if one were to include all conceivable data with all available terms to maturity in the optimization model, then the optimal value of the objective function, say ϵ^0, will represent the level of arbitrage of the computed solution. If $\epsilon^0 = 0$, then there is no arbitrage. The condition $\epsilon^0 > 0$ means the existence of arbitrage and the value of ϵ^0 is its level. The sufficient condition for arbitrage can also assist in the choice of specific input parameters and functions $\{\Omega, h(\cdot, \cdot)\}$, referring again to Definition 3.1 and Assumption 3.1. One goal could be to select an observation model for the data so as to minimize ϵ^0.

Another issue concerning the sufficient condition is its strength. At first it does appear as a very strong condition, and so could have limited use. Indeed, for some current time

t and *all* possible combinations of future times to maturity T_1, T_2 and $W(T_1, T_2)$ there should exist a solution to the optimization problem $\hat{\omega}(t)$ such that (6.5) holds.

Let us take a look at what appears in the stochastic case. There, the nonarbitrage condition is the following:

$$\frac{\mu(t, T_1) - r(t)P(t, T_1)}{v(t, T_1)} = \frac{\mu(t, T_2) - r(t)P(t, T_2)}{v(t, T_2)} \tag{6.12}$$

which should hold for any maturities T_1, T_2; see, for example, Rebonato [56, (7.12)]. Here μ is the real world drift of the price of a discount bond, $r(t)P(t, T)$ is the risk-neutral drift and $v(t, T)$ is the volatility of the bond price. This equation leads to the well-known concept of *market price of risk*, namely that there should exist a function $\lambda(t, r)$, possibly dependent on r and t, but *independent of maturity*, satisfying

$$\lambda(t, r) = \frac{\mu(t, T) - r(t)P(t, T)}{v(t, T)}. \tag{6.13}$$

So by the stochastic route we have arrived at an analogous condition to our sufficient condition, which states that there should exist some market characteristic that possibly depends on current time but does not depend on the time to maturity.

7

Characteristics of Moments in Linear Dynamical Systems under Uncertainty with Perturbations

From the theory of stochastic processes applied to the law of motion of a risky asset over time, there exist unique characteristics such as drift and volatility for each stochastic processes model. An issue with our approach to modeling asset prices with linear dynamical systems under nonstochastic uncertainty and perturbations arises about the existence of companion or analogous concepts of 'drift' and 'volatility'. We address this issue next.

7.1 MEAN PATH SOLUTIONS TO DYNAMICAL SYSTEMS (2.17)

Drift in a stochastic process describes the mean (first moment) behavior of the stochastic process. By analogy, the *mean function* of the estimate of uncertainty embedded in our approach should have the following three properties.

1. The mean function should be a solution to the differential system (2.17) for the spot rate, and it should approximate observed data well. In our application, the integral of an optimal solution should approximate the observed yields.
2. The influence or *force* of uncertainty on the mean function estimate should be absent or at least minimal.
3. A mean function should be uniquely determined.

Consider the analog of the Vasicek model (9.8), with perturbations (3.22) and (3.34)–(3.36). We assume now that β is fixed, say $\beta = \hat{\beta} < 0$, and that the accuracy obtained in approximating the observed data is within ϵ. Let

$$\Omega^\epsilon = \{\omega \mid |\hat{R}(t, t + T) - p(t, \omega | T)| \leqslant \epsilon, \forall t \in T^N\}. \tag{7.1}$$

Note that the set Ω^ϵ consists of only those members of Ω for which an estimated trajectory exists within an ϵ approximation of the observed data, in the sense of the L_1 norm.

Motivated by properties 1–3 we construct the following optimization problem:

$$V(\hat{\beta}, \epsilon) = \min_{\omega \in \Omega^\epsilon} \frac{1}{T^N} \int_{T^N} w^2(\tau) \, d\tau,$$

$$r_{0*} \leqslant r_0 \leqslant r_0^*; \, \alpha \geqslant 0; \, w_i \in \mathbf{R}, \, i = \overline{1, N}. \tag{7.2}$$

In Chapter 3 we considered two classes of perturbation functions $\{w(t), \, t \in T^N\}$: *impulse* specified in (3.22) and *point-impulse* specified in (3.34)–(3.36). These functions are among the unknown parameters in Ω and are included in any $\omega \in \Omega$. For both of these cases the perturbation functions can be characterized by real-valued constants $\{w_i\}_{i=\overline{1,N}}$, namely those appearing in (7.2). Note that in (7.2) there are no constraints on the perturbations. The objective function is strictly convex quadratic in the variables w_i and the constraints are of linear semi-infinite programming type.

Assume that ϵ is chosen so that (7.2) has an optimal solution $\omega^0(\epsilon, \hat{\beta})$ which necessarily will be unique. The unique solution corresponds to the estimate of the spot rate having minimal possible values of the perturbations in a sum of squares sense, for the fixed parameters β and ϵ.

Definition 7.1 *A feasible solution $\omega \in \Omega$ to (7.2) is termed an ϵ-approximation of the observed data. If $\omega^0(\epsilon, \hat{\beta})$ is the optimal solution, then the function $\mu_T(t) = r(t|\hat{\beta}, \epsilon) = h(t, \omega^0(\epsilon, \hat{\beta}))$, $t \in T^N$ is termed the mean path of the spot rate.*

The *mean path* corresponds to the unique estimate of the spot rate that comes from an ϵ-approximation with minimal possible influence of the perturbations. This estimate describes the mean tendency with maximal possible stable behavior.

In [48] Medvedev and Cox showed that within the framework of affine stochastic models for the term structure of interest rates with constant parameters, observations of the yield rates process do not in general uniquely determine the parameters of the model. In our approach we obtain a unique estimate of the spot rate for some fixed specification of the parameter β and preassigned error of the estimation. Naturally, the question arises, how does the estimated trajectory of the spot rate depend on the choices of these two parameters, namely β and the maximum admissible error?

7.1.1 Numerical Experiments on Generating Spot Rate Trajectories

The following experiment shows the dependence of the spot rate trajectory on different values of β with a fixed estimation error of $\epsilon = 0.001$.

We observe the 3-month Treasury bill rate auction average taken from the St. Louis Federal Reserve Bank's file wtb3mo for the period of observation defined by 2/7/97 through 2/6/98. The computations were for

$$\beta \in \{-0.001, -0.01, -1, -5, -10, -100\}.$$

All estimates of the spot rate trajectories are close to each other. Figure 7.1 provides an illustration of estimated spot rate trajectories for the two extreme cases, namely $\beta = -0.001$ and $\beta = -100$. Hence, the parameter β determines the type of spot rate function that is generated. For large negative values of β we obtain a spot rate trajectory that is approximately an impulse function. When values of β are chosen close to zero, then the spot rate trajectory is approximately piecewise linear.

7.2 MINIMAX AMPLITUDE

We now examine the linear dynamical system under uncertainty for the purpose of estimating the amplitude of possible values around some characteristic of the estimate of the spot rate. It is natural to choose the *mean reversion limit* of the estimated spot

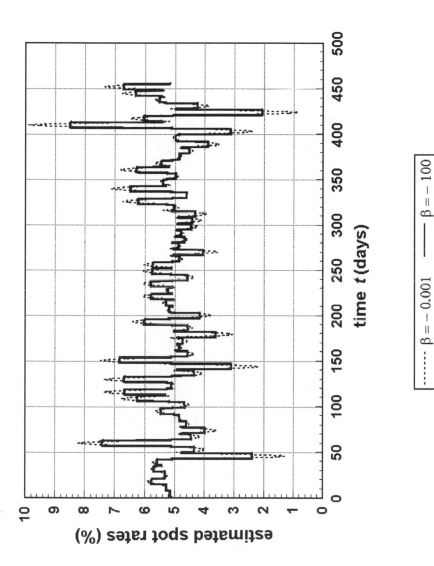

Figure 7.1 Comparison of estimated spot rates for different values of β

rate for one such characteristic. By our conservative *minimax* approach we automatically generate lower, guaranteed bounds for this type of amplitude. Upper bounds are more difficult because these bounds will depend on realized values (e.g. implied bounds) of the perturbations.

We begin by freeing the parameter β while keeping the accuracy of the approximation fixed at ϵ. We seek an estimate of the amplitude according to the following optimization problem:

$$\sigma_\epsilon^0 = \min_{\omega \in \Omega} \max_{t \in T^N} \left| r(t|\omega) - \left| \frac{\alpha}{\beta} \right| \right|. \tag{7.3}$$

Problem (7.3) is equivalent to

$$\min_{\omega \in \Omega} \sigma_\epsilon \text{ subject to}$$

$$|\hat{R}(t, t + \mathcal{T}) - p(t, \omega | \mathcal{T})| \leqslant \epsilon, \ \forall t \in T^N,$$

$$\left| r(t|\omega) + \frac{\alpha}{\beta} \right| \leqslant \sigma_\epsilon, \ \forall t \in T^N, \tag{7.4}$$

$$r_{0*} \leqslant r_0 \leqslant r_0^*; \ \alpha \geqslant 0; \ \beta \leqslant -\gamma; \ w_i \in \mathbf{R}, \ i = \overline{1, N},$$

where γ is sufficiently small.

Definition 7.2 *We term the optimal value σ_ϵ^0 the minimax amplitude of the estimate of the spot rate.*

The value σ_ϵ^0 has the following interpretation. For any estimate $r(\cdot|\cdot)$ of the spot rate $r(\cdot)$ that stems from an ϵ-approximation of the observed data, the maximum deviation of the values of the spot rate coming from an ϵ-approximation around the mean reversion limit on the whole interval cannot be less than σ_ϵ^0. It is natural to expect that different types of perturbations for the spot rate will give different values of σ_ϵ^0. This means that we can use the value of σ_ϵ^0 as a criterion for the choice of perturbations to use in a given situation. We should choose a perturbation of the spot rate that gives the minimal value of σ_ϵ^0 among all available classes of perturbations.

7.3   CHAPTER NOTES

In this chapter we introduced two characteristics of the solution to the dynamical system under uncertainty that facilitate the estimation of the dynamics of the observed data.

The mean path of the spot rate corresponds to a trajectory of the dynamical system for the spot rate that is based on the minimal possible values of perturbations for some preassigned level of estimation error. In this sense such an estimate is more 'certain' upon comparison with others that generate the same estimation error. Such an estimate of the dynamical system under uncertainty could be interpreted as an analog of the drift in a stochastic process.

The second characteristic, termed *minimax amplitude*, allows one to estimate the lower bound of the maximal deviation of possible values of the spot rate from its mean-reversion limit. Under this approach applied to observed data the maximal absolute deviation of any possible value of the spot rate could not be less than the minimax amplitude value.

All estimates introduced in this chapter were obtained by fixing some predetermined level ϵ of the error of estimation. Another way of modeling such estimates includes using penalty functions in the optimal observation problem. In this approach the level of estimation errors is not fixed a priori but obtained a posteriori from the solution of the optimization problem. Moreover, different values of the penalty coefficient yield different values of the level of the estimation error. Observation models of this type will be described in Chapter 9. They are more flexible and allow the modeler to easily construct estimates of the dynamical system for different levels of estimation errors. A sensitivity analysis between the penalty coefficient and the level of the estimation error will be presented in Chapter 9.

8
Backtesting with Treasury Auction Data

8.1 DATA AND ESTIMATION

A *universal data period* for 3-month Treasury averages begins with **1/5/90** and continues through **12/26/97**. This 8-year period is the *universal period*. The source of data for estimation, forecasting and backtesting is the St. Louis Federal Reserve Bank's file, **wtb3mo**, the 3-MONTH TREASURY BILL RATE AUCTION AVERAGE PERCENT. A graphical representation of the observed data is given in Figure 8.1.

Within the universal data period is a sequence of 375 observation periods of 6 months duration (26 weeks) beginning with 1/5/90–6/29/90. These periods move forward one week at a time, so the second period is 1/12/90–7/6/90, continuing through the last observation period, 3/7/96–8/29/97. There are 52 Fridays in each year except 1993 (which has 53) and 10 Fridays in 1997 corresponding to observation periods. Table 8.1 summarizes these choices.

For each observation period we compute optimal, data-dependent parameters defining our estimated yield function applicable to the given observation period, and state the error of the estimated yields to the observed auction yields. We use an analog of the Vasicek model with daily impulse perturbations with error of estimation 0.001.

Table 8.1 Definition of the weeks in the universal period

Number of period	Observation period 26 Fridays inclusive
1	1/5/90–6/29/90
2	1/12/90–7/6/90
3	1/19/90–7/13/90
...	... ...
371	2/7/97–8/1/97
372	2/14/97–8/8/97
373	2/21/97–8/15/97
374	2/28/97–8/22/97
375	3/7/97–8/29/97

8.1.1 Forecasting

Following the last week of an observation period, we compute a forecast of the yield of a 3MO constant maturity bond for each week in the 17 Friday forecast period, denoted generically 'Forecast (Friday)' with the variable date designation 'Friday' ranging over the forecast period. Lower and upper bounds for the true auction yield, denoted 'Auction (Friday)', are also forecasted. These bounds are denoted 'Lower (Friday)' and 'Upper (Friday)'. The difference 'Upper (Friday) − Lower (Friday)' computed towards the end of the forecast period is termed the 'Range' for the given forecast period.

The word alias is used for backtesting because all data have occurred in the past. As we move an observation period forward, we act as though we encounter a future

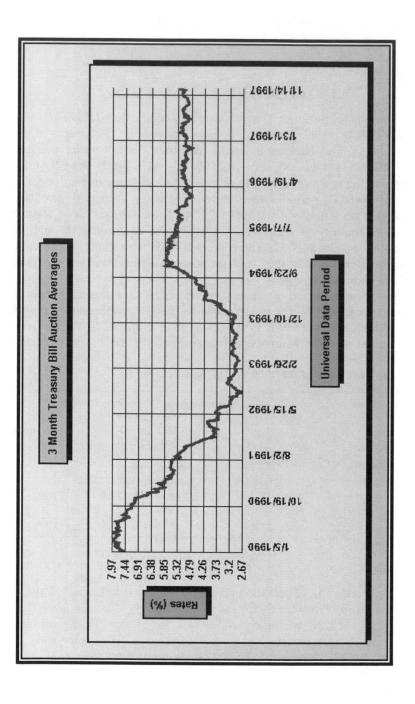

Figure 8.1   Observed 3-month Treasury bill auction averages: 1/5/90–12/26/97

Table 8.2 The 375 forecast periods over the time interval 1/5/90–12/26/97

Number of period	Current time	Forecast period 17 Fridays (excluding 7/4/97)
1	6/29/90	7/6/90–10/26/90
2	7/6/90	7/13/90–11/3/90
3	7/13/90	7/20/90–11/9/90
. . .		
367	7/7/97	7/11/97–10/31/97
368	7/11/97	7/18/97–11/7/97
369	7/18/97	7/25/97–11/14/97
370	7/25/97	8/1/97–11/21/97
371	8/1/97	8/8/97–11/28/97
372	8/8/97	8/15/97–12/5/97
373	8/15/97	8/22/97–12/12/97
374	8/22/97	8/29/97–12/19/97
375	8/29/97	9/5/97–12/26/97

Note that 7/4/97 is a Friday so that the data date is the following Monday 7/7/97

forecasting period. The alias current time is the last week of a given forecasting period, and the forecast begins with the very next Friday inclusive for 17 weeks. The current time for the first observation period is Friday 6/29/90, and the first forecast begins with Friday 7/6/90. The first alias forecast period continues through Friday 10/26/90. The last observation period is 3/7/97–8/29/97, and so the last alias forecasting period is 9/5/97 12/26/97. Just as there are 375 observation periods, there are also 375 forecasting periods. For convenience we list some of them in Table 8.2.

8.1.2 Reliability of Forecasts

Along with computing the forecasted yield curve, upper and lower bound forecasted curves are also computed. For a given forecast period let N denote the number of times the true auction yields, contained in the universal data set, lie within the forecasted bounds. Since there are 17 Fridays in each forecast period, N divided by 17 defines the **reliability** of the forecast for the given forecast period, and shall be termed the **reliability proportion** for the respective forecast period. See Figures 8.2 and 8.3.

8.1.3 Range of Forecasts

By the range of forecasts we shall mean the difference in percent between the upper and lower bound at a point in time near the end of a given forecast period. As a rule ranges differ among different forecast periods. See Figures 8.4 and 8.5.

8.1.4 Precision of Forecasts

Let FP denote a given forecast period. We use the following performance quantities for forecasting, referring again to Friday as our generic date in a given week. Perfect forecasts during all the forecast periods would generate a reliability curve uniformly at 100%, while the range curve would be uniform at 0%. Each respective bar chart would have a unique bar of height 100 at the extreme left of the chart.

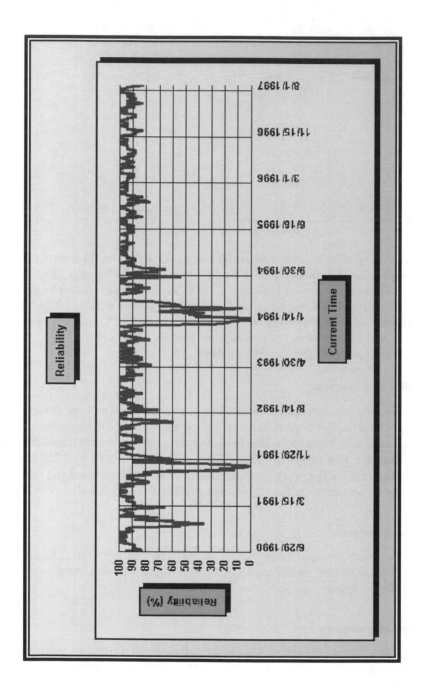

Figure 8.2   Reliability proportions for the respective forecast period

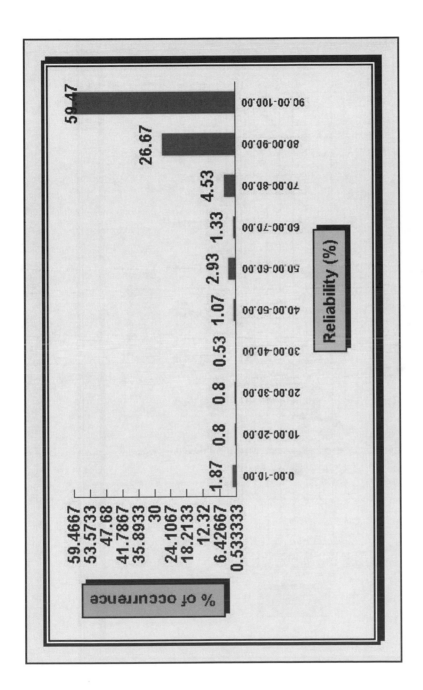

Figure 8.3 Reliability proportions for the respective forecast period by percentage occurrences

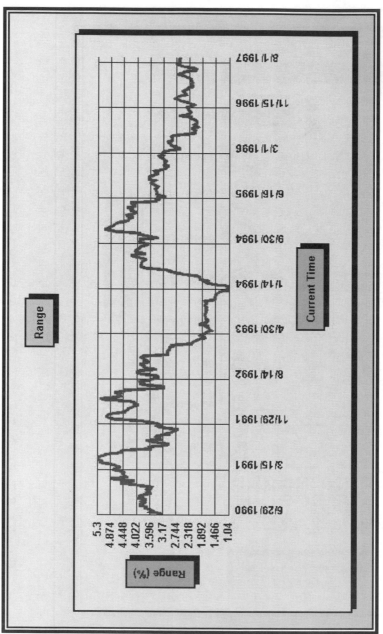

Figure 8.4 Range of upper and lower bounds of the forecasts

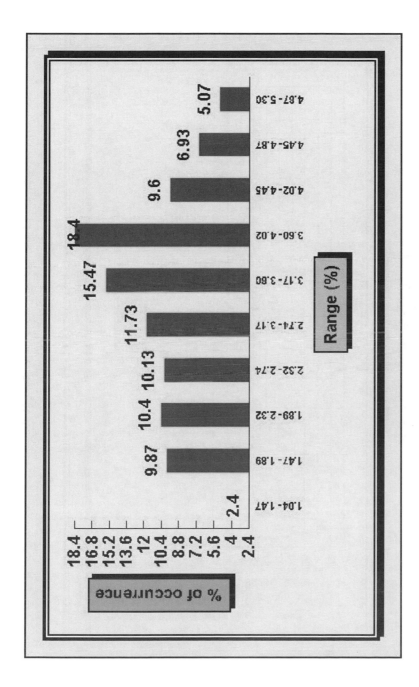

Figure 8.5 Range of upper and lower bounds of the forecasts, percentage occurrences

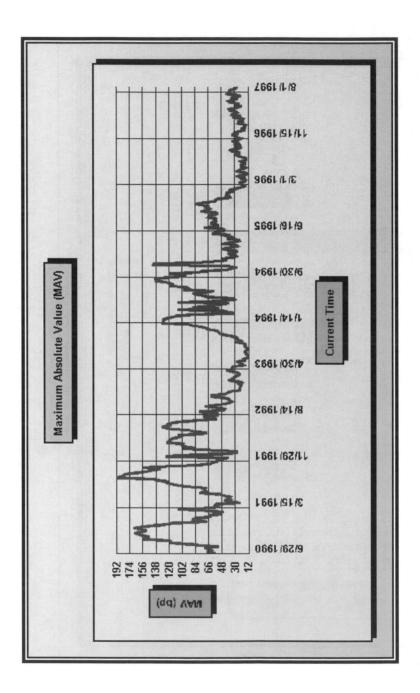

Figure 8.6   Maximum absolute value in basis points over a forecast period

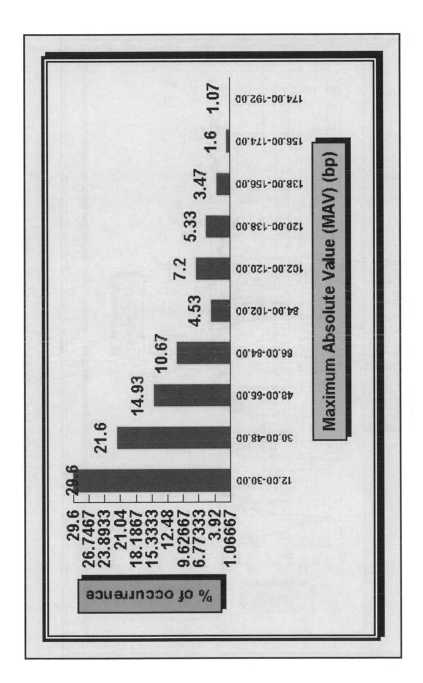

Figure 8.7 Maximum absolute value in basis points over a forecast period by percentage occurrences

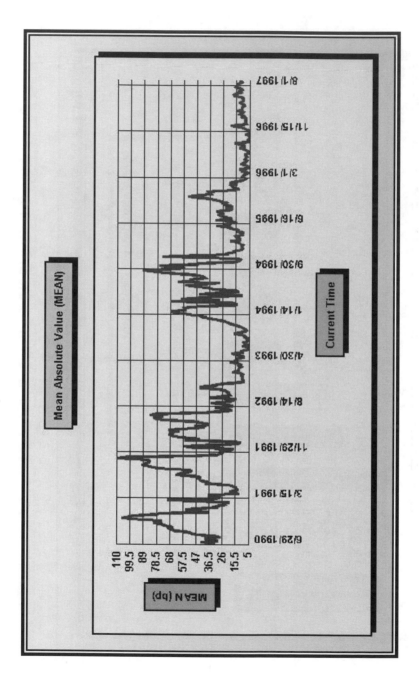

Figure 8.8   Mean absolute value over a forecast period

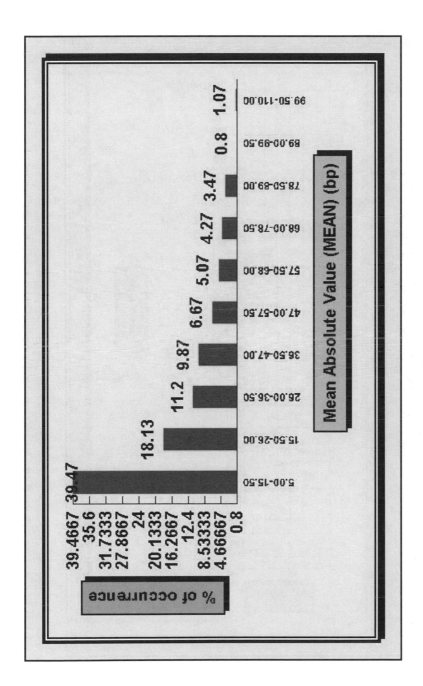

Figure 8.9 Mean absolute value over a forecast period, percentage occurrences

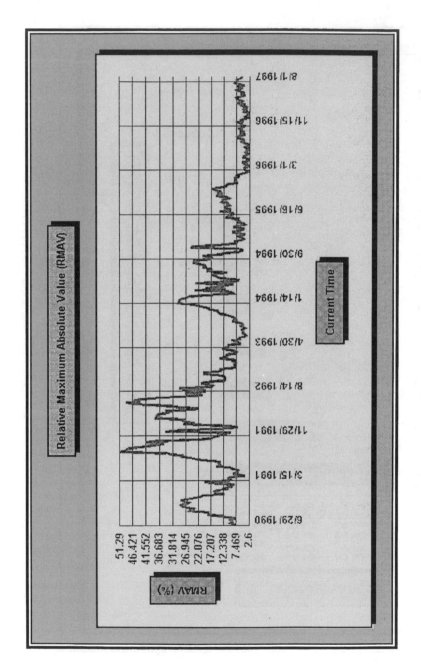

Figure 8.10   Relative maximum absolute value over a forecast period

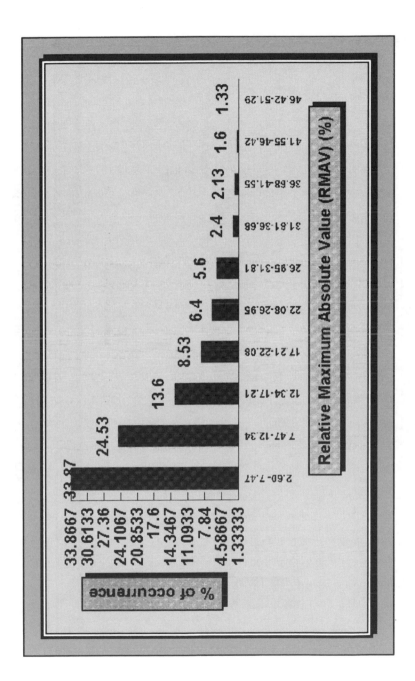

Figure 8.11   Relative maximum absolute value over a forecast period, percentage occurrences

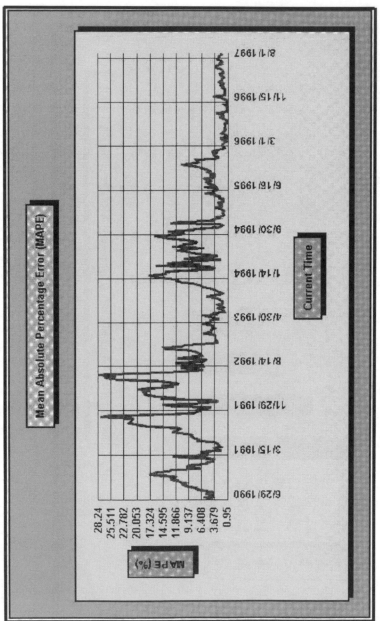

Figure 8.12   Mean absolute percentage error over a forecast period

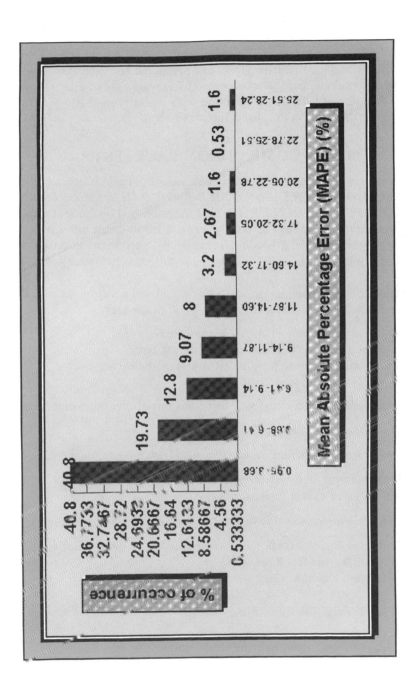

Figure 8.13   Mean absolute percentage error over a forecast period, percentage occurrences

Perfect forecasts during all forecasting periods would have the maximum absolute value, the mean absolute value, the relative absolute value and the mean absolute percentage curves all residing on the horizontal axes of their respective figures. Each corresponding bar chart would have a unique bar of height 100 at the extreme left.

As a by-product of computing weekly estimates of 3MO constant maturity yields, estimates of 3MO constant maturity yields are computed for each day in a forecast period. *Forecast(day)* shall denote the computed forecasted yield to maturity prevailing at the current date *day* of a zero coupon bond with maturity date *day* + 3*MO*, where *day* ranges over all the Fridays in a fixed forecast period.

8.2 A COMPARISON BACKTEST

We make a comparison between computed estimates of daily 3MO constant maturity yields with the *3-MONTH TREASURY BILL RATE DAILY FIGURES SECONDARY MARKET NOT SEASONALLY ADJUSTED* published by the St. Louis Fed, file **dtb3**. We emphasize that even for the weekly series, auction yields differ from *reported* secondary market yields. This is a comparative study only because no observations from the secondary market are used in the computations, only weekly US Treasury auction yields.

For each measure listed below we present a line graph and a histogram over the entire universal period. Each of the six series consists of 375 numbers.

1. The maximum absolute value (MAV) of the forecast error.
2. The mean absolute value (MEAN) of the forecast error.
3. The relative maximum absolute value (RMAV) of the forecast error.
4. The mean absolute percentage error (MAPE).

Let *FP* denote a given forecast period. The definitions of these measures now follow.

(a) Maximum absolute value over a forecast period:

$$MAV(FP) = \max \text{ absolute value } (Forecast(Friday) - Auction(Friday))$$

over all Fridays in the observation period. See Figures 8.6 and 8.7.

(b) Mean absolute value over a forecast period:

$$MEAN(FP) = \text{absolute value sum } (Forecast(Friday) - Auction(Friday))$$

over all Fridays in the observation period divided by 17 (number of Fridays in the forecast period). See Figures 8.8 and 8.9.

(c) Relative maximum absolute value over a forecast period:

$$RMAV(FP) = \max \text{ absolute value } \left\{ \frac{Forecast(Friday) - Auction(Friday)}{Auction(Friday)} \right\}$$

over all Fridays in the forecast period. See Figures 8.10 and 8.11.

(d) Mean absolute percentage error over a forecast period:

$$MAPE(FP) = \text{sum} \left\{ \frac{Forecast(Friday) - Auction(Friday)}{Auction(Friday)} \right\}$$

over all Fridays in the forecast period divided by 17 (number of Fridays in the forecast period) multiplied by 100 to obtain percentages. See Figures 8.12 and 8.13.

Over the 8-year universal backtesting period the computed daily 3MO Treasury bill rate estimates based on observed weekly Treasury auction data are reasonably close to the Treasury bill rates determined and reported by the secondary market.

A Forward Rates-based Dynamical System Model

9.1 EXTRACTING FORWARD RATES CURVES FROM THE TERM STRUCTURE OF INTEREST RATES

In the next two chapters we develop two different approaches for modeling financial data. Of course, other alternatives could be suggested, but those we have developed could be used as starting points for modeling more complicated financial systems.

In this chapter we develop a differential equations model under uncertainty for the forward rate. Observed data take two forms: (a) prices of Treasury bonds and notes or (2) yields of Treasury bills. We also assume that the observed data could include errors of observation.

9.1.1 The Observation Model

As a rule, observed financial data are discrete. This is in contrast to analog data that arise in various physical phenomena. A major financial application begins with the construction of an observation model based on daily prices (or yields), S_i, $i = 0, 1, \ldots$, where i denotes the day of observation. The modeling procedure extends the discrete observed data to the class of piecewise constant functions by fixing the values to be constant within a given day, as we presented in Figure 2.3:

$$S(t) = S_i, \ t \in T_i = [i - 1, i], i = 1, 2, \ldots \quad (9.1)$$

Throughout this book piecewise constant functions have been termed *impulse functions*. A definition on the characteristics of data is essential for our approach.

Definition 9.1 *Data for which all observation intervals T_i have the same length and are contiguous are termed homogeneous. Data for which (i) the time interval lengths differ or (ii) there are several observed values for the same time of observation or (iii) some time intervals T_i are not contiguous are termed heterogeneous.*

In order to accommodate heterogeneous data the impulse function (9.1) is generalized as follows:

$$S(t) = S_i, \ t \in T_i = [\tau_{i-1,i}, \tau_{i,i}], i = 1, 2, \ldots \quad (9.2)$$

For convenience we shall use the notation T_i to denote either (9.2) or the special case (9.1).

Real market data frequently tend to be heterogeneous. Table 9.1 illustrates bonds and notes data from the Treasury quotes section of the *Wall Street Journal, Interactive*

Table 9.1 Treasury quotes: bonds and notes 03/14/00

Rate	Maturity (MO/year)	Bid	Ask	Chg	Ask yield
$5\frac{1}{2}$	Mar 00 N	99:30	100:00		5.375
$6\frac{7}{8}$	Mar 00 N	100:01	100:03		4.58
$5\frac{1}{2}$	Apr 00 N	99:29	99:31		5.74
$5\frac{5}{8}$	Apr 00 N	99:29	99:31		5.75
$6\frac{3}{4}$	Apr 00 N	100:01	100:03		5.89

Edition for 14 March 2000. The letter 'N' denotes notes while the two digits after the colon are the number of 32nd's in the fraction accompanying the integer part of the price. In addition, the March entries correspond to the common date 3/31/00, which is approximately 17 days after the day of observation 3/14/00. The specific days for the April entries are respectively 4/15/00, 4/30/00 and 4/30/00.

Using formula (9.2), we have the following correspondences for the observed prices of Table 9.1:

- $T_1 = [\tau_{0,1}, \tau_{1,1}] = [16, 17]$, corresponding to 3/31/00;
- $T_2 = [\tau_{1,2}, \tau_{2,2}] = [16, 17]$, corresponding to 3/31/00;
- $T_3 = [\tau_{2,3}, \tau_{3,3}] = [31, 32]$, corresponding to 4/15/00;
- $T_4 = [\tau_{3,4}, \tau_{4,4}] = [46, 47]$, corresponding to 4/30/00;
- $T_5 = [\tau_{4,5}, \tau_{5,5}] = [46, 47]$, corresponding to 4/30/00.

For the time up to and including 14 March 2000 Treasury quotes bill yields were reported by days as illustrated in Table 9.2, where $\tau = 0$ corresponds to 15 March 2000.

Using the formula (9.2) again, we have the following correspondences for the observed prices of Table 9.2:

- $T_1 = [\tau_{0,1}, \tau_{1,1}] = [1, 2]$;
- $T_2 = [\tau_{1,2}, \tau_{2,2}] = [8, 9]$;
- $T_3 = [\tau_{2,3}, \tau_{3,3}] = [15, 16]$;
- $T_4 = [\tau_{3,4}, \tau_{4,4}] = [22, 23]$;
- $T_5 = [\tau_{4,5}, \tau_{5,5}] = [29, 30]$;
- $T_6 = [\tau_{5,6}, \tau_{6,6}] = [36, 37]$.

This specification is illustrated in Figure 9.1 for observed yields.

Table 9.2 Treasury quotes: bills 03/14/00

Maturity	Days to maturity	Bid	Ask	Chg	Ask yield
16 Mar 00	1	5.72	5.64	−0.02	5.725
23 Mar 00	8	5.09	5.01	−0.12	5.09
30 Mar 00	15	5.32	5.24	−0.06	5.32
6 Apr 00	22	5.05	4.97	−0.11	5.05
13 Apr 00	29	5.15	5.07	−0.04	5.16
20 Apr 00	36	5.47	5.43	−0.04	5.54

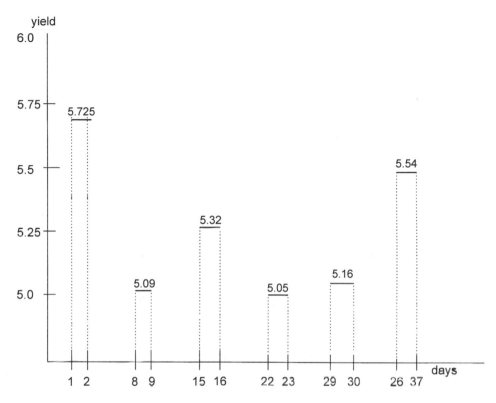

Figure 9.1 Heterogeneous data: x-axis for days to maturity: current time $t = 0$

9.1.2   The Optimal Observation Problem

In this section we present a general description of the optimal observation problem. We will give a more detailed description according to the observed data in sections to follow.

Assume that for some current moment of time there are N observed yields (prices) R_i, having times to maturity T_i^*:

$$R_i = R(t, T_i^*), \quad T_i^* > t, i = \overline{1, N}. \tag{9.3}$$

From Definition 9.1 and (9.3) the first step is to construct an impulse function based on the discrete data observations:

$$\hat{R}(T | t) = \hat{R}(t, T) = R_i, \quad \text{for all } T \in T_i = [T_i^* - 1, T_i^*], i = \overline{1, N}. \tag{9.4}$$

Denote $f(\cdot)$ as a forward rate function. Then the observed function $R(t, T)$ can be written more formally as follows:

$$R(t, T) = R(T, f(\cdot) | t). \tag{9.5}$$

An interesting statement appeared in the literature [34]:

'While yield is a bond specific property, the term structure of interest rates defines a market-wide property: the set of interest rates operating at a given instant of time.'

In a dynamical systems approach this is interpreted to imply a relation between the observed function $\hat{R}(t, T)$ and the real function $R(t, T)$ for each fixed current time t with respect to the time to maturity T. More precisely:

$$R(T, f(\cdot)|t) = \hat{R}(T|t) + \xi_i(T|t), \quad \forall T \in T_i, \ i = \overline{1, N}, \tag{9.6}$$

where $\xi_i(T|t)$ is the pricing error for Treasury issue i. Relation (9.6) serves as the structural equation for estimating the forward rate function $f(\cdot)$ with respect to the observed yields to maturity (or prices) of different Treasury issues. It motivates formulating optimality criteria such as 'find a forward rate curve that gives minimal errors of pricing, in some sense'.

As in previous chapters, we will apply the following rules intrinsic to our continuing approach for constructing the dynamical systems optimization problem.

1. Describe the desired admissibility properties of the function $f(\cdot)$.
2. Choose a criterion for the quality or 'goodness' of the estimation (e.g. least squares or a minimax criterion).
3. Choose a norm 'scoring' function for measuring the degree of uncertainty (e.g. the expectation).

The admissibility class of functions for the forward rates remains the same as in Section 3.2, namely the class of bounded piecewise continuous functions. In addition, upon selecting the minimax estimation criterion we obtain the following optimization model for the 'goodness' or 'scoring' of the estimation.

Minimax (Guaranteed) Model

Introduce the notation

$$\epsilon_i(f(\cdot)) = \max_{T \in T_i} |\xi_i(T|t)| = \max_{T \in T_i} |R(T, f(\cdot)|t) - \hat{R}(T|t)|.$$

Now, seeking a function $f^0(\cdot)$ that minimizes $\Sigma_i^N \epsilon_i^2(f(\cdot))$ over all admissible functions $f(\cdot)$ leads to the following infinite optimization problem:

$$\min_{f(\cdot)} \sum_{i=1}^N \epsilon_i^2 \text{ subject to}$$

$$\hat{R}(T|t) \leqslant R(T, f(\cdot)|t) + \epsilon_i, \tag{9.7}$$

$$\hat{R}(T|t) \geqslant R(T, f(\cdot)|t) - \epsilon_i, \quad \forall T \in T_i, \ i = \overline{1, N}.$$

Note that (9.7) seeks the minimum of the worst possible error over all times to maturity. A less conservative criterion having more of a median character can be readily obtained by replacing the objective function in (9.7) with the following one:

$$\sum_{i=1}^N \int_{T_i} \xi_i^2(\tau|t) \, d\tau,$$

where $\xi_i(\cdot\,|\,t))$ satisfies (9.6). Building on results presented in [39] a linear differential equation under uncertainty is presented next.

9.1.3 A Linear Differential Equation under Uncertainty Model for the Forward Rate Curve

We saw in Chapter 1 that there are useful relationships that can be obtained when differentiating the yield function or the logarithm of the price function with respect to the *time to maturity T*, see (1.60) and (1.63). These relationships motivate a differential equation for the forward rate, where the current time t is actually fixed, and differentiation occurs with respect to the *time to maturity T*:

$$\frac{df}{dT}(T\,|\,t) = \alpha(t) + \beta(t)f(T\,|\,t) + w(T\,|\,t), \quad \forall T \geqslant t, \, f(t, t) = r(t), \qquad (9.8)$$

where $w(T\,|\,t)$ is an unknown function of the perturbations acting on the model, and the coefficients $\alpha(t)$, $\beta(t)$ and the spot rate $r(t)$ satisfy the following constraints:

$$0 < \alpha_*(t) \leqslant \alpha(t) \leqslant \alpha^*(t), \ \ \beta_*(t) \lesssim \beta(t) \lesssim \beta^*(t) < 0,$$
$$0 < r_*(t) \lesssim r(t) \leqslant r^*(t). \qquad (9.9)$$

Now the perturbation functions need to be specified. For simplicity, we consider here the class of *impulse functions*. Let

$$\tilde{T} = \{\tilde{\tau}_0, \tilde{\tau}_1, \ldots, \tilde{\tau}_L\}, \ \text{where} \ \tilde{\tau}_{i-1} < \tilde{\tau}_i, \, i = \overline{1, L}; \, \tilde{\tau}_0 = t, \, \tilde{\tau}_L = \tau_N. \qquad (9.10)$$

Define the function $w(T\,|\,t)$ by

$$w(T\,|\,t) = w_i(t), \ \ w_*(t) \leqslant w_i(t) \leqslant w^*(t) \ \text{for all} \ T \in \tilde{T}_i \doteq [\tilde{\tau}_{i-1}, \tilde{\tau}_i], \, i = \overline{1, L}, \qquad (9.11)$$

where $w_*(t)$, $w^*(t)$ are preassigned bounds for the perturbations, and where similar notation to (9.2) for heterogeneous data has been employed.

Substituting (9.11) into (9.8) and applying the Cauchy formula gives an explicit expression for the forward rate function:

$$f(T, \omega(t)\,|\,t) = r(t)e^{\beta(t)(T-t)} + \frac{\alpha(t)}{\beta(t)}(e^{\beta(t)(T-t)} - 1)$$

$$+ \frac{e^{\beta(t)T}}{\beta(t)} \sum_{j=1}^{i-1} (e^{-\beta(t)\tilde{\tau}_{j-1}} - e^{-\beta(t)\tilde{\tau}_j})w_j(t) + w_i(t)\frac{e^{\beta(t)(T-\tilde{\tau}_{i-1})} - 1}{\beta(t)}, \ \ T \in \tilde{T}_i, \qquad (9.12)$$

where the parameter vector $\omega(t)$ is given by

$$\{r(t), \alpha(t), \beta(t); w_i(t), i = \overline{1, L}\}.$$

Rewrite the parameter admissible set (9.9)–(9.11) in the following form:

$$\Omega(t) = \{\omega(t): \alpha_*(t) \leqslant \alpha(t) \leqslant \alpha^*(t), \ \beta_*(t) \leqslant \beta(t) \leqslant \beta^*(t),$$
$$r_*(t) \leqslant r(t) \leqslant r^*(t), \ w_*(t) \leqslant w_i(t) \leqslant w^*(t), \, i = \overline{1, L}\}. \qquad (9.13)$$

In the following sections we consider several models depending on the type of observed data.

9.1.4 A Yield-based Optimal Observation Problem

Assume that the observed data (9.3) represent yield R_i, having time to maturity T_i^*:

$$R_i = R(t, T_i^*), \quad T_i^* > t, \, i = \overline{1, N}. \tag{9.14}$$

From (9.4) it follows that the function $R(t, T)$ has the form

$$
\begin{aligned}
R(T, f(\cdot)\,|\,t) = R(T, \omega(t)\,|\,t) &= \frac{1}{T-t} \int_t^T f(s, \omega\,|\,t)\, ds \\
&= \frac{1}{T-t} \left(\frac{e^{\beta(t)(T-t)}}{\beta(t)} r(t) + \left(\frac{e^{\beta(t)(T-t)} - 1}{\beta^2(t)} - \frac{T-t}{\beta(t)} \right) \alpha(t) \right. \\
&\quad + \sum_{j=1}^{i-1} \left(\frac{e^{\beta(t)(T-\tilde{\tau}_{j-1})} - e^{\beta(t)(T-\tilde{\tau}_j)}}{\beta^2(t)} - \frac{\tilde{\tau}_j - \tilde{\tau}_{j-1}}{\beta(t)} \right) w_j(t) \\
&\quad + \left. \left(\frac{e^{\beta(t)(T-\tilde{\tau}_{i-1})} - 1}{\beta^2(t)} - \frac{T - \tilde{\tau}_{i-1}}{\beta(t)} \right) w_i(t) \right)
\end{aligned}
$$

$$T \in \tilde{T}_i, \, i = \overline{1, L}. \tag{9.15}$$

The following notation for the coefficients in (9.15) simplifies the mathematical expressions:

$$
\begin{aligned}
a_r(T, \beta(t)) &= \frac{1}{T-t} \frac{e^{\beta(t)(T-t)}}{\beta(t)}, \\
a_\alpha(T, \beta(t)) &= \frac{1}{T-t} \left(\frac{e^{\beta(t)(T-t)} - 1}{\beta^2(t)} - \frac{T-t}{\beta(t)} \right), \\
a_j(T, \beta(t)) &= \frac{1}{T-t} \left(\frac{e^{\beta(t)(T-\tilde{\tau}_{j-1})} - e^{\beta(t)(T-\tilde{\tau}_j)}}{\beta^2(t)} - \frac{\tilde{\tau}_j - \tilde{\tau}_{j-1}}{\beta(t)} \right), \\
\bar{a}_i(T, \beta(t)) &= \frac{1}{T-t} \left(\frac{e^{\beta(t)(T-\tilde{\tau}_{i-1})} - 1}{\beta^2(t)} - \frac{T - \tilde{\tau}_{i-1}}{\beta(t)} \right).
\end{aligned} \tag{9.16}
$$

Substituting (9.15) with the expressions for the coefficients (9.16) into (9.7) leads us to the following nonlinear semi-infinite programming problem:

$$\min_{\omega(t)} \sum_{i=1}^{N} \epsilon_i^2 \quad \text{subject to}$$

$$\hat{R}(T \mid t) \leqslant a_r(T, \beta(t)) r(t) + a_\alpha(T, \beta(t)) \alpha(t) + \sum_{j=1}^{i-1} a_j(T, \beta(t)) w_j(t) + \bar{a}_i(T, \beta(t)) w_i(t) + \epsilon_i,$$

$$\hat{R}(T \mid t) \geqslant a_r(T, \beta(t)) r(t) + a_\alpha(T, \beta(t)) \alpha(t) + \sum_{j=1}^{i-1} a_j(T, \beta(t)) w_j(t) + \bar{a}_i(T, \beta(t)) w_i(t) - \epsilon_i,$$

$$\forall T \in T_i, \, i = \overline{1, N}; \, \omega(t) \in \Omega(t); \, \epsilon_i \geqslant 0, \, i = \overline{1, N}.$$

$$(9.17)$$

Here $\Omega(t)$ is the parameter admissible set (9.13).

In general (9.17) may not have a unique solution. We alter this formulation to achieve uniqueness while simultaneously focusing on some reasonable additional objective function goals.

In Section 7.1 we presented the effects of some limiting behavior of $\beta(t)$ on the spot rate. Applying these features for the forward rate equation (9.12) yields: (a) for $\beta(t) = 0$ the forward rate is piecewise linear, while (b) for $\beta(t) \to -\infty$ it becomes an impulse, namely piecewise constant. For convenience, therefore, we fix $\beta(t) = \beta^* < 0$, generating simplifying linear constraints in (9.17) with respect to the parameter vector $\omega(t)$.

We introduce the following additional objective function goals which are consistent with the theory of finance.

Goal I   The spot rate $r(t)$ should be as close as possible to the observed yield R_1 having the shortest term to maturity.

Goal II   The mean reversion ratio should be as close as possible to the yield R_N having the largest term to maturity.

Goal III   The perturbations acting on the forward rate curve should be as small as possible (stability).

Introduce the following values:

$$\gamma_1 = (\hat{R}(T_1) - r(t))^2, \quad \gamma_2 = \left(\hat{R}(T_N) + \frac{\alpha}{\beta^*} \right)^2, \quad \gamma_3 = \sum_{i=1}^{L} w_i^2(t).$$

Their meanings are as follows:

- γ_1 is a measure of the distance of the yield of shortest observed maturity from the spot rate at the current time;
- γ_2 is a measure of the distance of the yield of the largest observed maturity to the mean reversion ratio $-\alpha/\beta^*$, where recall $\beta^* < 0$;
- γ_3 is simply the sum of the squared errors of the perturbations.

Denote

$$a_r(T) = a_r(T, \beta^*), \; a_\alpha(T) = a_\alpha(T, \beta^*),$$
$$a_j(T) = a_j(T, \beta^*), \; \bar{a}_j(T) = \bar{a}_i(T, \beta^*), \, i = \overline{1, N};$$
$$\Omega^*(t) = \{\Omega(t) : \beta(t) = \beta^*\}.$$

An application of Goals I–III to problem (9.17) yields the following quadratic semi-infinite programming problem with linear constraints:

$$\min_{\omega \in \Omega, \beta = \beta} \gamma_1 + \gamma_2 + \gamma_3 + \theta \sum_{i=1}^{N} \epsilon_i^2 \text{ subject to}$$

$$\hat{R}(T \mid t) \leqslant a_r(T)r(t) + a_\alpha(T)\alpha(t) + \sum_{j=1}^{i-1} a_j(T)w_j(t) + \bar{a}_i(T)w_i(t) + \epsilon_i,$$

$$\hat{R}(T \mid t) \geqslant a_r(T)r(t) + a_\alpha(T)\alpha(t) + \sum_{j=1}^{i-1} a_j(T)w_j(t) + \bar{a}_i(T)w_i(t) - \epsilon_i,$$
(9.18)

$$\omega(t) \in \Omega^*(t); \forall T \in T_i, \; \epsilon_i \geqslant 0, \; i = \overline{1, N},$$

where θ is a penalty coefficient whose selection is usually aided by a sensitivity analysis, namely a 'tuning' of the model. Problem (9.18) has a unique solution. Regarding θ, if one wants to achieve the smallest error in pricing, then θ should be chosen sufficiently large. This choice will however lead to very flat forward rate and yield curves. If achieving smoothness of both curves is important, then θ should be sufficiently small. But in this case the errors of pricing will increase. We present the numerical results in Section 9.1.8.

9.1.5   A Price-based Optimal Observation Problem

Assume that the observed data (9.4) represent the prices of the bond or notes, having times to maturity T_i^*, coupon rate c_i and frequency of coupon payments x_i:

$$P_i = P(T_i^* \mid t, c_i, x_i), \quad T_i^* > t, \; i = \overline{1, N}.$$
(9.19)

Denote by $P(t, T_i)$ the price of a zero-coupon bond at current time t with time to maturity $T_i > t$. The price P_i of the bond at time t, with time to maturity T_i^*, having coupon rate c_i with frequency of coupon payments x_i could be expressed by the following equation:

$$P_i = 100P(t, T_i^*) + \sum_{j=1}^{L_i} c_i x_i P(t, t_{ij}), \quad T_i^* > t, \; i = \overline{1, N},$$
(9.20)

where t_{ij} denotes the time of coupon payments.

Using formula (1.62) for the price of a zero-coupon bond:

$$P(t, T) = \exp\left(-\int_t^T f(t, s)\, ds\right)$$

and the equation for the forward rate (9.12) from (9.20) follows:

$$P_i(T, \omega(t)) = P_i(T, \omega(t) \mid t, c_i, x_i) = P_i(T, f(\cdot) \mid t, c_i, x_i),$$

$$P_i(T, f(\cdot) \mid t, c_i, x_i) = 100 \, \exp\left(\int_t^T f(t, s)\, ds\right) + \sum_{j=1}^{L_i} c_i x_i \exp\left(\int_t^{t_{ij}} f(t, s)\, ds\right),$$

$$T \in T_i = [T_i^* - 1, T_i^*], \; i = \overline{1, N}.$$

Using the coefficient notation given in (9.16), this equation can be rewritten as follows:

$$P_i(T, \omega(t)) = 100 \exp \left(a_r(T, \beta(t))r(t) + a_\alpha(T, \beta(t))\alpha(t) + \sum_{k=1}^{i-1} a_k(T, \beta(t))w_k(t) \right.$$
$$\left. + \bar{a}_i(T, \beta(t))w_i(t) \right) + \sum_{j=1}^{L_i} c_j x_j \exp \left(a_r(t_{ij}, \beta(t))r(t) + a_\alpha(t_{ij}, \beta(t))\alpha(t) \right.$$
$$\left. + \sum_{k=1}^{j-1} a_k(t_{ij}, \beta(t))w_k(t) + \bar{a}_j(t_{ij}, \beta(t))w_j(t) \right), \quad T \in T_i, \, i = \overline{1, N}. \tag{9.21}$$

According to (9.7) the optimal observation problem for price observation has the following form:

$$\min_{f(\cdot)} \sum_{i=1}^{N} \epsilon_i^2 \text{ subject to}$$
$$\hat{P}_i(T \mid t) \leqslant P_i(T, \omega(t)) + \epsilon_i, \quad \hat{P}_i(T \mid t) \geqslant P_i(T, \omega(t)) - \epsilon_i, \quad \forall T \in T_i, \tag{9.22}$$
$$\omega(t) \in \Omega(t); \, \epsilon_i \geqslant 0, \, i = \overline{1, N}.$$

The problem (9.22) is a nonlinear semi-infinite programming problem. As in previous sections, we need to reformulate the problem in order to achieve a unique solution. Fixing $\beta(t) = \beta^* < 0$ gives the convexity of the constraints. The values R_0 and R_∞ denote the corresponding smallest and largest observed yields to maturity. The outcome of building a model under the same assumptions as given in the previous section yields the following optimization problem:

$$\min (r(t) - R_0)^2 + \left(\frac{\alpha_t}{\beta^*} + R_\infty \right)^2 + \sum_{i=1}^{L} w_i^2(t) + \theta \sum_{i=1}^{N} \epsilon_i^2 \text{ subject to}$$
$$\hat{P}_i(T \mid t) \leqslant P_i(T, \omega(t)) + \epsilon_i, \quad \hat{P}_i(T \mid t) \geqslant P_i(T, \omega(t)) - \epsilon_i, \quad \forall T \in T_i, \tag{9.23}$$
$$\omega(t) \in \Omega^*(t); \, \epsilon_i \geqslant 0, \, i = \overline{1, N}.$$

9.1.6   A Bid–ask Optimal Observation Problem

Up to now we have assumed that we are observing some fixed price of the Treasury securities. As a rule, observed data contents are not 'some' fixed price but two prices — 'bid' and 'ask' prices. The optimal observation problem for price observation could be reformulated taking into account such observed data.

Assume that for each Treasure security i having time to maturity T_i^*, coupon rate c_i and frequency of payment x_i we are observing two prices: 'bid' price $P_i^b = P^b(t, T_i^* \mid c_i, x_i)$ and 'ask' price $P_i^a = P^a(t, T_i^* \mid c_i, x_i)$, $T_i^* > t$, $i = \overline{1, N}$. Construct the functions $\hat{P}_i^b(T \mid t)$ and $\hat{P}_i^a(T \mid t)$ by (9.4). Without loss of generality we assume that $P_i^a > P_i^b$ for every i, $i = \overline{1, N}$. In this case problem (9.23) could be reformulated as follows:

$$\min (r(t) - R_0)^2 + \left(\frac{\alpha_t}{\beta*} + R_\infty \right)^2 + \sum_{i=1}^{L} w_i^2(t) + \theta \left(\sum_{i=1}^{N} \epsilon_{bi}^2 + \sum_{i=1}^{N} \epsilon_{ai}^2 \right) \text{ subject to}$$

$$\widehat{P_i^b}(T|t) \leqslant P_i(T, \omega(t)) + \epsilon_{bi}, \ \widehat{P_i^a}(T|t) \geqslant P_i(T, \omega(t)) - \epsilon_{ai}, \ \forall T \in T_i,$$

$$\omega(t) \in \Omega(t); \ \epsilon_{bi} \geqslant 0, \ \epsilon_{ai} \geqslant 0, \ i = \overline{1, N},$$

where ϵ_{bi} and ϵ_{ai} are pricing errors for the Treasury issue i.

9.1.7   A General Optimal Observation Problem

Combining the yield-based and price-based optimal observation problems leads us to a more general and more complex optimization problem to solve.

Let us assume that we simultaneously observe yields (9.14) $R_i = R(t, T_i^*)$, $T_i^* > t$, $i = \overline{1, N}$ and prices (9.19) $P_i = P(T_i^*|t, c_i, x_i)$, $T_i^* > t$, $i = \overline{1, M}$. Using expressions for the estimate of yield (9.15) and price (9.21) we come to the following nonlinear semi-infinite programming problem:

$$\min_{\omega \in \Omega, \beta = \hat{\beta}} \gamma_1 + \gamma_2 + \gamma_3 + \theta \sum_{i=1}^{N} \epsilon_{Ri}^2 + \theta \sum_{i=1}^{N} \epsilon_{Pi}^2 \text{ subject to}$$

$$\hat{R}_i(T|t) \leqslant a_r(T)r(t) + a_\alpha(T)\alpha(t) + \sum_{j=1}^{i-1} a_j(T)w_j(t) + \bar{a}_i(T)w_i(t) + \epsilon_{Ri},$$

$$\hat{R}_i(T|t) \geqslant a_r(T)r(t) + a_\alpha(T)\alpha(t) + \sum_{j=1}^{i-1} a_j(T)w_j(t) + \bar{a}_i(T)w_i(t) - \epsilon_{Ri},$$

$$\hat{P}_i(T|t) \leqslant P_i(T, \omega(t)) + \epsilon_{Pi}, \ \hat{P}_i(T|t) \geqslant P_i(T, \omega(t)) - \epsilon_{Pi}, \ \forall T \in T_i,$$

$$\omega(t) \in \Omega(t); \ \epsilon_{Pi} \geqslant 0, \ i = \overline{1, M}; \ \epsilon_{Ri} \geqslant 0, \ i = \overline{1, N}.$$

9.1.8   A Tradeoff Between Smoothness of the Estimation and Accuracy

In Section 9.1.4 we remarked that the penalty coefficient θ controls the accuracy of the estimation. A more accurate estimation appears to produce a flatter trajectory of the forward rate. Let us illustrate this tendency with the example taking observed yields of bills. Input data were taken from the *Wall Street Journal* for 22 June 2000. The observed function $\hat{R}(T|t)$, $t = 06/22/00$ is represented in Figure 9.2. The results of solving problem (9.18) for different values of θ are shown in Table 9.3 where

Table 9.3   Comparison of penalty coefficient and accuracy of estimation

θ	ϵ_{max}	ϵ_{med}	s	$r(t)$	$\alpha(t)$	R_∞
1	0.8342822105	0.1698981646	<1	4.970788066	4.444066931	8.888133862
100	0.4440194792	0.0659306042	<1	5.127043489	3.79566141	7.59132282
1000	0.2589348855	0.0426494485	1	4.90493658	3.755088755	7.51017751
10^6	0.0404633704	0.0112100198	1	4.61919023	3.477769698	6.955539396
10^{10}	0.0250015122	0.0016725627	2	4.719148476	3.486769861	6.973539722

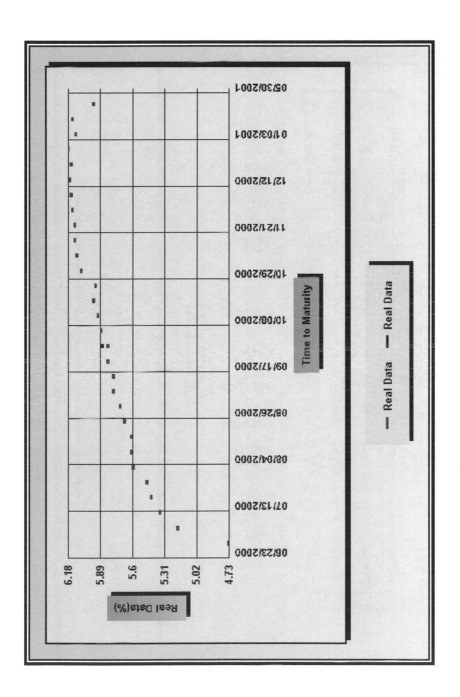

Figure 9.2 Observations on Treasury bill yields

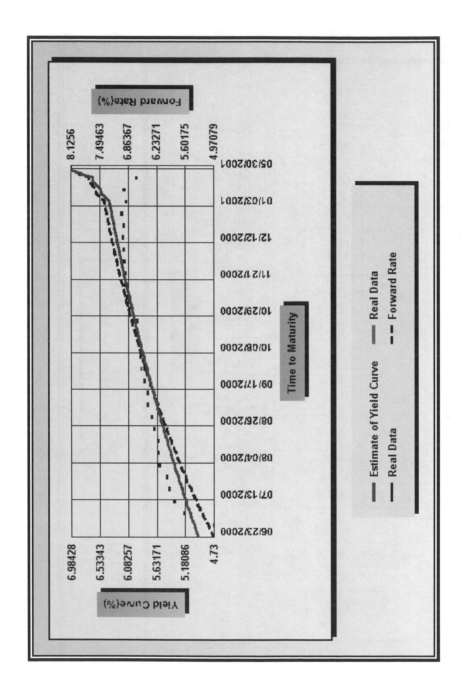

Figure 9.3   Penalty parameter $\theta = 1$

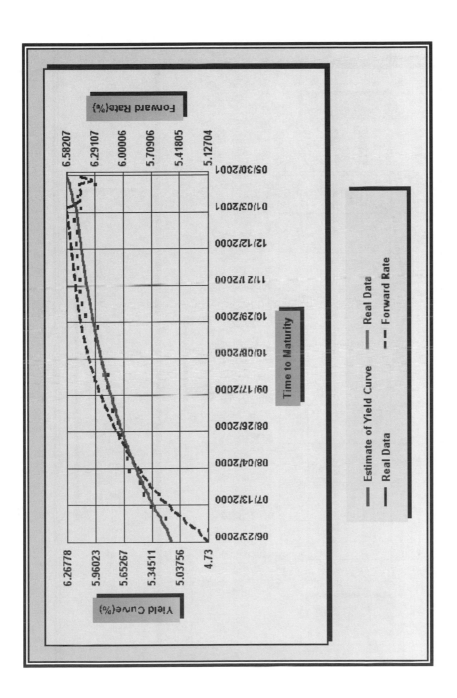

Figure 9.4 Penalty parameter $\theta = 100$

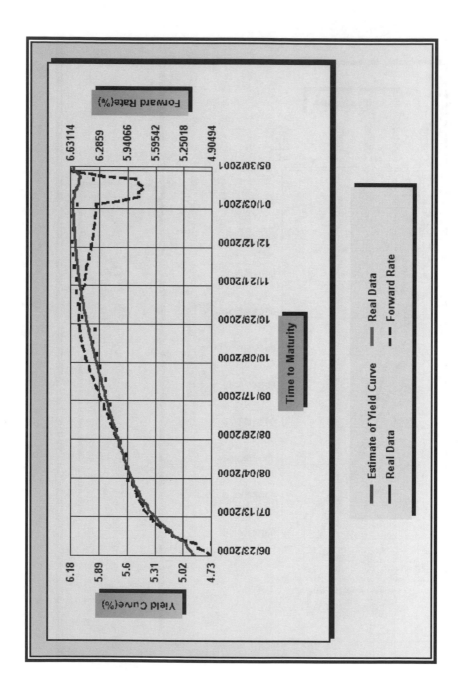

Figure 9.5 Penalty parameter $\theta = 1000$

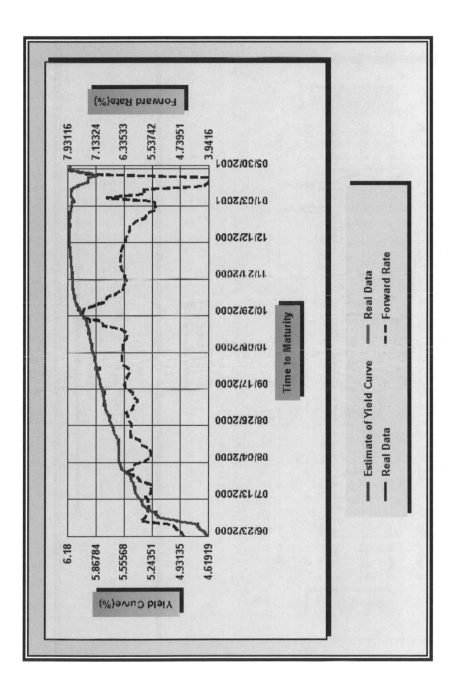

Figure 9.6 Penalty parameter $\theta = 10^6$

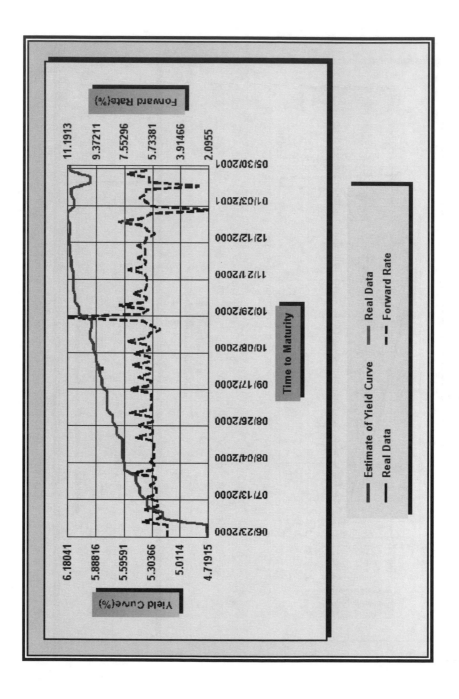

Figure 9.7 Penalty parameter $\theta = 10^{10}$

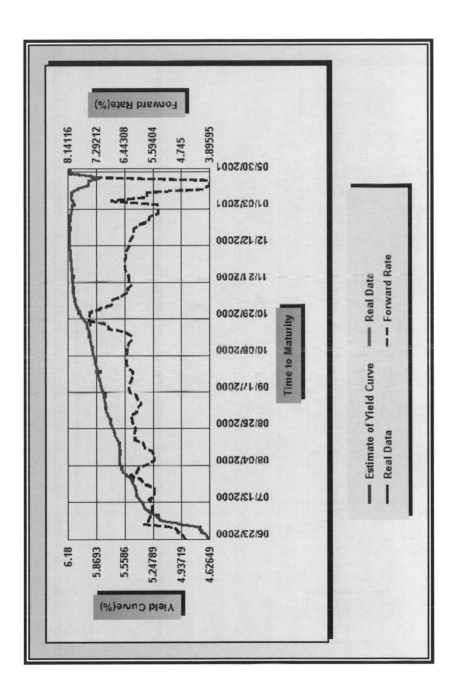

Figure 9.8 Parameter $\beta = -0.01$

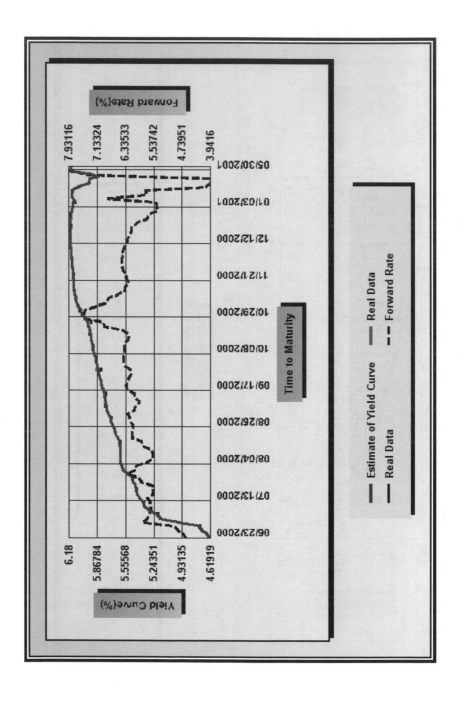

Figure 9.9   Parameter $\beta = -0.5$

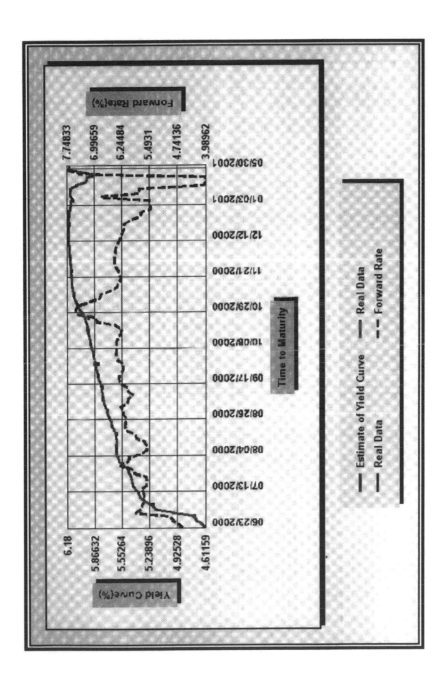

Figure 9.10   Parameter $\beta = -0.1$

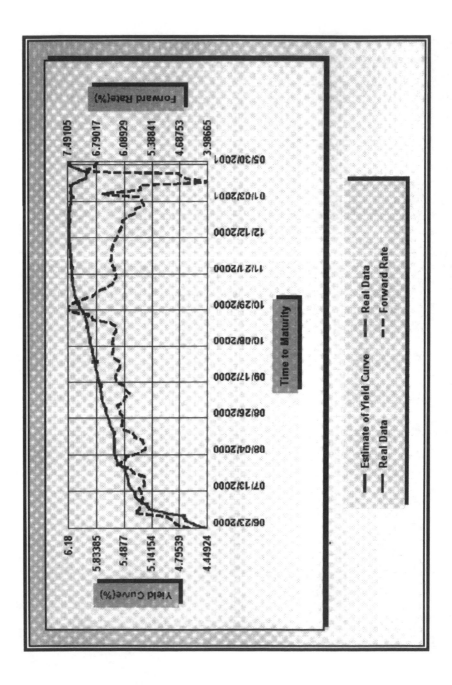

Figure 9.11   Parameter $\beta = -10$

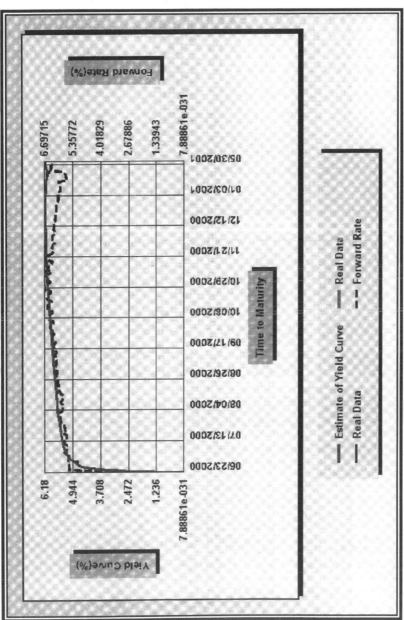

Figure 9.12 Parameter $\beta = -100$

Table 9.4 Comparison of parameter β and accuracy of estimation

β	ϵ_{max}	ϵ_{med}	s	$r(t)$	$\alpha(t)$	R_{∞}
-0.01	0.040462187	0.0112144359	1	4.626489815	0.5254032518	8.888133862
-0.5	0.0404633704	0.0112100198	1	4.61919023	3.477769698	6.955539396
-1	0.0404762378	0.0112089943	1	4.611594088	6.49179795	6.49179795
-10	0.0425440595	0.0117473923	1	4.449241077	60.84743456	6.084743456
-100	0.0947402772	0.031376675	1	0	605.01917	6.0501917

$\epsilon_{max} = \max \ \epsilon_i, \ i = \overline{1, N}$ is the maximal error of the computed estimate,

$\epsilon_{med} = \dfrac{1}{N} \displaystyle\sum_{i=1}^{N} |\epsilon_i|, \ i = \overline{1, N}$ is the median (middle) error of the computed estimate,

$$(9.24)$$

s is the CPU time (s). We have chosen $\beta^* = -0.5$ here.

Figures 9.3–9.7 represent the estimates of yield curve and forward rate for five different values of θ listed in the first column of Table 9.3.

Table 9.4 represents numerical results for different values of the parameter β. We used $\theta = 10^6$ here.

Figures 9.8–9.12 represent the estimates of yield curve and forward rate for five values of β listed in the first column of Table 9.4.

9.2 CHAPTER NOTES

This chapter is devoted to an implementation of term structure of interest rate models based on the differential equation under uncertainty for the forward rate. For modeling the forward rate we have chosen the differential equation of Vasicek type. The models proposed in this chapter are based on daily observations of the prices of bonds and notes, in addition to US Treasury bill yields. Such series usually include the set of data for some fixed day of observation and differ by their time to maturity. The dynamics of the observed data lead us to formulate a differential equation for the forward rate where differentiation is taken with respect to time to maturity for a fixed given current time. Another feature of the models presented in this chapter is that the level of the estimation error is defined from the solution of the optimization problem. This was made possible by introducing a penalty coefficient in the objective function of the optimization problem. As the value of the penalty coefficient increases, the value of the estimation error decreases. Increasing the penalty coefficient leads to a flatter trajectory of the estimated forward rate. A sensitivity analysis of features of the model is presented at the end of this chapter.

A General Integro-differential Term Structure Model

10.1 A DYNAMICAL LINEAR DIFFERENTIAL EQUATIONS SYSTEM FOR FORWARD RATES

In the previous chapters we developed models for estimating the term structure of interest rates for some fixed current moment of time or some fixed terms to maturity. In this chapter we develop a more general class of differential systems under uncertainty with perturbations to model processes according to two time characteristics, namely real time and time to maturity. In this extension the basic differential equation is formulated with respect to bond prices. But similar to our previous models we use classes of perturbation functions to model uncertainty, although this time the perturbations are applied to bond prices themselves. It will not be necessary to describe again the optimal observation model because it is basically the same one presented in previous chapters.

The main goal of this chapter is to construct a general dynamical system of differential equations for the term structure of interest rates, a system having the characteristic that it does not depend on a specific concrete model for forward rates or spot rates. It is therefore constructed as a differential system in a most general form for bond prices.

Throughout this chapter we will adopt the following notation:

$P(t, T)$: price at time t of a discount bond with principal $1 maturing at time T;
$f(t, T_1, T_2)$: forward rate at time t for the future period $[T_1, T_2]$;
$F(t, T)$: instantaneous forward rate at time t for a contract maturing at time T;
$r(t)$: spot rate at time t, see (1.50) and (1.52);
$w(t, T)$: external input perturbations acting on bonds having price $P(t, T)$ at time t;
$\nu(t)$: external input perturbations acting on the short-term risk-free interest rate at time t.

In Section 1.4 we used lowercase f for initial modeling of the instantaneous forward rate. Because we have a more complex system now, we henceforth use capital F.

We start with the following differential equation process for $P(t, T)$:

$$dP(t, T) = r(t)P(t, T)\, dt + w(t, T)\, dt. \tag{10.1}$$

Suppose upper and lower bound functions $w^*(\cdot, \cdot)$, $w_*(\cdot, \cdot)$ are known for the perturbation function $w(\cdot, \cdot)$:

$$w_*(t, T) \leqslant w(t, T) \leqslant w^*(t, T).$$

The forward rate $f(t, T_1, T_2)$ is related to the discount bond prices as follows:

$$f(t, T_1, T_2) = \frac{\log P(t, T_1) - \log P(t, T_2)}{T_2 - T_1}.$$

From (10.1) we obtain

$$d \log P(t, T_i) = \frac{1}{P(t, T_i)} (r(t)P(t, T_i) + w(t, T_i))\, dt = \left(r(t) + \frac{w(t, T_i)}{P(t, T_i)} \right) dt.$$

It follows that

$$df(t, T_1, T_2) = -\frac{1}{T_2 - T_1} \left(\frac{w(t, T_2)}{P(t, T_2)} - \frac{w(t, T_1)}{P(t, T_1)} \right) dt. \qquad (10.2)$$

If we substitute $T_1 = T$ and $T_2 = T + \Delta T$ in (10.2) and take limits as $\Delta \to 0$, then $f(t, T_1, T_2)$ converges to $F(t, T)$ and we obtain

$$dF(t, T) = \lim_{\Delta T \to 0} df(t, T, T + \Delta T) = -\lim_{\Delta T \to 0} \left(\frac{w(t, T + \Delta T)}{P(t, T + \Delta T)} - \frac{w(t, T)}{P(t, T)} \right) \frac{1}{\Delta T} dt$$

$$= -\frac{\partial}{\partial T} \frac{w(t, T)}{P(t, T)} dt = -\frac{(\partial w(t, T)/\partial T)P(t, T) - w(t, T)(\partial P(t, T)/\partial T)}{P(t, T)^2} dt$$

$$= \left(-\frac{\partial w(t, T)}{\partial T} \frac{1}{P(t, T)} + \frac{1}{P(t, T)} \frac{\partial P(t, T)}{\partial T} \frac{w(t, T)}{P(t, T)} \right) dt$$

$$= -\frac{\partial w(t, T)/\partial T}{P(t, T)} dt + \frac{\partial \log P(t, T)}{\partial T} \frac{w(t, T)}{P(t, T)} dt$$

$$= \left(-\frac{w(t, T)}{P(t, T)} F(t, T) - \frac{1}{P(t, T)} \frac{\partial w(t, T)}{\partial T} \right) dt.$$

From the above equation it follows that

$$dF(t, T) = \left(-\frac{w(t, T)}{P(t, T)} F(t, T) - \frac{1}{P(t, T)} \frac{\partial w(t, T)}{\partial T} \right) dt. \qquad (10.3)$$

10.2   DYNAMIC MODELING OF THE TERM STRUCTURE OF INTEREST RATES

We now describe how the differential equation determines the spot rate $r(t)$ from the forward rate and the initial interest rate structure.

Remark 10.1   *When convenient, we use the standard partial derivative notation*

$$Z_\eta(\tau, t) = \frac{\partial Z(\tau, t)}{\partial \eta} \quad and \quad Z_{\eta\varsigma}(\tau, t) = \frac{\partial^2 Z(\tau, t)}{\partial \eta \partial \varsigma}.$$

On the other hand, when the maturity term T is fixed we use another subscript notation, for example, $P_T(t) = P(t, T)$. In the latter case there should be no confusion because the subscripted function has only one argument, usually t.

Since

$$F(t,\,t) = F(0,\,t) + \int_0^t dF(\tau,\,t) \quad \text{and} \quad r(t) = F(t,\,t), \quad \text{see (1.64),}$$

it follows that

$$r(t) = F(0,\,t) + \int_0^t \left[-\frac{w(\tau,\,t)}{P(\tau,\,t)} F(\tau,\,t) - \frac{1}{P(\tau,\,t)} \frac{\partial w(\tau,\,t)}{\partial t} \right] d\tau.$$

Differentiating with respect to t we obtain

$$
\begin{aligned}
dr(t) = & \left[\frac{\partial F(0,\,t)}{\partial t} - \frac{w(t,\,t)}{P(t,\,t)} F(t,\,t) - \frac{1}{P(t,\,t)} \frac{\partial w(t,\,t)}{\partial t} \right. \\
& - \int_0^t \left[\frac{\partial w(\tau,\,t)/\partial t}{P(\tau,\,t)} F(\tau,\,t) + \frac{w(\tau,\,t)}{P(\tau,\,t)} \frac{\partial F(\tau,\,t)}{\partial t} - \frac{w(\tau,\,t)}{P(\tau,\,t)^2} \frac{P(\tau,\,t)}{\partial t} F(\tau,\,t) \right. \\
& \left. \left. + \frac{\partial^2 w(\tau,\,t)/\partial t^2}{P(\tau,\,t)} - \frac{1}{P(\tau,\,t)^2} \frac{\partial w(\tau,\,t)}{\partial t} \frac{\partial P(\tau,\,t)}{\partial t} \right] d\tau \right] dt \\
= & \left[F_t(0,\,t) - w(t,\,t)r(t) - w_t(t,\,t) - \int_0^t \left[\frac{w_t(\tau,\,t)}{P(\tau,\,t)} F(\tau,\,t) + \frac{w(\tau,\,t)}{P_t(\tau,\,t)} F_t(\tau,\,t) \right. \right. \\
& \left. \left. - \frac{w(\tau,\,t)}{P^2(\tau,\,t)} P_t(\tau,\,t) F(\tau,\,t) + \frac{w_{tt}(\tau,\,t)}{P(\tau,\,t)} - \frac{w_t(\tau,\,t)P_t(\tau,\,t)}{P^2(\tau,\,t)} \right] d\tau \right] dt. \quad (10.4)
\end{aligned}
$$

From (10.1), (10.3) and (10.4) we obtain the following system describing the term structure of interest rates:

$$\dot{P}(t,\,T) = r(t)P(t,\,T) + w(t,\,T)$$

$$\dot{F}(t,\,T) = -\frac{w(t,\,T)}{P(t,\,T)} F(t,\,T) - \frac{1}{P(t,\,T)} \frac{\partial w(t,\,T)}{\partial T}$$

$$\dot{r}(t) = F_t(0,\,t) - w(t,\,t)r(t) - [w(\tau,\,t)|_{\tau=t}] - \int_0^t \left[\frac{w_t(\tau,\,t)}{P(\tau,\,t)} F(\tau,\,t) + \frac{w(\tau,\,t)}{P(\tau,\,t)} F_t(\tau,\,t) \right.$$

$$\left. - \frac{w(\tau,\,t)}{P^2(\tau,\,t)} P_t(\tau,\,t) F(\tau,\,t) + \frac{w_{tt}}{P(\tau,\,t)} - \frac{w_t(\tau,\,t)P_t(\tau,\,t)}{P^2(\tau,\,t)} \right] d\tau, \quad t \in [0,\,T],\ T \in [0,\,T^*];$$

$$ \tag{10.5}$$

$$P(0,\,T) = P(T), \quad F(0,\,T) = F(T), \quad r(0) = F(0,\,0); \quad T \in [0,\,T^*].$$

Remark 10.2 Impulse Perturbations of Prices. *Assume that the function $w(\cdot,\,\cdot)$ for generating price perturbations belongs to the class of impulse functions*

$$w(t,\,T) = w_{ij}, \quad t \in T_i,\ T \in T_j,\ i \leqslant j.$$

Then the differential equation for the spot rate has the special form

$$\dot{r}(t) = F_t(0,\,t) - w_{ii}r(t) - \int_0^t \left[\frac{w(\tau,\,t)}{P(\tau,\,t)} F_t(\tau,\,t) - \frac{w(\tau,\,t)}{P^2(\tau,\,t)} F(\tau,\,t) \right] d\tau,$$

for all $t \in T_i,\ i = \overline{1,\,N}$.

In some sense the model (10.5) could be considered to be an analog of the well-known HJM model [27]. In the HJM model it is assumed that the structure of stochastic volatility, $\sigma(t, T)$, is known. According to our model (10.5) this would mean that the structure of price perturbations $w(t, T)$ should be known. The function $w(t, T)$ could be estimated by observing bond prices with different times to maturity. Another unknown function in the system (10.5) is the yield curve $F(t)$, which is actually included among the initial conditions in (10.5). Such functions could be obtained by the methods described in previous chapters. There is another difficulty in using models of this HJM analog type. In the stochastic case, in general, the HJM model is non-Markov, and it appears that Monte Carlo simulation is needed to effectively implement this model. We underscore that our model (10.5) has no closed form solution. This means that solving the optimal observation problem numerically will require numerical integrations on (10.5) during each iteration.

There are several ways to eliminate computational difficulties in solving (10.5). One of them would be to replace the integro-differential equation for the spot rate by another differential equation, adding additional conditions to the system. Another way that is consistent with our approach could be to choose some functional class for the spot rate function. In the following section we will consider several such modifications. We will consider (10.1) for some fixed term to maturity T. Actually, this is consistent with real data, which as we have discussed in Chapter 2 have a discrete nature. By combining the differential equations for all observed bonds with different terms to maturity in one observation problem, it is possible to obtain the estimates of the price perturbation function $w(t, T)$. Then applying this function for a term to maturity T different from the observed data, it is easy to reconstruct the corresponding differential equations for the price and the forward rate for that particular maturity time T.

10.3   THE TERM STRUCTURE OF INTEREST RATES FOR A FIXED MATURITY

Suppose that the maturity term T is fixed so that we do not have the previous relation between the spot rate and the forward rate, except for the special relation (10.7) below. Referring back to Remark 10.1 for notation in this case, namely for fixed T, we obtain

$$\dot{P}_T(t) = r(t)P_T(t) + w_T(t),$$
$$\dot{f}_T(t) = -\frac{w_T(t)}{P_T(t)}f_T(t) - \frac{\partial w_T(t)}{\partial T}\frac{1}{P_T(t)}, \quad \forall t \in [0, T]. \tag{10.6}$$

System (10.6) has three unknown functions (the bond price, the spot rate and the forward rate) and two equations (one for price and one for the forward rate). Hence, we should supplement this system with a model describing the spot rate.

We have seen earlier that (1.64) is related to the forward rate as follows:

$$F(t, t) = r(t), \quad \forall t \in [0, T]. \tag{10.7}$$

Since, according to our assumption, values of $F(t, t)$ are known at only one point, $t = T$, we will need a model for the spot rate that satisfies the following terminal condition:

$$r(T) = f_T(T). \qquad (10.8)$$

We consider some cases for generating the spot rate $r(t)$, $t \in [0, T]$.

10.3.1   An Impulse Representation of the Spot Rate

Assume that the spot rate is described by the following impulse function:

$$r(t) = r_i, \quad r_{*i} \leqslant r_i \leqslant r_i^*, t \in T_i, i = 1, \ldots, N, \qquad (10.9)$$

where $T_i = [t_{i-1}, t_i]$, t_0 and $t_N = T$. Let $P_T(0) = P_{T0}$. Applying the Cauchy formula to (10.6) yields

$$P_T(t) = \exp\left(\int_0^t r(\tau)\, d\tau\right) P_{T0} + \int_0^t w_T(\tau) \exp\left(\int_\tau^t r(s)\, ds\right) d\tau. \qquad (10.10)$$

Suppose that the perturbations for the bond price are described by the following impulse function:

$$w_T(t) = w_i, \quad w_{*Ti} \leqslant w_i \leqslant w_{Ti}^*, t \in T_i, i = 1, \ldots, N. \qquad (10.11)$$

Substituting (10.9) and (10.11) into (10.10) yields

$$P_T(t) = P_{0T} \exp\left(\sum_{i=1}^{j-1}(t_i - t_{i-1})r_i + (t - t_{j-1})r_j\right) + \sum_{i=1}^{j-1}\int_{t_{i-1}}^{t_i}\exp\left(\int_\tau^t r(s)\, ds\right) d\tau\, w_i$$

$$+ \int_{t_{j-1}}^t \exp\left(\int_\tau^t r(s)\, ds\right) d\tau\, w_j = P_{0T}\exp\left(\sum_{i=1}^{j-1}(t_i - t_{i-1})r_i + (t - t_{j-1})r_j\right)$$

$$+ \sum_{i=1}^{j-1} w_i \int_{t_{i-1}}^{t_i}\exp\left\{(t_i - \tau)r_i + \sum_{k=i+1}^{j-1}(t_k - t_{k-1})r_k + (t - t_{j-1})r_j\right\} d\tau$$

$$+ w_j \int_{t_{j-1}}^t \exp(r_j(t - \tau)\, d\tau) = P_{0T}\exp\left(\sum_{i=1}^{j-1}(t_i - t_{i-1})r_i + (t - t_j)r_j\right)$$

$$+ \sum_{i=1}^{j-1} w_i \exp\left(\sum_{k=i+1}^{j-1}(t_k - t_{k-1})r_k + (t - t_{j-1})r_j\right)\int_{t_{i-1}}^{t_i}\exp(r_i(t_i - \tau))\, d\tau$$

$$+ w_{j-1}\frac{\exp(r_j(t - t_{j-1})) - 1}{r_j} = P_{T0}\exp\left(\sum_{i=1}^{j-1}(t_i - t_{i-1})r_i + (t - t_{j-1})r_j\right)$$

$$+ \sum_{i=1}^{j-1}\frac{w_i}{r_i}\exp\left(\sum_{k=i+1}^{j-1}(t_k - t_{k-1})r_k + (t - t_{j-1})r_j\right)(\exp(r_i(t_i - t_{i-1})) - 1)$$

$$+ \frac{w_j}{r_j}(\exp(r_j(t - t_{j-1})) - 1), \quad t \in T_j, j = 1, \ldots, N.$$

Hence, in model (10.9), (10/10) for price perturbations, the price of a bond with maturity T has the form:

$$P_T(t) = \exp(r_j(t - t_{j-1}))\left(P_{T0}a_j + \sum_{i=1}^{j-1} \frac{w_i}{r_i} b_{ij}(\exp(r_i(t_i - t_{i-1})) - 1) + \frac{w_j}{r_j}\right) - \frac{w_j}{r_j},$$

$$t \in T_j, j = 1, \ldots, N, \text{ where } a_j = \exp\left(\sum_{i=1}^{j-1} r_i(t_i - t_{i-1})\right), b_{ij} = \exp\left(\sum_{k=i+1}^{j-1} r_k(t_k - t_{k-1})\right).$$

10.3.2   A Piecewise Linear Representation of the Spot Rate

Assume that the spot rate is modeled by the following piecewise linear function:

$$r(t) = r_{j-1} + a_j(t - t_{j-1}), \quad a_j = \frac{r_j - r_{j-1}}{t_j - t_{j-1}}, r_{*j} \le r_j \le r_j^*, t \in T_j, j = 1, \ldots, N, \quad (10.12)$$

with perturbations for prices of type (10.11).

Substituting (10.12), (10.11) into (10.10) yields

$$P_T(t) = P_{T0} \exp\left\{\sum_{i=1}^{j-1}\int_{t_{i-1}}^{t_i}(r_{i-1} + a_i(\tau - t_{i-1}))\,d\tau + \int_{t_{j-1}}^{t}(r_j + a_j(\tau - t_{j-1}))\,d\tau\right\}$$

$$+ \sum_{i=1}^{j-1} w_i \int_{t_{i-1}}^{t_i} \exp\left\{w_i\left[\left[\int_{\tau}^{t_i}(r_{i-1} + a_i(s - t_{i-1}))\,ds + \sum_{k=i+1}^{j-1}\int_{t_{k-1}}^{t_k}(r_k + a_k(s - t_{k-1}))\,ds\right]\right.\right.$$

$$+ \int_{t_j}^{t}(r_{j-1} + a_j(s - t_{j-1}))\,ds\right\} + w_j \int_{t_{j-1}}^{t}\exp\left\{\int_{\tau}^{t}(r_j - a_j(s - t_{j-1}))\,ds\right\}d\tau$$

$$= P_{T0} \exp\left\{\sum_{i=1}^{j-1}\left[\frac{a_i}{2}(t_i - t_{i-1})^2 + r_{i-1}(t_i - t_{i-1})\right] + \frac{a_j}{2}(t - t_{j-1})^2 + r_{j-1}(t - t_{j-1})\right\}$$

$$+ \sum_{i=1}^{j-1} w_i \int_{t_{i-1}}^{t_i}\exp\left\{\left[\frac{a_i}{2}(t_i^2 - \tau^2) - a_i t_{i-1}(t_i - \tau) + r_{i-1}(t_i - \tau)\right]\right.$$

$$+ \sum_{k=i+1}^{j-1}\left[\frac{a_i}{2}(t_k - t_{k-1})^2 + r_k(t_k - t_{k-1})\right] + \left[\frac{a_{j-1}}{2}(t - t_{j-1})^2 + r_{j-1}(t - t_{j-1})\right]\right\}$$

$$+ w_j \int_{t_{j-1}}^{t}\exp\left\{\frac{a_{j-1}}{2}(t^2 - \tau^2) + (r_{j-1} - a_j t_{j-1})(t - \tau)\right\}d\tau$$

$$= P_{T0}a_j(t) + \sum_{i=1}^{j-1} w_i \exp\left\{\sum_{k=i+1}^{j-1}\left[\frac{a_k}{2}(t_k - t_{k-1})^2 + r_{k-1}(t_k - t_{k-1})\right]\right.$$

$$+ \left[\frac{a_{j-1}}{2}(t - t_{j-1})^2 + r_{j-1}(t - t_{j-1})\right]\right\}\int_{t_{i-1}}^{t_i}\exp\left\{\frac{a_i}{2}(t_i^2 - \tau^2) + (r_{i-1} - a_i t_{i-1})(t_i - \tau)\right\}d\tau$$

$$+ w_j \int_{t_{j-1}}^{t}\exp\left\{\frac{a_{j-1}}{2}(t^2 - \tau^2) + (r_{j-1} - a_j t_{j-1})(t - \tau)\right\}d\tau$$

$$= P_{T0}a_j(t) + \sum_{i=1}^{j-1} w_i b_{ij}(t)\sqrt{\frac{\pi}{2a_i}}\,g\left(\frac{a_i(t_i - t_{i-1}) + r_{i-1}}{\sqrt{2a_i}}\right)\exp\left\{\frac{(a_i(t_i - t_{i-1}) + r_{i-1})^2}{2a_i}\right\}$$

$$- \sqrt{\frac{\pi}{2a_i}}\,g\left(\frac{r_{i-1}}{\sqrt{2a_i}}\right)\exp\left\{\frac{(a_i(t_i - t_{i-1}) + r_{i-1})^2}{2a_i}\right\}$$

$$+ \sqrt{\frac{\pi}{2a_j}}\exp\left\{\frac{(a_j(t - t_{j-1}) + r_{j-1})^2}{2a_j}\left(g\left(\frac{a_j(t - t_{j-1}) + r_{j-1}}{2a_j}\right) - g\left(\frac{r_{j-1}}{\sqrt{2a_i}}\right)\right)\right\}w_j,$$

where

$$a_j(t) = \exp\left\{ \sum_{i=1}^{j-1} \left[\frac{a_i}{2}(t_i - t_{i-1})^2 + r_{i-1}(t_i - t_{i-1}) \right] + \frac{a_j}{2}(t - t_{j-1})^2 + r_{j-1}(t - t_{j-1}) \right\},$$

$$b_{ij}(t) = \exp\left\{ \sum_{k=i+1}^{j-1} \left[\frac{a_k}{2}(t_k - t_{k-1})^2 + r_{k-1}(t_k - t_{k-1}) \right] + \frac{a_j}{2}(t - t_{j-1})^2 + r_{j-1}(t - t_{j-1}) \right\},$$

$$g(x) = \frac{2}{\sqrt{\pi}} \int_0^x \exp(-t^2)\, dt.$$

10.3.3 A Vasicek-type Spot Rate Model

Consider the spot rate of Vasicek type but generated by a linear differential equation under uncertainty:

$$\dot{r}(t) = \alpha + \beta r(t) + \nu(t), \quad r(0) = r_0,\, \nu_*(\tau) \leqslant \nu(\tau) \leqslant \nu^*(\tau),\, \tau \in [0, T], \tag{10.13}$$

where $\nu^*(\cdot)$ and $\nu_*(\cdot)$ are known functions which model the external input perturbations of the spot rate.

In addition, assume upper and lower bounds are known for the unknown parameters of (10.13):

$$\alpha_* \leqslant \alpha \leqslant \alpha^*, \quad \beta_* \leqslant \beta \leqslant \beta^*, \quad r_{0*} \leqslant r_0 \leqslant r_0^*. \tag{10.14}$$

Combining (10.6) with (10.13), (10.14) and taking into account that $P_T(0) = p_0$ and $f_T(0) = f_{T0}$, where p_0 and f_{T0} are known numbers, we obtain the following LDU describing the term structure of interest rates for a fixed maturity T:

$$
\begin{aligned}
&\dot{P}_T(t) = r(t)P_T(t) + w_T(t),\\
&\dot{r}(t) = \alpha + \beta r(t) + \nu(t),\\
&\dot{f}_T(t) = -\frac{w_T(t)}{P_T(t)} f_T(t) - \frac{\partial w_T(t)}{\partial T}\frac{1}{P_T(t)}, \quad \forall t \in [0, T],\\
&P_T(0) = p_0,\, r(0) = r_0,\, f_T(0) = f_{T0};\\
&w_{*T}(t) \leqslant w_T(t) \leqslant w_T^*(t),\, \nu_*(t) \leqslant \nu(t) \leqslant \nu^*(t),\, \forall t \in [0, T];\\
&\alpha_* \leqslant \alpha \leqslant \alpha^*,\, \beta_* \leqslant \beta \leqslant \beta^*,\, r_{0*} \leqslant r_0 \leqslant r_0^*.
\end{aligned}
\tag{10.15}
$$

In addition, from (10.8) and the definition of bond prices a solution of dynamical system under uncertainty (10.15) is subject to the following terminal conditions:

$$r(T) = f_T(T) \quad \text{and} \quad P_T(T) = 1.$$

10.4 CHAPTER NOTES

In this chapter we develop a general model of the term structure of interest rates that does not depend on some predefined differential system either for the spot rate or the forward rate. The formulation begins with a general differential equation for Treasury security prices (10.1) that includes perturbations and is then extended to the integro-differential system (10.5). It seems that by its very nature a model of this type has several features similar to the well-known HJM model. At first, in order to obtain an optimal solution of system (10.5), the structure of the perturbation surface $w(t, T)$ should be estimated, while in the HJM model the structure of the volatility function $\sigma(t, T)$ should be known or estimated. Secondly, system (10.5) has no closed form solution. This leads to numerical integration methods required during each iteration of an algorithm for solving the (10.5)-based optimization model. Stochastic models of HJM type are non-Markovian in general, and this leads to using Monte Carlo simulation procedures for solving such models. Finally, we have presented several simplified models derived from the general model that facilitate computation.

Applications to Pricing Futures Fairly and Trading Futures Contracts

11.1 AN EQUATION FOR THE FAIR FUTURE PRICE OF TREASURY BILLS

We begin with an extension of the standard forward rate calculation with respect to two consecutive yields for the period embracing the future forward period. We studied this procedure in Chapter 1 with respect to LIBOR rates and forward rates, going back to (1.12). We now see how the procedure applies to US Treasury bill rates and futures rates, for example the 90-day SYCOM rates regularly reported in the *Wall Street Journal* and elsewhere. The interest rate at which one can sell a Treasury bill is the *bid yield*. It is less than the interest rate at which one can buy a Treasury bill, termed the asked price or, in particular, the *ask yield*. Now, Treasury futures settle to the offered side of the market, the ask yield. Consider two periods each less than one year, S days in the short period and L days in the long period, with the third period being the time between them, the so-called future period:

- R_L = ask yield for the long period;
- R_S = ask yield for the short period;
- F = forward rate for the period between the short and the long consisting of $L - S$ days;
- $days_L$ = actual number of days in the long period;
- $days_S$ = actual number of days in the short period;
- $days_F$ = actual number of days covered by the forward period.

Definition 11.1 *The forward offered rate F is fair if and only if*

$$[1 + R_L(days_L/360)] = [1 + R_S(days_S/360)] \times [1 + F(days_F/360)]. \tag{11.1}$$

For the illustration of (11.1) we see that the *current time* is Thursday 7/13/00, and we focus on future dates of 3/1/01 and 5/31/01. The number of days between 7/13/00 and 3/1/01 is $days_S = 231$, while the number of days between 7/13/00 and 5/31/01 is $days_L = 322$. In summary, from Table 11.1 we find:

- $R_L = 6.08$;
- $R_S = 5.86$;
- F = sought for ask forward rate for the period between the short and the long;
- $days_L$ = days in [7/13/00, 5/31/01] = 322;
- $days_S$ = days in [7/13/00, 3/1/01] = 231;
- $days_F = 91$.

Table 11.1 Excerpts from the *Wall Street Journal, Interactive Edition* Treasury bills data as of Wednesday 7/12/00: current time = 7/13/00 with 7 days to maturity corresponding to the first yield entry

Maturity	Bid	Ask yield
20 Jul 00	5.88	5.89
27 Jul 00	5.54	5.63
03 Aug 00	5.80	5.82
. . .	. . .	. . .
16 Nov 00	5.97	6.16
. . .	. . .	. . .
01 Feb 01	5.92	6.17
01 Mar 01	5.63	5.86
31 May 01	5.77	6.08

Table 11.2 Excerpts from the *Wall Street Journal, Interactive Edition* 90-day bill (SYCOM)

Contr.	Date	Settle
ASRU00	Sep 00	9380
ASRZ00	Dec 00	9366
ASRH01	Mar 01	9360
. . .	. . .	. . .
. . .	. . .	. . .

According to (11.1), the futures fair ask price satisfies

$$\left(1 + 0.0608\frac{322}{360}\right) = \left(1 + 0.0586\frac{231}{360}\right) \times \left(1 + F\frac{91}{360}\right), \tag{11.2}$$

from which we find $F = 0.0640$. From Table 11.2 we find a very close correlation, namely that the future SYCOM price is $640 = 10\,000 - 9360 = 6.40\%$, which is exact. This is not always the case.

11.2 ESTIMATING ARBITRAGE OPPORTUNITIES FOR A USER-SELECTED FUTURE TIME INTERVAL

A software documentation of the forward rate model of Chapter 9 appears in Chapter 15. Typical input data to the model appear in Figure 15.1, where for illustration the current time is 6/30/00. A continuous trajectory of the US Treasury yield curve is computed that passes as closely as possible to the observed data. Simultaneously, an estimated forward rates curve is computed corresponding to that trajectory.

The main graphical output of the computation appears in Figure 15.2 where we see: (a) the estimate of the yield curve, (b) the real data and (c) the forward rate curve. In addition Figure 15.3 gives a view of the corresponding 'spectral analysis', namely the histogram of the full range of the computed forward rates as an indication of the volatility of the forward rates. There are also smoothed variations of the forward rate curve in other graphical displays.

To illustrate how a user may apply the software in an interactive manner let us suppose that today is Wednesday 7/12/00, the day we receive data from the *Wall Street Journal, Interactive Edition* section 'Treasury Quotes: Treasury Bills'. We find the first yield given corresponds to the maturity date 7/20/00 while the last data date is 5/31/01, establishing a 315-day future period, see Table 11.1.

11.2.1 Illustrative Use of the Estimated Forward Rates

As a rule, 90-day future bill rates are posted for only Sep, Dec, Mar and Jan, approximately from the 19th to the 23rd. But what if your customers want the 90-day forward rate during the period 16 Nov 00 to 14 Feb 01? Both the bid and ask prices for 16 Nov 00 are published on 7/12/00, 5.97 and 6.16 respectively. The closest date to your 14 Feb 01 ending date for which there are published spot rates is 01 Feb 01, 13 days short.

11.2.2 The Estimated Nonarbitrage Future Price Interval

The computed interval for the offered settled forward rate for 16 Nov 00–14 Feb 01 for which no arbitrage is possible is [5.180, 6.204]. The computed futures fair offered rate is 5.741. We note that the 90-day bill (SYCOM) has the rate 6.20 for Sep 00 and 6.34 for Dec 00. The Treasury bills asked rates for 01 Feb 01 and 01 Mar 01 are respectively 6.17 and 5.86. These calculations basically involve relationship (11.1), and as a rule are straightforward.

In the context of these data and dates, the user merely needs to specify the 'User Future Period' by giving its beginning date (at least 27 Jul 00) and its ending date (not later than 31 May 01). For the 'User Future Period' we can compute the range of its forward rate for which there is no arbitrage opportunity. Of course, all of these dates will change as we progress into the future, but the procedure will be the same.

In the next section we give results of daily computations and estimations for a 27-day period starting with 09 Aug 00. We anticipate that readers will be interested in performing similar experiments.

11.3 AN INTEREST RATE–FUTURES RATE SCENARIO AT THE CLOSE OF 8/14/00

Imagine that it is the close of the business day on Monday 14 August 2000, and we have received published data on US Treasury bills rates. We find it convenient to refer to 8/14/00 as a 'data date'. We see the first date for which a rate appears is 17 Aug 00 listed with days to maturity 2. This means that the current time is 8/15/00 which is consistent with days to maturity 2 and settlement conditions. The very first entry of Treasury bills data appearing on 14 Aug 00 appears in Table 11.3 as one particular excerpt from the entire table, where we are not interested in the rates having two days to maturity.

Assume there are three dates that are important to us: 8/15/00, 12/21/00 and 3/23/01. We can obtain T-bills rates data for 12/21/00 as seen in Table 11.4.

Table 11.3 First data entry for T-bills rates published close of 8/14/00

Maturity	Days to maturity	Bid	Ask	Chg	Ask yield
17 Aug 00	2	6.16	6.08	+0.11	6.17

Table 11.4 Data entry 21 Dec 00 for T-bills rates published close of 8/14/00

Maturity	Days to maturity	Bid	Ask	Chg	Ask yield
21 Dec 00	128	6.03	6.01	+0.01	6.23

We wish to make a short-term loan from the current time of 8/15/00 to the future date 12/21/00, a 128 loan period at the bid rate of 6.03%, which is the best we can obtain as lenders. We record this initial transaction together with the conclusion at termination of the loan in Table 11.5.

We ask next whether a trade with futures over the future period 12/21/00 to 3/23/01 could increase our return over the loan rate of 6.03%. The published T-bills data on 8/14/00 does not have an entry for the ending date of the future period, 3/23/01. The closest date to 3/23/01 for which a rate is given is 01 Mar 01.

Here is where our dynamical estimation procedure applies. Based on current Treasury bills rates published on 8/14/00, we estimate the future annualized ask rate to maturity date 3/23/01 ('out-of-sample') to be 6.15%. We next assume a bid–ask spread of 0.22 to 0.25 to obtain an estimated bid rate for 3/23/01. For specificity we take this to be 5.90%. We also have a published futures rate with which we can initiate a transaction, namely the 90-day futures SYCOM settle–ask price for Dec 00 of 6.69%, namely 9331. This means that the futures annualized yield for the 92-day future period [12/21/00, 3/23/01] is 6.69%, and we can buy a futures contract for 9331 on 8/15/00. To examine the merits of this transaction, one could use our estimated bid yield of 5.90% under the assumption that it will be realized sometime on or before the termination date of the futures contract, 12/21/00. Should this assumption be valid, then we can sell the futures contract purchased on 8/15/00 for 9409, and there would be a capital gain. Table 11.6 summarizes the transaction.

The gain on the long futures contract augments the return on the 8/15/00 loan of $9 790 100. This amount now grows to $10 019 933 in 128 days for an annualized return of 6.60. If our estimate of the 3/23/01 ask yield price holds between now and 12/21/00, then it is possible to increase the return of our 128-day loan by 57 basis points.

Table 11.5 Making a 128-day loan, current time = 8/15/00

At time	8/15/00
Loan	$9 790 100 for 128 days at 6.03
At time	12/21/00
Receive	$10 000 000 = 9 790 100 $(1 + 0.0603 \frac{128}{360})$ from the 128-day loan
Interest received	$209 900

Table 11.6 Results from a long Dec 00 futures contract purchased at the settle–ask 8/14/00 price 9331, sold at the estimated price 9401

At time	8/15/00
Buy	$10 000 000 Dec 00 futures at 9331
At time	12/21/00
Receive	$19 933 = (9409 − 9331) × 1000 × $\frac{92}{360}$

Table 11.7 Yield data underlying a forward rate calculation for [12/21/00, 3/23/01]

At time	8/18/00	the 125-day to 12/21/00	ask rate is	6.21
At time	8/18/00	the 125-day to 12/21/00	bid rate is	6.02
At time	8/18/00	the 217-day to 3/23/01	est. ask rate is	5.74051
At time	8/18/00	the 217-day to 3/23/01	est. bid rate is	5.49051
		assuming a bid–ask spread of 0.25 at 3/23/01		

Assume the bid–ask spread for the fair forward rate (12/21/00–3/23/01) is the mean of the two spreads above

The fair offered forward rate for [12/21/00, 3/23/01] according to these data and (11.1) is 4.9949

11.4 AN INTEREST RATE–FUTURES RATE SCENARIO FOR THE DATA DATE OF 8/17/00

Let us move ahead a few days to a data date of 8/17/00, this means that the current time is 8/18/00, and assume the market bid yield and ask yield are respectively 6.02 and 6.21. It will be clear when a figure is a percentage, so it will not be necessary to always be explicit.

A bank is contemplating now making a 125-day loan from the current time of 8/18/00 to 12/21/00. For this data date the published 92-day futures settle–ask rate for Dec 00 (which we take to 12/21/00) is 6.74. As a check on our arithmetic, we may carry more decimals than one usually does in practice.

Just as before we estimate the ask yield for the future date 3/23/01. This now is the annualized yield for the 217-day period 8/18/00–3/23/01. The result is an ask yield of 5.74051 (the rate at which we borrow). The bid–ask spreads for yields having maturities near to 3/23/01 were about 0.25, and so we assume the same for the date 3/23/01. This means that the bid yield to maturity is 5.49051 (the rate at which we can lend). In the standard way according to (11.1) we combine the estimate of the ask yield from 8/18/00 to 3/23/01 with the published ask yield from 8/18/00 to 12/21/00 to compute the 'fair forward ask yield' that applies to the 92-day future period, 12/21/00–3/23/01. We find that the estimated fair forward offered rate is 4.9949. Hence the futures estimated fair offered rate at date 12/21/00 is 9500.51. Table 11.7 summarizes the pertinent yield data and assumptions we have made to calculate a forward rate consistent with them, recognizing again that for the farthest future date, 3/23/01, the yield is estimated by the forward rate model in Chapter 9.

Table 11.8   An illustrative two-arbitrage transaction for market futures rate 6.74 for [12/21/00, 3/23/01]

At time	8/18/00
Loan	$9 795 252.02 for 125 days at 6.02
Buy	$10 000 000 futures at 9326 = (10 000 − 674)
Borrow	$9 795 252.02 for 217 days at 5.74051
At time	12/21/00
Receive	$10 000 000 from 125-day loan made at 8/18/00 = 9 795 252.02$(1 + 0.0602\frac{125}{360})$
Receive	$44 597 from long futures bought on 8/18/00 at 9326, sold at termination for 9500.51 = $(9500.51 − 9326) \times 1000 \times \frac{92}{360}$
Loan	$10 044 597 for 92 days at (fair ask price − spread) = 4.99491 − 0.22 = 4.77491
At time	3/23/01
Bank receives	$10 167 166.67 = 10 044 597$(1 + 0.0477491\frac{92}{360})$ from the 92-day loan
Bank repays	217-day loan $10 134 192.41 = 9 795 252.02$(1 + 0.0574051\frac{217}{360})$
Arbitrage profit	$32 974

Table 11.9   An illustrative two-arbitrage transaction for market futures rate 3.425 for [12/21/00, 3/23/01]

At time	8/18/00
Borrow	$9 788 926.28 for 125 days at the ask yield 6.21
Sell	$10 000 000 futures at 9657.5 = (10 000 − 342.5)
Lend	$9 788 926.28 for 217 days at the bid yield 5.49051
At time	12/21/00
Borrow	$9 959 880 for 92 days at the fair ask rate 4.9949
Repay	$10 000 000 on the 125-day loan taken at 8/18/00 = 9 788 926.28$(1 + 0.0621\frac{125}{360})$
Receive	$40 120 from the short futures sold on 8/18/00 for 9657.5, bought at termination for 9500.51 = $(9657.5 − 9500.51) \times 1000 \times \frac{92}{360}$
	Note that the short futures receipts plus the loan proceeds covers the 10 000 000 12/21/00 debt obligation
At time	3/23/01
Bank receives	$10 112 896.42 = 9 788 926.28$(1 + 0.0549051\frac{217}{360})$ from the 217-day loan
Bank repays	$10 087 015.32 = 9 959 880$(1 + 0.049949\frac{92}{360})$ on the 92-day futures loan
Arbitrage profit	$25 881

Table 11.8 gives the details of the transactions that yield $32 974 arbitrage profits under these assumptions. The $32 974 arbitrage level would decrease if we decreased the given market yield to maturity 6.74. A little experimentation aided by a spread sheet will show that when the 6.74 is decreased to about 5.46527, the arbitrage figure will vanish. We term this figure the *high end of the nonarbitrage interval*. It is well defined, and can be computed by a formula. For illustrative purposes a computation suffices. But what about the 'other end' of the market yield, namely where we start with a sufficiently small market 92-day futures rate? Let us illustrate with a series of trans-actions in Table 11.9 analogous to Table 11.8.

The $25 881 arbitrage level would decrease if we increased the given market yield to maturity 3.425. Again, a little experimentation aided by a spread sheet will show that

Table 11.10   For each data day an estimate is made for bid–ask yields for the date 3/23/01 to use in computing an estimate of a 'fair futures rate' for future period 12/21/00–3/23/01. Based on this result a 'nonarbitrage interval' is computed for each of the data days. Est. means estimated, arb. means arbitrage

Data date 2000	Current time 2000	Published		3/23/01 Est.		92-Day futures 12/21/00	Est. fair futures rate	Nonarb. ask interval	
		Bid yield	Ask yield	Bid	Ask			Low	High
8/9	8/10	5.970	6.17	5.782	6.032	6.620	5.702	5.113	6.207
8/10	8/11	5.980	6.18	5.720	5.970	6.610	5.543	4.955	6.046
8/11	8/14	6.020	6.220	5.862	6.112	6.660	5.831	5.252	6.327
8/14	8/15	6.030	6.230	5.900	6.150	6.690	5.909	5.332	6.403
8/15[a]	8/16	6.040	6.240	5.762	6.012	6.670	5.574	5.000	6.067
8/16	8/17	6.030	6.230	5.755	6.005	6.750	5.576	5.005	6.056
8/17	8/18	6.020	6.210	5.491	5.741	6.740	4.995	4.425	5.465
8/18	8/21	6.020	6.210	5.559	5.809	6.740	5.169	4.607	5.631
8/21	8/22	6.010	6.210	5.775	5.827	6.690	5.214	5.098	5.597
8/22	8/23	5.980	6.170	5.595	5.845	6.720	5.312	4.755	5.772
8/23	8/24	5.990	6.170	5.686	5.936	6.740	5.521	4.967	5.962
8/24	8/25	5.990	6.170	6.028	6.278	6.720	6.290	5.740	6.728
8/25	8/28	6.010	6.190	6.068	6.318	6.750	6.352	5.809	6.784
8/28	8/29	6.050	6.230	6.074	6.324	6.760	6.316	5.776	6.747
8/29	8/30	6.050	6.230	6.152	6.402	6.780	6.487	5.950	6.916
8/30	8/31	6.050	6.230	6.138	6.388	6.740	6.455	5.920	6.882
8/31	9/1	6.070	6.250	6.128	6.378	6.560	6.409	5.877	6.834
9/1	9/5	6.030	6.200	6.048	6.298	6.550	6.295	5.772	6.696
9/5	9/6	6.040	6.210	5.951	6.206	6.550	6.090	5.558	6.492
9/6	9/7	6.010	6.180	5.914	6.164	6.640	6.038	5.520	6.435
9/7	9/8	5.990	6.160	6.016	6.266	6.660	6.274	5.759	6.670
9/8	9/11	5.940	6.100	6.069	6.319	6.660	6.449	5.942	6.824
9/11	9/12	5.940	6.100	5.997	6.247	6.640	6.299	5.786	6.674
9/12	9/13	5.890	6.050	5.950	6.200	6.650	6.275	5.755	6.629
9/13	9/14	5.900	6.060	5.926	6.176	6.610	6.198	5.698	6.568
9/14	9/15	5.970	6.140	5.950	6.200	6.670	6.161	5.664	6.545
9/15	9/18	5.960	6.130	5.940	6.190	6.690	6.153	5.624	6.541

[a] We will use this three-period term structure to illustrate hedging strategies and martingales in Chapter 12.

when the 3.425 is increased to about 4.42496, the arbitrage figure will vanish. We term this figure the *low end of the nonarbitrage interval*. It is well defined, and also can be computed by a formula.

Thus with a little algebra we can compute a range of yields for which such transactions do not generate profits of the type illustrated in Table 11.8, taking a long futures position for profitability, and Table 11.9, taking a short futures position. For the case at hand, the estimated nonarbitrage futures price interval is [4.425, 5.465], as indicated to the far right in the shaded row of Table 11.10.

Actually, by using a formula based upon calculations illustrated in Tables 11.8 and 11.9, nonarbitrage intervals have been computed for the 27 days of real data presented in Table 11.10. The intervals are traced against actual 90-day SYCOM data over this 27-day period during the summer of 2000 in Figure 11.1.

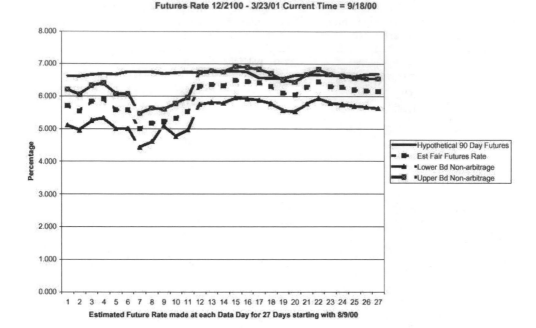

Figure 11.1   Nonarbitrage intervals, 27 days US T-bill yield data

11.5   CHAPTER NOTES

In this application we have followed the standard (discrete) interest rate definitions and day count conventions reviewed in Chapter 1 expressions (1.9)–(1.12). Actually, this portion of our approach to the term structure readily follows [5, Chapter 2], where it appears under the title 'Basic Interest Rate Building Blocks'. Our (11.1) appears with the same notation in this reference, but applied to the LIBOR rate. Our 'ask' prices are analogous to these, but of course Treasury prices for our illustrations. Our 'bid' prices are analogous to the LIBID prices, which are the rates at which the London Bank is willing to borrow. These correspondences were necessary so that we could use the estimates of future US Teasury yields to maturity at times where such yields were not readily available in the public press.

In Section 11.2 we have basically used (11.1) to illustrate the use of estimated forward rates (obtained from our model) for discovering possible arbitrage opportunities.

In Section 11.3, we elaborated upon the concept appearing in [5, Chapter 2], entitled 'The High Payoff of Keeping Future Prices in Line'. Actually, we are illustrating in terms of our modeling a role of futures trading that has long been recognized by practitioners, e.g. citing [5, p. 50]:

'Our experience suggests that bankers are very interested indeed in opportunities to reduce the costs of funds or raise the rate of return on investments.'

Finally, Section 11.4 provides the results of a 27 consecutive day experiment related to arbitrage interval calculations appearing in [5, Appendix B]. In the authors' terminology we have calculated what they term 'a strong above fair futures nonarbitrage bound' and 'a strong below fair futures nonarbitrage bound' for each of the 27 days beginning with the data date of 8/9/00. For each day with US Treasury bills we are computing the bounds analogous to those that appear in [5, Exhibit B.3], but where there they are the following: 2MO LIBOR, LIBID and 5MO LIBOR, LIBID.

It is interesting that in [5] over 100 pages are devoted to formal legal documents, namely:

- Code of Standard Wording;
- Interest Rate and Currency Exchange Definitions;
- Interest Rate Swap Agreement (an actual one);
- Standard Form Agreements.

The calculations given in this chapter are meant to be illustrative of an application of our approach, but do not necessarily reflect how actual borrowing and lending would occur or at what rates. For actual practice one would need to adhere to the precise definitions of "Bid", "Ask", and "Ask Yield" for U.S. Treasury Bill data.

Using Term Structure Estimation in Dynamic Interest Rate Models and Hedging Strategies

12.1   A SIMPLE TERM STRUCTURE HAVING THREE YIELDS TO MATURITY

We refer back to Table 11.10 for the illustrative yet simple term structure we will use. Actually, some of this term structure data required estimation by our model, so in this sense this chapter reports another application. With respect to yields to maturity, we will continue to use the $\mathcal{R}$ notation, see (1.5), for long-term rates including one-period rates, when they are discrete. Thus, we write $\mathcal{R}(t, T) = \mathcal{R}_{t,T-t}$, the latter designating days to maturity as a subscript $T - t$. In this application we demonstrate the approach beginning with a simple three-yield term structure corresponding to current time 8/16/00 appearing in Figure 14.1. Since the periods are of varying length, it is more convenient to state these rates as *annualized rates*. For the data date of 8/15/00 with current time 8/16/00 the 3/23/01 yield to maturity was not yet published and had to be estimated with the forward rate model of Chapter 10.

The annualized yields for these three bonds are presented in Table 12.1. Analogous to $P(t, T)$, see (1.49), for continuous compounding we denote the price of a bond at time t maturing at time T under discrete compounding by $\mathcal{P}(t, T)$. This is consistent with the applications presented in this chapter. More specifically:

$$\mathcal{P}_1 = \mathcal{P}(8/16/00, 12/21/00) = \frac{100}{1 + 0.0624 \times 0.35278} = 97.84608,$$

$$\mathcal{P}_2 = \mathcal{P}(8/16/00, 3/23/01) = \frac{100}{1 + 0.06012 \times 0.61111} = 96.45620, \qquad (12.1)$$

$$\mathcal{P}_3 = \mathcal{P}(8/16/00, 5/31/01) = \frac{100}{1 + 0.0616 \times 0.80278} = 95.28791.$$

We will be considering hedging bond $\mathcal{P}_2$ with bonds $\mathcal{P}_1$ and $\mathcal{P}_3$. In preparation for the analysis we will be denoting the amount of bonds $\mathcal{P}_1$ by x_1 and the number of units of bonds $\mathcal{P}_3$ by x_3.

12.2   ON THE CONSISTENCY OF INTEREST RATE MOVEMENTS WITH THE TERM STRUCTURE

Let r denote an annualized interest rate for a given period according to the definition of pure average long-term rate (1.5). An *Up* movement of the annualized interest rate to

Table 12.1 Four dates, time between dates and annualized yields to maturity

Time	Days ‖ years	Time	Days ‖ years	Time	Days ‖ years
8/16/00	127 ‖ 0.35278	12/21/00	92 ‖ 0.25556	3/23/01	69 ‖ 0.19167 5/31/01
	$\mathcal{AR}_{8/16/00,127} = 1.0624$				
			$\mathcal{AR}_{8/16/00,220} = 1.06012$		
					$\mathcal{AR}_{8/16/00,289} = 1.0616$

Table 12.2 Annualized one-period rate changes for three periods. Current time 8/16/00: first $Up = 0.633$, $Down = 0.367$; second $Up = 0.35736$, $Down = 0.64264$ with period-by-period rates $\mathcal{R}_1$, $\mathcal{R}_{2,U}$, $\mathcal{R}_{2,D}$, $\mathcal{R}_{3,UU}$, $\mathcal{R}_{3,UD}$, $\mathcal{R}_{2,DD}$ in *italics*

0.35278 years 8/16–12/21/00	0.2556 years 12/21/00–3/23/01	0.1917 years 3/23/01–5/31/01
		Up 0.35736 1.1383 $\mathcal{R}_{3,UU} = 1.02651$
	Up 0.633 1.1019 $\mathcal{R}_{2,U} = 1.02604$	
1.0624 $\mathcal{R}_1 = 1.02201$		*Down* 0.64264 1.06548 $\mathcal{R}_{3,UD} = 1.01255$
	Down 0.367 1.0229 $\mathcal{R}_{2,D} = 1.00585$	
		Down 0.64264 1.01472 $\mathcal{R}_{3,DD} = 1.00282$

the next period's annualized r^+ is determined by the relation $r^+ = 1 + r \times Up$, where Up denotes a specified number. Thus, if $\mathcal{AR}_1$ denotes the annualized long-term interest for a 127-day rate and $Up = 0.57$, then the next period's annualized interest is $1 + (\mathcal{AR}_1 - 1) \times 1.57$. For the *Down* change replace 1.57 with $1 - 0.57$. For our introductory example we choose one Up number for the first period change in annualized interest and another for the second period change in annualized rate. Our illustrative example will take the two Up's to be 0.633 for the first change with respect to period 8/16/00–12/21/00 and 0.3574 with respect to the period 12/21/00–3/23/01. With these numbers we generate the interest tree given in Table 12.2.

In Figure 15.3 we present a histogram of occurrences of forward rate values for an example and compute the standard deviation according to (15.1). We now choose the first Up change to be approximately that standard deviation.

Let us define the following bond prices associated with $\mathcal{P}_2$:

$\tau^+ = 12/21/00$ $\mathcal{P}_2$ price from an Up move $= 100/(1 + 0.0229 \times 0.25556) = 99.41816$,
$\tau^- = 12/21/00$ $\mathcal{P}_2$ price from a $Down$ move $= 100/(1 + 0.1019 \times 0.25556) = 97.4626$.

$$(12.2)$$

Table 12.3 $\mathcal{P}_2$ bond values at specific times corresponding to *Up/Down* changes

8/16/00	12/21/00
	$\mathcal{P}^+(12/21/00, 3/23/00)$ $$\tau^+ = 99.41816 = \frac{100}{1 + 0.0229 \times 0.25556} \text{ in (12.2)}$$
$\mathcal{P}(8/16/00, 3/23/01)$ 96.4562	
	$\mathcal{P}^-(12/21/00, 5/31/01)$ $$\tau^- = 97.46260 = \frac{100}{1 + 0.1019 \times 0.25556} \text{ in (12.2)}$$

Table 12.4 $\mathcal{P}_1$ bond values at specific times corresponding to *Up/Down* changes

8/16/00	12/21/00	3/23/01
		$\mathcal{P}^{++}(3/23/01, 5/31/01)$ $$99.71872 = \frac{100}{1 + 0.01472 \times 0.19167}$$
	$\mathcal{P}^+(12/21/00, 5/31/01)$	
$\mathcal{P}(8/16/00, 5/31/01)$ 95.28791		$\mathcal{P}^{+-}(3/23/01, 5/31/01)$ $$98.76044 = \frac{100}{1 + 0.06548 \times 0.19167}$$
	$\mathcal{P}^-(12/21/00, 5/31/01)$	
		$\mathcal{P}^{--}(3/23/01, 5/31/01)$ $$97.41744 = \frac{100}{1 + 0.13831 \times 0.19167}$$

Note that τ^+, τ^- (also appearing in Table 12.3) are known with perfect certainty at time 12/21/00 because at that time the bonds become a one-period bond with known payoff 100 depending on the interest rate movement. Similarly, the prices $\mathcal{P}$ with superscripts in Table 12.4 at time 3/23/01 are also known with perfect certainty. From the term structure the present values $\mathcal{P}_1$, $\mathcal{P}_2$ are also known with perfect certainty. But a seeming paradox arises in that the period rates appearing in *italics* in Table 12.2 are not consistent with the term structure, as a rule. They do not act as forward rates even though they are of course rates associated with the three respective periods of different lengths. For example

$$\mathcal{P}_2 \times 1.02201 \times 1.02604 = 101.14662, \text{ not the terminal } 100,$$

$$\mathcal{P}_3 \times 1.02201 \times 1.02604 \times 1.02651 = 102.57046, \text{ not the terminal } 100.$$

12.3   A LINEAR PROGRAMMING ANALYSIS OF A HEDGING OPPORTUNITY

Let x_1 denote the dollar level of $\mathcal{P}(8/16/00, 12/21/00)$ bonds purchased. Let x_3 denote the units of bond $\mathcal{P}(8/16/00, 5/31/01)$ purchased. Both purchases are made at the current time 8/16/00. There will be no confusion if we denote the bond prices in Table 12.3 by the shortened notation $\mathcal{P}$ alone or together with the appropriate combination of $+$ and $-$ superscripts. We seek the minimum current investment in these instruments at 8/16/00 which will cover the bond values of $\mathcal{P}(8/16/00, 3/23/01)$ at time 12/21/00. At time 12/21/00 the x_1 bonds are worth

$$\mathcal{R}_1 x_1, \quad \text{where } \mathcal{R}_1 = (1 + (\mathcal{R}_{8/16/00,127} - 1) \times 0.35278) = 1.02201 x_1.$$

At time 12/21/00 the bond $\mathcal{P}(8/16/00, 5/31/01)$ has one of two values, at this time 'unknown', namely

$$\mathcal{P}^+ = \mathcal{P}^+(12/21/00, 5/31/01) \quad \text{or} \quad \mathcal{P}^- = \mathcal{P}^-(12/21/00, 5/31/01).$$

There are two interest rates for the second period 12/21/00–3/23/01 depending on an *Up* or *Down* movement:

$$\mathcal{R}_{2,U} = 1 + 0.019 \times 0.2556 = 1.02604,$$

$$\mathcal{R}_{2,D} = 1 + 0.0229 \times 0.2556 = 1.00583.$$

We are considering what is termed a *hedge* of $\mathcal{P}(8/16/00, 3/23/01)$ by the two bonds, $\mathcal{P}(8/16/00, 12/21/01)$ and $\mathcal{P}(8/16/00, 5/31/01)$, see (12.1) and Table 12.1. Our interpretation begins with a behavior principle that is analogous to an investor in $\mathcal{P}_2$ who seeks a fair price for $\mathcal{P}_2$ at the current time 8/16/00 by asking for the least to be required at 8/16/00 so that by 12/21/00 the value of $\mathcal{P}_2$ will be covered by the portfolio constructed in 8/16/00. This leads to the ASK linear programming problem.

The BID problem on the other hand has the following interpretation. It is based on the behavior of a security issuer who seeks the maximum loan value that can be obtained for $\mathcal{P}_2$ at 8/16/00 subject to solvency conditions at time 12/21/00, namely that the respective values of the $\mathcal{P}_1$ and $\mathcal{P}_3$ portfolio do not exceed the value of $\mathcal{P}_2$ at 12/21/00:

The ASK hedging program	*The BID hedging program*
$v_{\text{ask}} = \min_{\{x_1, x_3\}} x_1 + x_3 \mathcal{P}_3$	$v_{\text{bid}} = \max_{\{x_1, x_3\}} x_1 + x_3 \mathcal{P}_3$
subject to	subject to
$\mathcal{R}_1 x_1 + x_3 \mathcal{P}^+ \geqslant \tau^+,$	$\mathcal{R}_1 x_1 + x_3 \mathcal{P}^+ \leqslant \tau^+,$
$\mathcal{R}_1 x_1 + x_3 \mathcal{P}^- \geqslant \tau^-,$	$\mathcal{R}_1 x_1 + x_1 \mathcal{P}^- \leqslant \tau^-,$

(12.3)

with respective dual linear programming problems:

$\max_{\{y^+, y^-\}} y^+ \tau^+ + y^- \tau^-$	$\min_{\{y^+, y^-\}} y^+ \tau^+ + y^- \tau^-$
subject to	subject to
$y^+ \mathcal{R}_1 + y^- \mathcal{R}_1 = 1,$	$y^+ \mathcal{R}_1 + y^- \mathcal{R}_1 = 1,$
$y^+ \mathcal{P}^+ + y^- \mathcal{P}^- = \mathcal{P}_3,$	$y^+ \mathcal{P}^+ + y^- \mathcal{P}^- = \mathcal{P}_3,$
$y^+, y^- \geqslant 0.$	$y^+, y^- \geqslant 0.$

(12.4)

The primal and dual optimal solutions to ASK primal and dual linear programs are given in (12.5) and (12.6), where the subscript 'opt' denotes optimality. The data for our illustrative example are consistent with the following assumption, for without it the hedging problem would not make economic sense.

Assumption 12.1 $\mathcal{P}^+ > \mathcal{R}_1 \mathcal{P}_3 > \mathcal{P}^-$.

Finally, observe as usual bond prices move inversely to bond yields:

$$\text{Optimal primal hedging portfolio}$$

$$x_1^{\text{opt}} = \frac{\mathcal{P}^+ \tau^- - \tau^+ \mathcal{P}^-}{(\mathcal{P}^+ - \mathcal{P}^-)\mathcal{R}_1} \quad \text{and} \quad x_3^{\text{opt}} = \frac{\tau^+ - \tau^-}{\mathcal{P}^+ - \mathcal{P}^-}, \tag{12.5}$$

$$\text{Optimal dual variables}$$

$$y_{\text{opt}}^+ = \frac{1}{\mathcal{R}_1} \pi^+ \quad \text{and} \quad y_{\text{opt}}^- = \frac{1}{\mathcal{R}_1} \pi^-, \tag{12.6}$$

where

$$\pi^+ = \frac{\mathcal{R}_1 \mathcal{P}_3 - \mathcal{P}^-}{\mathcal{P}^+ - \mathcal{P}^-} \quad \text{and} \quad \pi^- = \frac{\mathcal{P}^+ - \mathcal{R}_1 \mathcal{P}_3}{\mathcal{P}^+ - \mathcal{P}^-}.$$

Observe the very important fact that $\{\pi^+, \pi^-\}$ is a discrete probability distribution, termed the *risk neutral probability distribution*.

Actually, the optimal solution is also optimal for both the ASK and the BID problems, and so the bid and ask values are the same.

Lemma 12.1 $\mathcal{P}_1 = v_{\text{ask}}$.

Proof. We use an arbitrage argument. If $\mathcal{P}_1 > v_{\text{ask}}$, then sell $\mathcal{P}_1$ bonds at time 8/16/00 and buy the portfolio $\{x_1^{\text{opt}}, x_2^{\text{opt}}\}$ for v_{ask}, which is assumed to be less than $\mathcal{P}_1$. Pocket the difference. If $\mathcal{P}_1 < v_{\text{ask}}$, then consider that the hedger is willing to pay v_{ask}, since this amount is the minimum over all conceivable portfolios which will cover 12/21/00 obligations. Therefore, buy $\mathcal{P}_1$ bonds at time 8/16/00 and sell them to the investor for $v_{\text{ask}} > \mathcal{P}_1$. Pocket the difference. □

We are now faced with the action we should take at 12/21/00 with respect to the values $\mathcal{P}^{++}$, $\mathcal{P}^{+-}$, $\mathcal{P}^{+-}$ of bond $\mathcal{P}_3$ known with perfect certainty at time 3/23/01. The hedger still holds the bonds $\mathcal{P}_1$ and $\mathcal{P}_3$, but their values need to be updated to time 12/21/00. There is a pair of values $\mathcal{P}^{++}$, $\mathcal{P}^{+-}$ associated with an *Up* interest move and a pair of values $\mathcal{P}^{+-}$, $\mathcal{P}^{+-}$ associated with a *Down* interest move. We formulate the linear program associated with the *Down* move first. It is analogous to those developed in (12.3) and (12.4), but we will concentrate only on the ASK dual linear programming problem pair:

$$\text{Period two Down } \mathcal{R}_{2,D} \text{ ASK hedging program}$$

$$v_{D\text{-ask}} = \min_{\{x_1, x_3\}} \mathcal{R}_1 x_1 + \mathcal{R}_1 \mathcal{P}_3 x_3$$

subject to

$$\mathcal{R}_1 \mathcal{R}_{2,D} x_1 + \mathcal{R}_{2,D} \mathcal{P}^+ x_3 \geqslant \mathcal{P}^{+-},$$

$$\mathcal{R}_1 \mathcal{R}_{2,D} x_1 + \mathcal{R}_{2,D} \mathcal{P}^- x_3 \geqslant \mathcal{P}^{--}, \tag{12.7}$$

with the following dual linear programming problem:

$$\max_{\{y^+, y^-\}} \mathcal{P}^{+-} y^+ + \mathcal{P}^{--} y^-$$

subject to

$$\mathcal{R}_1 \mathcal{R}_{2,D} y^+ + \mathcal{R}_1 \mathcal{R}_{2,D} y^- = \mathcal{R}_1,$$

$$\mathcal{R}_{2,D} \mathcal{P}^+ y^+ + \mathcal{R}_{2,D} \mathcal{P}^- y^- = \mathcal{R}_1 \mathcal{P}_3, \tag{12.8}$$

$$y^+, \ y^- \geqslant 0.$$

Analogous to the optimal solution for the first period problem (12.5) we derive the following optimal solutions for the second period problem:

Period two Down $\mathcal{R}_{2,D}$ optimal primal hedging portfolio

$$x_1^{\text{opt}} = \frac{\mathcal{P}^+ \mathcal{P}^{--} - \mathcal{P}^{+-} \mathcal{P}^-}{(\mathcal{R}_{2,D} \mathcal{P}^+ - \mathcal{R}_{2,D} \mathcal{P}^-) \mathcal{R}_1} \quad \text{and} \quad x_3^{\text{opt}} = \frac{\mathcal{P}^{+-} - \mathcal{P}^{--}}{\mathcal{R}_{2,D}(\mathcal{P}^+ - \mathcal{P}^-)}, \tag{12.9}$$

Period two Down $\mathcal{R}_{2,D}$ optimal dual variables

$$y_{\text{opt}}^+ = \frac{1}{\mathcal{R}_{2,D}} \pi^+ \quad \text{and} \quad y_{\text{opt}}^- = \frac{1}{\mathcal{R}_{2,D}} \pi^-,$$

where π^+ and π^- are defined in (12.6).

For completeness we include the linear programming dual pair for an *Up* interest rate move now involving the period two bond values $\mathcal{P}^{++}$, $\mathcal{P}^{+-}$:

Period two Up $\mathcal{R}_{2,U}$ ASK hedging program

$$v_{U\text{-ask}} = \min_{\{x_1, x_3\}} \mathcal{R}_1 x_1 + \mathcal{R}_1 \mathcal{P}_3 x_3$$

subject to

$$\mathcal{R}_1 \mathcal{R}_{2,U} x_1 + \mathcal{R}_{2,U} \mathcal{P}^+ x_3 \geqslant \mathcal{P}^{++}, \tag{12.10}$$

$$\mathcal{R}_1 \mathcal{R}_{2,U} x_1 + \mathcal{R}_{2,U} \mathcal{P}^- x_3 \geqslant \mathcal{P}^{+-},$$

$$\max_{\{y^+, y^-\}} \mathcal{P}^{++} y^+ + \mathcal{P}^{+-} y^-$$

subject to

$$\mathcal{R}_1 \mathcal{R}_{2,U} y^+ + \mathcal{R}_1 \mathcal{R}_{2,U} y^- = \mathcal{R}_1,$$

$$\mathcal{R}_{2,U} \mathcal{P}^+ y^+ + \mathcal{R}_{2,U} \mathcal{P}^- y^- = \mathcal{R}_1 \mathcal{P}_3, \tag{12.11}$$

$$y^+, \ y^- \geqslant 0.$$

Analogous to the optimal solution for the second period *Down* interest rate movement solutions (12.9) we obtain the following optimal solutions for the second period *Up* interest rate problem:

Period two Up $\mathcal{R}_{2,U}$ optimal primal hedging portfolio

$$x_1^{\text{opt}} = \frac{\mathcal{P}^+ \mathcal{P}^{+-} - \mathcal{P}^{++} \mathcal{P}^-}{(\mathcal{R}_{2,U} \mathcal{P}^+ - \mathcal{R}_{2,U} \mathcal{P}^-) \mathcal{R}_1} \quad \text{and} \quad x_3^{\text{opt}} = \frac{\mathcal{P}^{++} - \mathcal{P}^{+-}}{\mathcal{R}_{2,U}(\mathcal{P}^+ - \mathcal{P}^-)}, \tag{12.12}$$

Period two Up $\mathcal{R}_{2,U}$ optimal dual variables

$$y_{\text{opt}}^+ = \frac{1}{\mathcal{R}_{2,U}} \pi^+ \quad \text{and} \quad y_{\text{opt}}^- = \frac{1}{\mathcal{R}_{2,U}} \pi^-,$$

where π^+ and π^- are defined in (12.6).

Analogous to Lemma 12.1 we state (without giving an arbitrage proof) the following period two balancing relationship:

Lemma 12.2 $\mathcal{P}^+ = v_{D\text{-ask}}$ *and* $\mathcal{P}^- = v_{U\text{-ask}}$.

There is one remaining task, and that is to relate the present value of the three-period bond $\mathcal{P}_3$ in (12.1) to the next period's values $\mathcal{P}^+$, $\mathcal{P}^-$. This is almost a tautology, but for completeness we provide the primal linear programming problem for this case together with the primal and dual linear programming solutions. It is analogous to (12.3) and (12.4):

$$\min_{\{x_1, x_3\}} x_1 + x_3 \mathcal{P}_3$$

subject to

$$\mathcal{R}_1 x_1 + x_3 \mathcal{P}^+ \geqslant \mathcal{P}^+,$$

$$\mathcal{R}_1 x_1 + x_3 \mathcal{P}^- \geqslant \mathcal{P}^-. \tag{12.13}$$

Clearly this has the same form as (12.3), and in fact re-examining (12.5) yields

$$x_1^{\text{opt}} = 0, \quad x_3^{\text{opt}} = 1, \quad \text{with } y_{\text{opt}}^!, y_{\text{opt}}^- \text{ remaining the same as in (12.5).} \tag{12.14}$$

The most powerful property of linear programming applies to all the dual program pairs developed in this chapter, namely that for each dual pair the objective function values are equal. The practical impact of this property is that the probability distribution $\{\pi^+, \pi^-\}$ can be used to determine the values of all the portfolios. We collect these results in a corollary.

Corollary 12.1

$$\mathcal{P}_2 = \frac{1}{\mathcal{R}_1} [\pi^+ \tau^+ + \pi^- \tau^-], \tag{12.15}$$

$$\mathcal{P}^+ = \frac{1}{\mathcal{R}_{2,D}} [\pi^+ \mathcal{P}^{++} + \pi^- \mathcal{P}^{+-}], \tag{12.16}$$

$$\mathcal{P}^- = \frac{1}{\mathcal{R}_{2,U}} [\pi^+ \mathcal{P}^{+-} + \pi^- \mathcal{P}^{--}], \tag{12.17}$$

$$\mathcal{P}_3 = \frac{1}{\mathcal{R}_1} [\pi^+ \mathcal{P}^+ + \pi^- \mathcal{P}^-]. \tag{12.18}$$

Proof.   Relation (12.15) follows from the dual ASK program pair in (12.4) and Lemma 12.1. Relation (12.16) follows from the dual pair and the solutions in (12.7)–(12.9) and Lemma 12.2. Relation (12.17) follows from (12.10) and (12.11). Finally, (12.18) follows from (12.13) and (12.14).   □

Table 12.5 Risk neutral probabilities and period two bond values

π^+	π^-	$\mathcal{P}^+$	$\mathcal{P}^-$
0.56506	0.43494	98.72415	95.6846

Table 12.6 Relative error between the term structure and risk neutral prices

$\mathcal{P}_2$ of (12.1)	$\mathcal{P}_2$ of (12.15)	$\mathcal{P}_3$ of (12.1)	$\mathcal{P}_3$ of (12.18)
(a) 96.45620	(b) 96.444428	(c) 95.28791	(d) 95.30415
|(a) − (b)|/(a) 0.00012		|(c) − (d)|/(c) 0.00017	

For illustrative purposes we used the 'Goal Seek' routine in Excel's Tools software to determine the probabilities π^+ and π^-, but much more can be done in the direction of solving a nonlinear equation. Here is the summary that establishes the equilibrium given in Corollary 12.1.

12.3.1 Summary of Data Entries

- $\mathcal{P}^{++}$, $\mathcal{P}^{+-}$, $\mathcal{P}^{--}$ appear in Table 12.4;
- τ^+, τ^- both appear in Table 12.3;
- the two successive interest rate Up moves and $\mathcal{R}_1$, $\mathcal{R}_{2,U}$, $\mathcal{R}_{2,D}$ appear in Table 12.2;
- $\mathcal{P}_1$, $\mathcal{P}_2$, $\mathcal{P}_3$ appear in (12.1) with their annualized yields and times to maturity summarized in Table 12.1.

Observe that the values in Table 12.5 are computed simultaneously. As a cross-check, we see that they satisfy (12.6) to high accuracy.

Finally, we compare the values of $\mathcal{P}_2$ and $\mathcal{P}_3$ computed by the term structure, namely (12.1) against the values computed by the linear programming dual variables, (12.15) and (12.18) respectively (Table 12.6).

12.4 PRICING A SIMPLE BOND CALL OPTION USING AN INTEREST RATE TREE

For illustrative purposes we consider a call option on the three-period bond 8/16/16–5/31/01 having expiration date 3/23/01 and strike price $K = 98.5$. Let the value at the current time 8/16/00 be denoted by C. In contrast to our previous analysis this value is to be determined. It corresponds to $\mathcal{P}$ in Table 12.4. There are also values C^+, C^- that correspond to $\mathcal{P}^+$, $\mathcal{P}^-$ respectively in Table 12.4. Finally, also corresponding to Table 12.4 we have

$$
\begin{aligned}
C^{++} &= \max\{\mathcal{P}^{++} - K, 0\} \quad \text{replacing } \mathcal{P}^{++}, \\
C^{+-} &= \max\{\mathcal{P}^{+-} - K, 0\} \quad \text{replacing } \mathcal{P}^{+-}, \\
C^{--} &= \max\{\mathcal{P}^{--} - K, 0\} \quad \text{replacing } \mathcal{P}^{--}.
\end{aligned}
\tag{12.19}
$$

Table 12.7   Risk neutral probabilities and call option values by period

π^+	π^-	C	C^+	C^-	C^{++}	C^{+-}	C^{--}
0.56506	0.43494	0.49316	0.78157	0.14343	1.21872	0.14343	0.0000

Table 12.8   Six nodes of the bond price transition tree and link probabilities

8/16/00	transition	12/21/00	transition	3/23/01
				Node 6 $\mathcal{F} = \{1, 3, 6\}$
			π^+	
		Node 3 $\mathcal{F} = \{1, 3\}$		
	π^+		π^-	
Node 1				Node 5 $\mathcal{F} = \{1, 3, 5\}$ $= \{1, 2, 5\}$
	π^-		π^+	
		Node 2 $\mathcal{F} = \{1, 2\}$		
			π^-	
				Node 4 $\mathcal{F} = \{1, 2, 4\}$
		Filtration $\mathcal{F}_1$ values		Filtration $\mathcal{F}_2$ values

We may apply the linear programming duality-based, term-consistent probabilities π^+, π^- given in (12.6) immediately to compute the option price at 8/16/00. The computed option price appears as C in Table 12.7 along with the numerical values for the terms defined in (12.19) and intermediate option values. A linear programming duality development has rigorously provided a basis for defining what are classically termed the *risk neutral probabilities*. Therefore, we justify the results of Table 12.7 by properties of the analogous linear programming problems we have developed, but now for the option-based substitutions indicated in (12.19).

12.5   LINEAR PROGRAMMING DISCOUNTED DUAL VARIABLES AS MARTINGALE PROBABILITIES

In Table 12.8 we formally introduce a notation for all the paths available to reach the terminal nodes. Any such path reflects all the past history up to the time at which the terminal nodes appear. At time 12/21/00 there are only two terminal nodes. In this simple case there is a one-to-one relationship between nodes and paths. It is also convenient to use the word *claim* when referring to the value $\mathcal{P}^+$ or $\mathcal{P}^-$ at nodes within the terminal time. By a *filtration* we mean the ordered list of nodes associated with a particular link. The notation for a filter such as $\mathcal{F}_1$ has values in a general sense; not numbers but *paths*, namely:

$$\mathcal{F}_1 = \begin{cases} \{1, 3\} & \text{if the interest rate is } Up, \\ \{1, 2\} & \text{if the interest rate is } Down. \end{cases}$$

In preparation for an introductory probabilistic analysis let us change the notation from the previous section slightly. Let the present value of our three-period bond at the current time 8/16/00 be denoted by B_0. Then Corollary 12.1 (12.15) determines the claim at the current time as

$$B_0 = \frac{1}{\mathcal{R}_1}[\mathcal{P}^+\pi^+ + \mathcal{P}^-\pi^-].\qquad(12.20)$$

Define a *random variable* for the bond B_1 at time 12/21/00 by the numerical values it takes and the frequency with which these occur. The standard notation is as follows:

$$B_1 = \begin{cases} \mathcal{P}^+ & \text{with probability } \pi^+, \\ \mathcal{P}^- & \text{with probability } \pi^-. \end{cases}\qquad(12.21)$$

So, B_1 mirrors tossing a two-sided coin. Instead of 'heads' and 'tails' we have $\mathcal{P}^+$ and $\mathcal{P}^-$. If the coin were 'fair', we would expect $\pi^+ = \pi^- = 0.5$. Over many repeated tosses of our 'coin analog' the average value of B_1 is $\mathcal{P}^+\pi^+ + \mathcal{P}^-\pi^-$. We need to be more precise notationally about the probability distribution being used in computing what is also called the **expectation**, so we write more formally

$$E_\pi B_1 = \mathcal{P}^+\pi^+ + \mathcal{P}^-\pi^-.\qquad(12.22)$$

It is also useful to compute special expectations that depend on the histories (how we got where we are) associated with terminal nodes. Let's be formal to get things started. A vertical line | shall designate the past history or particular path, denoted by $\mathcal{F}$ with subscripts to identify the link traversed. The link defines the information over which we shall compute an expectation while ignoring all other information. Clearly, since $\mathcal{F}_0$ is just node 1 at the current time 8/15/00, we have

$$E_\pi(B_1\,|\,\mathcal{F}_0) = \mathcal{P}^+\pi^+ + \mathcal{P}^-\pi^-,\qquad(12.23)$$

which appeared in (12.22) under a simpler explanation. But there is a minor subtlety stemming from comparing (12.20) to (12.23):

$$E_\pi(\mathcal{R}_1^{-1}B_1\,|\,\mathcal{F}_0) = B_0,\qquad(12.24)$$

where we observe how one-period discounting automatically appears within the formula for the optimal linear programming dual variables in (12.6). While we have emphasized the filtrations in Table 12.8, there is also a probability distribution for the claim B_2, which is constructed by multiplications of the already available π's according to statistical independence, a property observed in ordinary successive coin tossing. B_2 has the following probability distribution:

$$B_2 = \begin{cases} \mathcal{P}^{++}, & \text{with probability } (\pi^+)^2, \\ \mathcal{P}^{+-}, & \text{with probability } 2\pi^+\pi^-, \\ \mathcal{P}^{--}, & \text{with probability } (\pi^-)^2. \end{cases}$$

Let us construct the conditional probability of B_2 given the period one filtration, $\mathcal{F}_1$, $E_\pi(B_2\,|\,\mathcal{F}_1)$. By definition the conditional random variable $(B_2\,|\,\mathcal{F}_1)$ takes on the two numerical values

$$\text{probability on arc } \overline{36} \times \text{node 6 claim}$$
$$+ \text{ probability on arc } \overline{35} \times \text{node 5 claim given } \{1, 3\} \tag{12.25}$$

and

$$\text{probability on arc } \overline{25} \times \text{node 5 claim}$$
$$+ \text{ probability on arc } \overline{24} \times \text{node 4 claim given } \{1, 2\}. \tag{12.26}$$

These numerical values stem from the direct calculations $\pi^+ \mathcal{P}^{++} + \pi^- \mathcal{P}^{+-}$ and $\pi^+ \mathcal{P}^{+-} + \pi^- \mathcal{P}^{--}$, respectively. But now the indicated probability π in $E_\pi(B_2 | \mathcal{F}_1)$ tells us what 'weights' to use in computing the final conditional expectation, namely π^+ and π^-. Hence

$$E_\pi(B_2 | \mathcal{F}_1) = \begin{cases} \pi^+ \mathcal{P}^{++} + \pi^- \mathcal{P}^{+-} & \text{with probability } \pi^+, \\ \pi^+ \mathcal{P}^{+-} + \pi^- \mathcal{P}^{--} & \text{with probability } \pi^-. \end{cases} \tag{12.27}$$

Now that there are claims for nodes 2 and 3 we face the same bid/ask problem as we did originally for the one-period replication, where original one-period claims appeared respectively on these nodes, see (12.3). Once again the unique dual optimal solution (12.6) arises because it is independent of node 2 and node 3 claims. These dual variable y^+ and y^- are used for determining the numerical values of the newly constructed random variable B_1, namely B_1 (12.21) is replaced by

$$B_1 = \begin{cases} \pi^+ \mathcal{P}^{++} + \pi^- \mathcal{P}^{+-} & \text{with probability } \pi^+, \\ \pi^+ \mathcal{P}^{+-} + \pi^- \mathcal{P}^{--} & \text{with probability } \pi^-. \end{cases} \tag{12.28}$$

Clearly, the probability distributions in (12.27) and (12.28) are identical, i.e.

$$E_\pi(\mathcal{R}^{-1} B_2 | \mathcal{T}_1) = B_1, \tag{12.29}$$

noting again the necessity of one-period discounting.

The tree could be extended to more future periods and the linear programming probability analysis would continue. For the three-period case, for example, the conditional probabilities would be augmented with

$$E_\pi(\mathcal{R}^{-1} B_3 | \mathcal{F}_2) = B_2 \tag{12.30}$$

and so on.

In general a probability distribution such as π^+, π^- that satisfies the collection of conditional probabilities is termed a *martingale*. Our main purpose is merely to show how martingales arise naturally through appropriate behavioral principles as modeled by linear programming.

12.6 CHAPTER NOTES

The topic of interest rate trees or lattices is essentially present in any book on fixed income securities, and we have focused on a simple illustration that uses the estimates we have computed from our term structure estimation methods. The development of finite martingale probability measures by means of linear programming duality theory appears in several references, although we have tried to emphasize a specific economic action of the ask problem 'player' and another action for the bid problem 'player'. Some of the references that use linear programming techniques include [5, exchange-traded options, p. 179], [14, option replication], [53, linear programming approach, p. 94], [54, two linear programs, p. 197], [55, linear pricing measure, p. 7], and [59, duality theorem of linear programming]. The list is necessarily incomplete. Our goal of using linear programming is twofold: (a) to provide economic interpretations that lead to nonarbitrage and (b) to establish a (another) rigorous approach for the existence of a risk neutral distribution of the up and down movements in an interest rate binomial tree. Our analysis has also benefited from a paper by Marsh [47].

A Review of Semi-infinite Optimization with a Focus on Finance

13.1 DUALITY OF THE LINEAR SEMI-INFINITE PROGRAMMING PROBLEM

Linear semi-infinite programming is a next level of extension of elementary finite linear programming where now finitely many variables occur in infinitely many linear inequalities [18, 24, 25, 30, 57] which for convenience we denote by *Program P*.

Program P Let T be an arbitrary nonempty set and $u = (u_1, \ldots, u_{n+1})$ be a finite list of real-valued functions on T and $b \in \mathbf{R}^n$.

$$\text{Find } v_P = \inf \ y^T b \tag{13.1}$$

from among $y \in \mathbf{R}^n$ satisfying $y^T u(t) \geqslant u_{n+1}(t)$, $\forall t \in T$.

Clearly if choose a finite subset $\{t_1, \ldots, t_k\}$ of T, then we obtain a finite linear programming approximation to P, namely

Program P_k

$$\text{Find } v_{P_k} = \inf \ y^T b \tag{13.2}$$

from among $y \in \mathbf{R}^n$ satisfying $y^T u(t_i) \geqslant u_{n+1}(t_i)$, $i = \overline{1, k}$.

Without sufficient regularity conditions, P_k may be a very bad approximation to P, and possibly useless.

Constructing the dual program of a finite linear programming is a pleasant task, and in this case yields the following:

Program D_k

$$\text{Find } v_{P_k} = \sup \sum_{i=1}^{k} u_{n+1}(t_i)\lambda_i \tag{13.3}$$

from among non-negative reals λ_i, $i = \overline{1, k}$ which satisfy $\Sigma_{i=1}^{k} u(t_i)\lambda_i = b$.

Now any finite linear programming approximation depends on a selection of a finite subset of the given *index set T*, and of course there are infinitely many such choices. To attempt to recover the given infinite problem by this procedure requires that we at least allow the finite subsets of T to be *freely chosen*. This is formulated mathematically with *generalized finite sequences*, a particular *function space*, in the dual program. There are close connections between this construction and George Dantzig's concept of *generalized linear programming with variable coefficients*, see [12]. Some of these relationships were explored in a paper published in the 1970s [38].

Program D   Same assumptions as in P.

$$\text{Find } v_D = \sup_{t \in \text{supp}\,\lambda} u_{n+1}(t)\lambda(t) \tag{13.4}$$

from among $\lambda \in \mathbf{R}^S$ satisfying $\Sigma_{t \in \text{supp}\,\lambda} u(t)\lambda(t) = b$, where $\Sigma_{t \in \text{supp}\,\lambda} u(t)\lambda(t)$ employs generalized finite sequences $\lambda \in \mathbf{R}^S$.

From a probabilist's point of view Program D is equivalent to the following:

Program DB

$$\text{Find } v_{DB} = \sup \int_T u_{n+1} d\alpha \tag{13.5}$$

from among all non-negative Borel measures α on a Borel set $T \subset \mathbf{R}^n$ subject to $\int_T u_i\, d\alpha = b_i$, $i = \overline{1, k}$ where u_i are Borel integrable functions, see [26].

Using analogous algebraic manipulations as in finite linear programming, one can verify that if y and λ are feasible respectively for Programs P and D, then

$$y^T b \geqslant \sum_{s \in \text{supp}\,\lambda} u_{n+1}(s)\lambda(s). \tag{13.6}$$

When both programs are feasible, as is assumed for (13.6), it follows that

$$v_P \geqslant v_D. \tag{13.7}$$

Termed the *duality inequality*, (13.7) becomes an equality when certain regularity conditions hold. The most widespread sufficient condition is that the functions $u(\cdot)$ are continuous on a compact set S, and the *Slater* condition holds, namely there exists $\hat{y}$ such that $\hat{y}^T u(t) > u_{n+1}(t)$ for all $t \in S$. This condition is also termed *superconsistency*, and is defined for the dual program D in a different way. As reviewed in [29, Theorem 6.11], one program is superconsistent if and only if its dual program has *bounded level sets*. Bounded level sets are necessary and sufficient to overcome the 'danger' we mentioned above with respect to using finite linear programming as an approximation to a linear semi-infinite program.

Rather that pursue duality theory in depth, we look to recent applications in finance which employ semi-infinite programs having index sets T appearing in a partitioned form, corresponding to units of time.

A basic structure for P in an index set-partitioned form is as follows:

$$\begin{aligned}
(\mathbf{PP}) \quad & \min c^T x \quad \text{subject to } b_*(t) \leqslant A(t)x \leqslant b^*(t); \\
& T = \bigcup_{i=1}^{L} T_i = [t_{i-1}, t_i], g_* \leqslant Gx \leqslant G^*, \text{ and } d_* \leqslant x \leqslant d^*,
\end{aligned} \tag{13.8}$$

where c, x, d^*, d_* are n-dimensional vectors, $b_*(\cdot)$, $b^*(\cdot)$ are m-dimensional functions, $A(\cdot)$ is an $m \times n$ matrix function, and G a $p \times n$ matrix, with g^*, g_* p-dimensional vectors.

13.2   ON THE SUPPORT PROBLEMS METHOD (*BELARUS*)

The basic references on the development of this method for solving semi-infinite programming problems are Kostyukova [41] and Medvedev [50], while related developments and implementations appear in [21], [49], [51] and [52].

Consider the linear semi-infinite programming problem

$$\max c^T x, \quad f(x, t) \leqslant 0,\, t \in T;\, d_* \leqslant x \leqslant d^*, \tag{13.9}$$

where

$$f(x, t) = a^T(t)x - b(t),\, t \in T = [t_*, t^*];\, x, c, d_*, d^* \in \mathbf{R}^n.$$

Here $a(\cdot) \in \mathbf{R}^n$ and $b(\cdot) \in \mathbf{R}$ are some analytical functions. Assume that the problem (13.9) satisfies the (classical) Slater condition according to the following definition:

Definition 13.1   *The linear system* (13.9) *satisfies the Slater condition if there exists $\bar{x}$, $d_* \leqslant \bar{x} \leqslant d^*$, for which it is satisfied strictly with $\bar{x}$.*

The **support problems method** is based on the principle of the 'subsequent' elimination of subsets of the index set T determined by points for which the constraints are violated. There are two main parts:

Part I   a technical procedure for forming, solving and analyzing the sequence of linear programming problems constructed with a small number of constraints termed *the support problems*;

Part II   a finishing procedure based on Newton-type procedures applied to the Karush–Kuhn–Tucker (KKT) first-order necessary optimality conditions.

In Part I the algorithm determines an approximate value of the optimal solution and also identifies the structure of the support set. On the other hand, a naive approach to Part I would be to solve problem (13.9) over a sufficiently fine mesh. The resulting linear programming problem has a small number of variables with a relatively large number of constraints. Such an approach encounters numerical difficulties as described, for example, in [29].

In contrast, Part I of the support problems algorithm is similar to Hettich's algorithm [28]. Let h_1 be the step size of the mesh over which the constraints of the problem (13.9) should be satisfied. Let $\hat{h} \geqslant h_1$ be an initial step size and $\bar{h}$, $h_1 \leqslant \bar{h} \leqslant \hat{h}$ be the step size for forming the support problem. Then we select all points from the mesh with the step size $\hat{h}$ at which the constraints are violated *and* the points in this mesh at which the constraints could be violated in the future. All of these points are adjoined to the set T_h. Thus, *the support problem* defined on the set T_h (derived from the problem (13.9) by replacing the interval T on a finite subset T_h) has considerably less constraints than arise in the naive approach. If $\bar{h} = \hat{h} = h_1$ and the constraints of the problem (13.9) are not violated on the mesh with step size h_1, then the algorithm terminates. Otherwise, this support problem is solved by the dual linear programming method adaptively.

Let T_a denote the set of points at which the constraints of the support problem are active. Select those points from $\bar{h}$ neighborhoods of the active points at which the constraints are violated or could be violated and add these points to the set T_h. Delete the points from the set T_h at which the constraints of the support problem are 'safely' satisfied. In this way a new support problem is constructed which differs from the previous support problem by only a few constraints. This problem is solved by the linear programming dual method beginning with the optimal solution for the previous support problem (usually only few iterations are needed). This process is repeated until the constraints of the problem (13.9) are violated only at the $\bar{h}$ neighborhood of the active points T_a. Then we perform the second part of the algorithm.

In Part II the finishing procedure equations constructed from the first-order KKT optimality conditions are solved by Newton's method. The procedure determines an optimal solution of problem (13.9) to within any preassigned accuracy (if solving the finishing procedure equations is successful). When the finishing procedure terminates, we set $\bar{h} = \hat{h} = h_1$. Otherwise, we decrease the values of $\bar{h}$ and $\hat{h}$ and return to Part I.

According to the classification of numerical linear semi-infinite programming methods given in [29], the support problems method should be referred to as a *hybrid method*. Its numerical implementation is similar to the three-phase algorithm of Gustafson [23].

In summary, the main features of the support problems method are:

1. in each iteration a linear program having a small number of constraints is solved where its size does not depend on a preassigned solution accuracy;
2. the initial starting solution for solving the support problem is an optimal solution of the previous support problem;
3. checking all the constraints to within a given accuracy is performed only after the finishing procedure is terminated.

13.3   EXTENDED SUPPORT PROBLEMS METHOD

In this section we assume that the Slater condition does not hold.

Assume that the set of feasible solutions of (13.9) is nonempty:

$$X = \{x \in \mathbf{R}^n: f(x, t) \leqslant 0, t \in T; d_* \leqslant x \leqslant d^*\}.$$

Define

$$J = \{1, 2, \ldots, n\}, \quad f^{(s)}(x, t) = \partial f(x, t)/\partial t^s,$$

$$a^{(s)}(t) = \{a_j^{(s)}(t) = d^s a_j(t)/dt^s, j \in J\};$$

$$N(q) = \varnothing \text{ if } q < 0, \quad N(q) = \{0, 1, \ldots, q\} \text{ if } q \geqslant 0; \tag{13.10}$$

$$p = p(x, t) \in \{0, 1, 2, \ldots\} \text{ — an integer such that}$$

$$f^{(s)}(x, t) = 0, s \in N(p-1); \quad f^{(p)}(x, t) \neq 0.$$

From (13.10) it follows that

$$p = p(x, t) \in \{0, 2, \ldots\}, \quad f^{(p)}(x, t) < 0 \quad \text{when} \quad t \notin \{t^*, t_*\};$$

$$p = p(x, t) \in \{0, 1, 2, \ldots\}, \quad f^{(p)}(x, t) < 0 \quad \text{when} \quad t = t_*; \tag{13.11}$$

$$p = p(x, t) \in \{0, 1, 2, \ldots\},$$

$$\begin{cases} f^{(p)}(x, t) < 0 & \text{if } p \text{ is even} \\ f^{(p)}(x, t) > 0 & \text{if } p \text{ is odd} \end{cases} \quad \text{when } t = t^*.$$

Definition 13.2   *The number $q = q(t)$ is called the motionless degree at the point $t \in T$ in problem* (13.9) *if*

$$f^{(s)}(x, t) = 0, \ s \in N(q(t)), \quad \forall x \in X \tag{13.12}$$

and there exists at least one feasible solution $\hat{x} \in X$ such that

$$f^{(q(t)+1)}(\hat{x}, t) \begin{cases} < 0 & \text{if } t \neq t^* \text{ or } t = t^*, \quad p \text{ is even,} \\ > 0 & \text{if } t = t^*, \quad p \text{ is odd.} \end{cases} \tag{13.13}$$

It follows from Definition 13.2 that

$$q(t) \in \{-1, 1, 3, 5, \ldots, p^*(t) - 1\} \quad \text{for } t \in \,]t_*, t^*[,$$
$$q(t) \in \{-1, 0, 1, 2, \ldots, p^*(t) - 1\} \quad \text{for } t \in \{t_*, t^*\}.$$

Here $p^*(t) = \max \ p(x, t), \ x \in X$.

If in problem (13.9) there exists $t \in T$ such that $q(t) \geqslant 0$, then the Slater condition does not hold.

Successive derivatives of the slack vectors has also occurred in [1, Section 4.5.2].

Let x be the nonzero feasible solution of the problem (13.9). Define

$$T(x) = \{t \in T: f(x, t) = 0\} = \{t_i, i \in I\},$$
$$I = I(x) = \{1, 2, \ldots, \bar{k} = k(x)\}; \quad p_i = p(x, t_i),$$
$$q_i = q(t_i), i \in I; \quad I_0 = \{i \in I: q_i + 1 = p_i\}, \quad I_* = I \backslash I_0;$$
$$I^* = \{i \in I: t_i = t^*, q_i + 1 \text{ is odd}\}, \quad I^0 = I \backslash I^*.$$

The following result has been proved in [41].

Theorem 13.1   *A feasible solution $x \in X$ is an optimal solution for the problem* (13.9) *if and only if the vector x is optimal for the following linear programming problem:*

$$\max \ c'z, \quad d_* \leqslant z \leqslant d^*,$$
$$f^{(s)}(z, t_j) = 0, \quad s \in N(q_j), j \in I, \tag{13.14}$$

$$f^{(q_j+1)}(z, t_j) \begin{cases} \leqslant 0 & \text{if } j \in I^0 \cap I_*, \\ \geqslant 0 & \text{if } j \in I^* \cap I_*. \end{cases} \tag{13.15}$$

The **extended support problems method** consists of the following three steps.

Step 1   Determine a feasible solution $\hat{x}$ for problem (13.9). In this step the linear semi-infinite programming problem with a floating number of variables is solved by the support problems method.

Step 2   Determine the motionless points $t_j \in T(\hat{x})$ and the corresponding motionless degrees $q_j, j \in I(\hat{x})$. In this step we find all points from the interval T for which $f(\hat{x}, t) = 0$ and solve the sequence of the linear programming problems defined at these points.

Step 3   Determine an optimal solution for (13.9). In this step the constraints (13.14), (13.15) are added to the constraints of the original problem (13.9). The augmented problem is solved by the support problems method.

13.4   A SIMPLE EXAMPLE

Consider the problem

$$\max -x_1, \quad -tx_1 - t^2 x_2 \leqslant 0, \text{ for all } t \in [0, 1], \ -10 \leqslant x_1, 1 \leqslant x_2.$$

Choose $\bar{x}_1 = 1$, $\bar{x}_2 = 1$ as a feasible solution. Then $T(\bar{x}) = \{t_1 = 0\}$. Since

$$f(x, 0) = 0, \ \forall x \in [-1, 1], \quad \text{and} \quad f^{(1)}(\bar{x}, 0) = -\bar{x}_1 \neq 0,$$

we conclude that $q(0) = 0$ and that the Slater condition is violated. Add the constraint $-x_1 \leqslant 0$ to problem (13.9) and solve the new problem by the support problems method. The optimal solution is $x^0 = (0, 1)$ having only one support point $t_{\sup} = 0$ which corresponds to the support matrix $A_{\sup} = (a_1^{(1)}(t_{\sup})) = (-1)$.

The method has been applied to nonlinear problems, but here we just present some preliminary numerical results.

13.5   NUMERICAL RESULTS ON SOLVING NONLINEAR SEMI-INFINITE PROGRAMMING PROBLEMS BY SUPPORT PROBLEMS METHOD

Problem 1

$$\min \tfrac{1}{3} x_1^2 + \tfrac{1}{2} x_1 + x_2^2 - x_2 \quad \text{subject to}$$
$$-x_1^2 - 2x_1 x_2 t \geqslant -\sin t, \quad \text{for all } t \in [0, 2];$$
$$-10 \leqslant x_j \leqslant 10, \quad j = 1, 2;$$
$$x_0 = (1, 2), \quad x^* = (-0.000948, 0.499636).$$

Problem 2

$$\min \tfrac{1}{3} x_1^2 + \tfrac{1}{2} x_1 + x_2^2 \quad \text{subject to}$$
$$x_1 t^2 + x_2^2 - (1 - x_1^2 t^2)^2 - x_2 \geqslant 0, \text{ for all } t \in [0, 1];$$
$$-10 \leqslant x_j \leqslant 10, \quad j = 1, 2;$$
$$x_0 = (1, -2), \quad x^* = (-0.75, -0.618034).$$

Problem 3

$$\min x_1^2 + x_2^2 + x_3^3 \quad \text{subject to}$$
$$-x_1 - x_2 e^{x_3 t} \geqslant e^{2t} - 2 \sin 4t, \text{ for all } t \in [0, 1];$$
$$-10 \leqslant x_j \leqslant 10, \quad j = 1, 2, 3;$$
$$x_0 = (1, 1, 1), \quad x^* = (-0.213313, -1.361450, 1.853547).$$

Problem 4

$$\min e^{x_1} + e^{x_2} + e^{x_3} \quad \text{subject to}$$
$$x_1 + x_2 t + x_3 t^2 \geqslant \frac{1}{1 + t^2}, \text{ for all } t \in [0, 1];$$
$$-10 \leqslant x_j \leqslant 10, \quad j = 1, 2, 3;$$
$$x_0 = (1, 0.5, 0), \quad x^* = (1.006605, -0.126880, -0.379725).$$

Problem 5

$$\min (x_1 - 2x_2 + 5x_2^2 - x_2^3 - 13)^2 + (x_1 - 14x_2 + x_2^2 + x_2^3 - 29)^2 \quad \text{subject to}$$
$$-x_1^2 - 2x_2 t^2 - e^{x_1 + x_2} \geqslant -e^t, \quad \text{for all } t \in [0, 1];$$
$$-10 \leqslant x_j \leqslant 10, \quad j = 1, 2;$$
$$x_0 = (1, 2), \quad x^* = (0.719961, -1.450487).$$

Problem 6

$$\min 1.21 e^{x_1} + e^{x_2} \quad \text{subject to}$$
$$e^{x_1 + x_2} \geqslant t, \quad \text{for all } t \in [0, 1];$$
$$-10 \leqslant x_j \leqslant 10, \quad j = 1, 2.$$
$$x_0 = (0.8, 0.9), \quad x^* = (-0.095310, 0.095310).$$

Problem 7

$$\min (x_1 - 2)^2 + (x_2 - 0.2)^2 \quad \text{subject to}$$
$$-\frac{5 \sin \pi t}{1 + t^2} x_1^2 + x_2 \geqslant 0, \quad \text{for all } t \in [0, 8];$$
$$-1 \leqslant x_1 \leqslant 1, \quad 0 \leqslant x_2 \leqslant 0.2;$$
$$x_0 = (0, 0.1), \quad x^* = (0.205237, 0.2).$$

Notationally, x_0 denotes the starting point and x^* the optimal solution. Other performance-type details of solving the seven problems by the support problems method are given in Table 13.1.

Analogous to notation given in previous chapters for presenting computational results we employ the following:

ITER	= number of iterations for solving the support problems;
NFUN	= number of times that the objective function and the constraint functions are evaluated during the process of solving the support problems;
NGRAD	= number of times the gradients of the objective function and the constraint functions are evaluated during the process of solving the support problems;
NQP	= number of QP subproblems solved during the process of solving the support problems;
ACCSP	= stopping tolerance for solving the support problems;
NSP	= number of support problems solved;
NCONFP	= maximum number of constraints in the generated support problems;
ITERFP	= number of iterations for solving the finishing procedure equations;
ACCFP	= stopping tolerance for solving the finishing procedure equations;
CPU	= elapsed CPU time (s).

The results are comparable to those published in [10], [11] and [62]. All experiments were run on a PC PENTIUM 120, and all are in BORLAND PASCAL 7.0.

All problems were relatively easy to solve because the structure of the optimal solutions was simple: there were only few active points that as a rule occurred at the endpoints of the interval T.

Table 13.1   Numerical tests with the support problems method

PROB	1	2	3	4	5	6	7
ITER	11	10	11	4	12	7	6
NFUN	13	10	11	4	18	7	6
NQP	11	10	10	4	12	7	6
NGRAD	11	10	10	4	12	7	6
ACCSP	10^{-3}	10^{-4}	10^{-1}	10^{-3}	10^{-2}	10^{-2}	10^{-2}
NSP	1	2	1	1	1	2	1
NCONSP	24	35	13	13	13	13	18
ITERFP	10	3	3	7	3	2	4
ACCFP	—	10^{-10}	10^{-10}	10^{-10}	10^{-10}	10^{-10}	10^{-10}
$f(x^*)$	−0.250473	0.19446	5.33468	4.301183	97.15885	2.20	3.2211750
CPU (s)	0.06	0.05	0.06	0.05	0.05	0.06	0.05

The classical interior-point, Slater condition does not hold for Problem 1. This is the reason why the finishing procedure failed. Current updated versions of the algorithm are underway for this case.

The question about stopping tolerance for solving the support problems is still open. The tolerance must be such that one may determine the structure of the optimal solution accurately. On the other hand, high accuracy in solving the support problems is not crucial because the solution of the finishing procedure equations provides the necessary accuracy.

A PASCAL translation of the SQP (successive quadratic programming) method FORTRAN implementation written by Schittkowski [60] was used throughout these preliminary computations.

13.6   CHAPTER NOTES

Semi-infinite programming is a natural extension of linear programming that allows finitely many variables to appear in infinitely many constraints. The many conferences and symposia on this topic that have occurred over the last 23 years confirm that the theoretical and practical manifestations and applications of this problem formulation are abundant and significant. The meetings to the best of our knowledge are the following:

1. Semi-infinite Workshop, Bad Honnef, Germany, 1978;
2. Semi-infinite Programming and Applications, Austin, TX Symposium, 1981;
3. Infinite Programming Symposium, Cambridge, UK, 1984;
4. Cluster Section, Systems and Management Science by Extremal Methods, Research Honoring Abraham Charnes at Age 70, Austin, TX, 1987;
5. Cluster Section, XIII World Conference on Operations Research, Lisbone, Portugal, 1993;
6. Cluster Section, IV International Conference on Parametric Optimization and Related Topics, Enschede, The Netherlands, 1995;
7. Semi-infinite Programming Workshop, Cottbus, Germany, 1996;

8. Cluster Section, XVI International Symposium on Mathematical Programming, Lausanne, Switzerland, 1997;

9. Cluster Section, International Conference on Nonlinear and Variational Inequalities, Hong Kong, 1998;

10. Semi-infinite Programming Symposium, Alicante, Spain, 1999;

11. Cluster Section, EURO VII, Budapest, Hungary, 2000;

12. Cluster Section, XVII International Symposium on Mathematical Programming, Atlanta, GA, 2000.

Software Documentation of the Term Structure, Constant Maturity Models

14.1 GETTING STARTED WITH THE PROGRAM
TermStructureCAD

The program *TermStructureCAD* signals the computational procedure for estimating and forecasting term structure of interest rates, denoted by TSIR, from observation of US Treasury constant maturity rates. The functional flexibility of the program is described next. Input data consist of US Treasury bill rates or constant maturity rates. There is flexibility to accept as input data either single rates with the same maturity or multiple rates with different terms of maturity. Models include one-factor and multi-factor (bilevel) types for description of the TSIR. Spot rate modeling is based on either the Vasicek or Dothan models. For the nondifferential equation spot rate models we use impulse functions. For modeling uncertainty we use perturbations of two types: impulse perturbations and point-impulse perturbations. An optimization employs several objective cost functions depending on the goals of the estimation. As a rule, minimax optimization is used for general estimation of TSIR, while minimizing the Euclidean norm of the perturbations is used for estimating the mean path of the spot rate such as in Chapter 7. Finally, minimax amplitude optimization seeks the minimal possible amplitude of the spot rate trajectory about its mean reversion limit revealed by observed data. The SQP method [60] is used for solving these optimization problems. The following steps in our analysis are a direct consequence of solving the estimation problem over the observation period accurately.

1. Calculating the estimated trajectory, the spot rate and the trajectory of its forecast for the forecast period immediately following the observation period.
2. Calculating the forecast of the trajectory of a specific constant maturity rate whether partially observable or not.
3. Calculating the forecast of an arbitrary yield curve.
4. Calculating the three-dimensional surface of the term structure of interest rates.

14.2 DEFINING THE ATTRIBUTES OF THE INPUT DATA

The main sheet defines attributes of the input data any of which the user may select. Moving from left to right the user should make the following choices:

- the time scale of the chosen input data;
- the period of observation;
- the type of data;
- the scale for the data (value vs. percent).

In the title box the user should indicate a convenient title for the experiment. If the input data are US Treasury yield curve rates, then the term to maturity must also be specified as in Figure 14.1.

After these choices have been made the user needs to load the files containing the input data. For example, if the user indicates US Treasury yield curve rates, then the input file will contain yields with different maturity terms, as illustrated in Figure 14.2.

In another example, it is necessary to indicate the term to maturity directly on the spreadsheet as demonstrated in Figure 14.3.

After the user has specified the data input files, the program automatically generates the main input file that itself will be used as an input for solving the optimal observation problem, see Figure 14.4.

14.3 SELECTING A MODEL FOR ESTIMATING THE TERM STRUCTURE

At this point the user should be prepared to select a model to be used for estimating the term structure of interest rates. Specifically, the user should set

- the type of underlying model (one-factor or bilevel);
- the type of spot rate model;
- the class of perturbations acting on the spot rate;
- the time scale for perturbation;
- the cost functional guiding the optimization.

Figure 14.5 illustrates a selection.

14.4 SELECTING PARAMETERS FOR THE OPTIMAL OBSERVATION PROBLEM

The user now comes to the point specifying the parameters that occur in the optimal observation problem. First is the selection of the stopping accuracy criterion for numerical computations. The second type of accuracy specification relates to the desired closeness of the solved-for trajectory of the estimated yield to the observed yield during the observation period. There is also added flexibility for the user to specify that the starting solution should be the previously computed one, for example, after the user has changed some of the initial specifications. Of course, one may also specify to completely restart the procedure. With this form the user can set the screen output during the course of solving the observation problem. By using the number of iterations as the control 'tick' computations can be terminated if it appears that an optimal solution cannot be achieved in reasonable time.

A specification of parameters appears in Figure 14.6.

14.5 SIGNALING TO SOLVE THE OBSERVATION PROBLEM

This part of the program solves the optimal observation problem. The viewing screen is divided into two parts. The bottom shows the current information about the performance and features of the actual, ongoing computations. The top part of the screen presents the current solution graphically, which depends on the choices the user

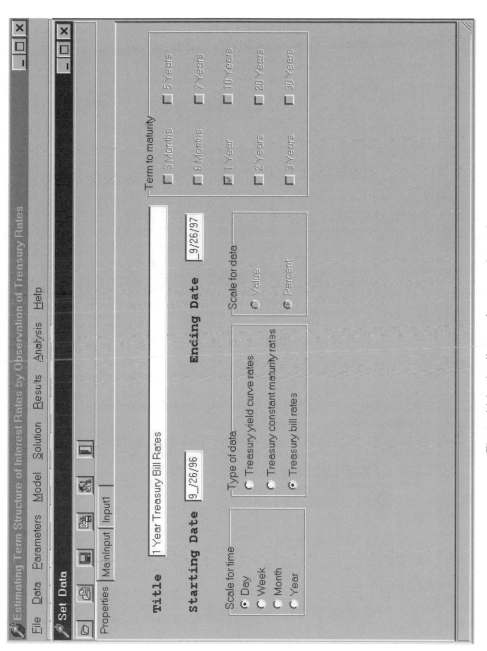

Figure 14.1 Attributes of program input data

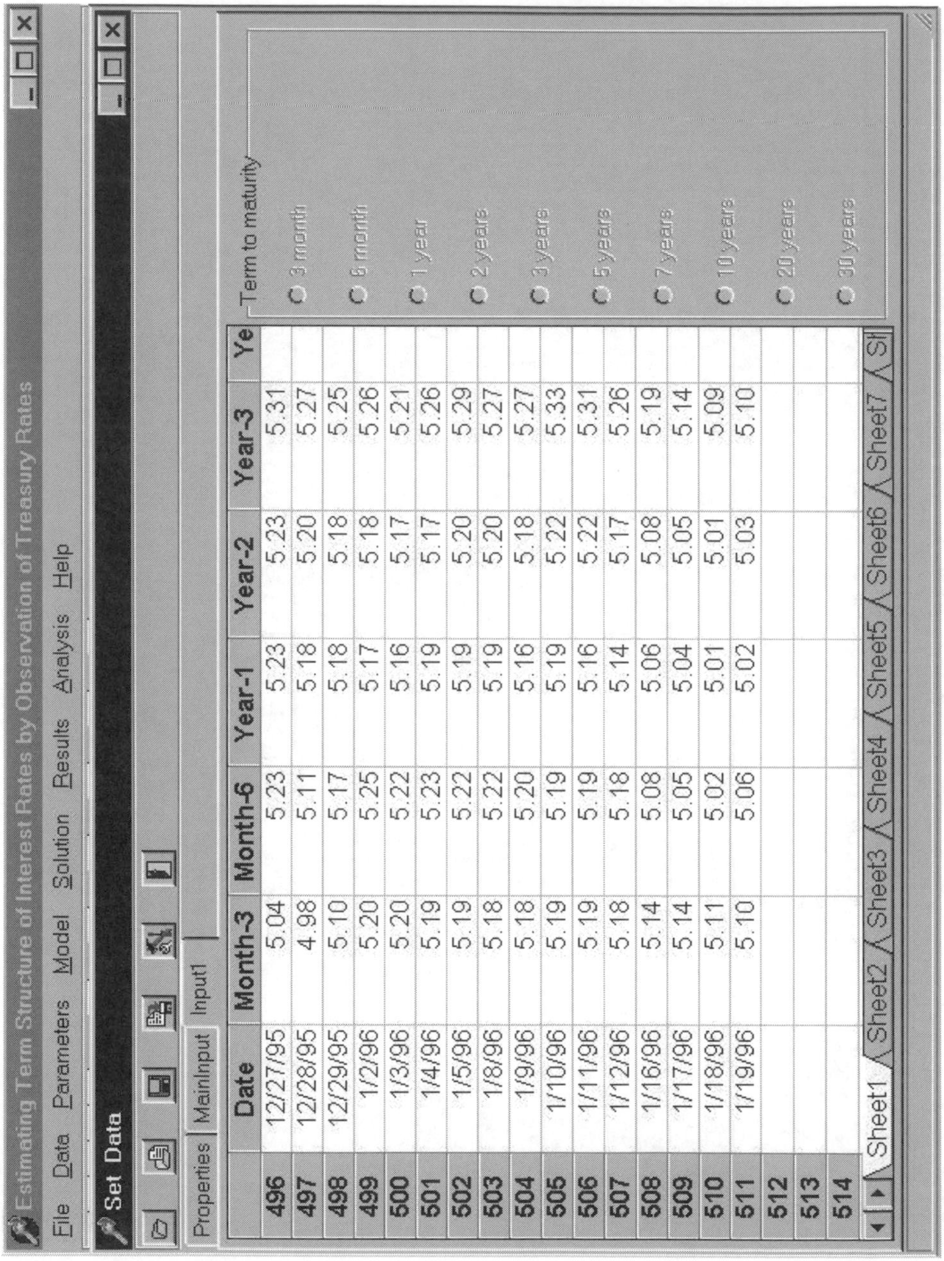

Estimating Term Structure of Interest Rates by Observation of Treasury Rates

File Data Parameters Model Solution Results Analysis Help

Set Data

Properties | MainInput | Input1

	Date	Month-3	Month-6	Year-1	Year-2	Year-3	Ye
496	12/27/95	5.04	5.23	5.23	5.23	5.31	
497	12/28/95	4.98	5.11	5.18	5.20	5.27	
498	12/29/95	5.10	5.17	5.18	5.18	5.25	
499	1/2/96	5.20	5.25	5.17	5.18	5.26	
500	1/3/96	5.20	5.22	5.16	5.17	5.21	
501	1/4/96	5.19	5.23	5.19	5.17	5.26	
502	1/5/96	5.19	5.22	5.19	5.20	5.29	
503	1/8/96	5.18	5.22	5.19	5.20	5.27	
504	1/9/96	5.18	5.20	5.16	5.18	5.27	
505	1/10/96	5.19	5.19	5.19	5.22	5.33	
506	1/11/96	5.19	5.19	5.16	5.22	5.31	
507	1/12/96	5.18	5.18	5.14	5.17	5.26	
508	1/16/96	5.14	5.08	5.06	5.08	5.19	
509	1/17/96	5.14	5.05	5.04	5.05	5.14	
510	1/18/96	5.11	5.02	5.01	5.01	5.09	
511	1/19/96	5.10	5.06	5.02	5.03	5.10	
512							
513							
514							

Term to maturity
- 3 month
- 6 month
- 1 year
- 2 years
- 3 years
- 5 years
- 7 years
- 10 years
- 20 years
- 30 years

Sheet1 / Sheet2 / Sheet3 / Sheet4 / Sheet5 / Sheet6 / Sheet7 / Sh

Figure 14.2 Input file with different maturity terms

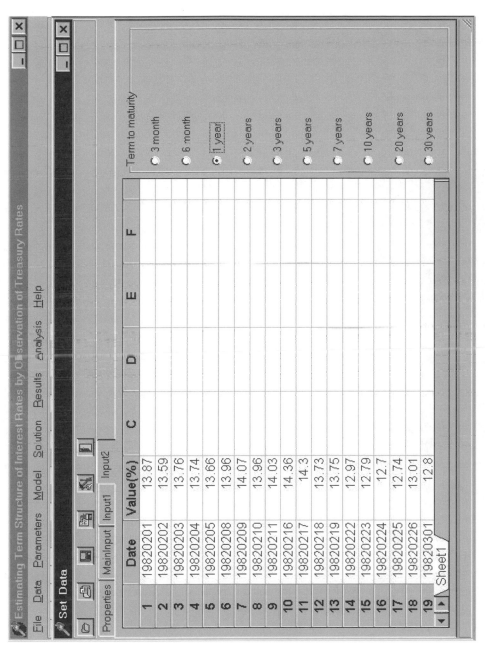

Figure 14.3 Choosing the term to maturity directly on the spreadsheet

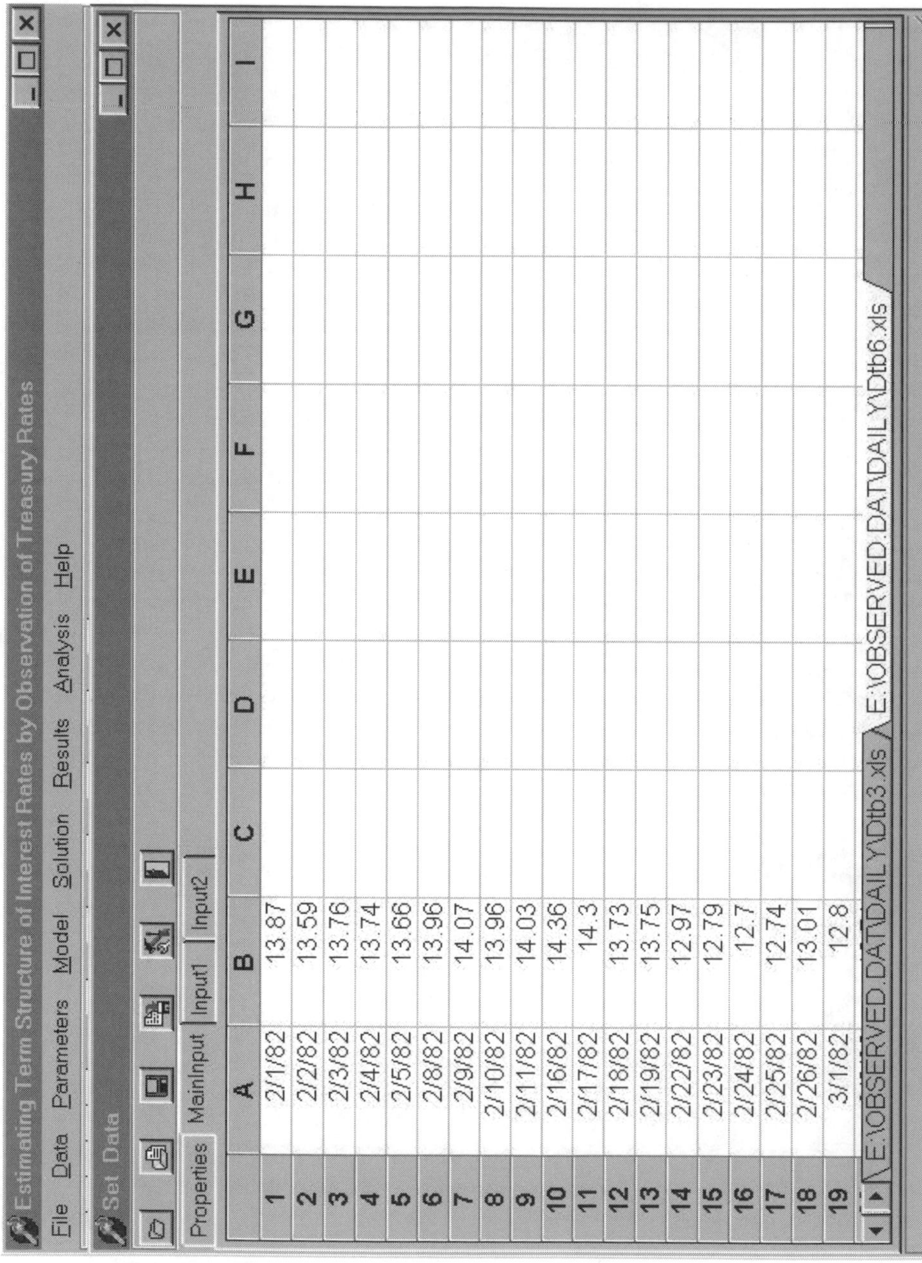

Figure 14.4   The main input automatically generated

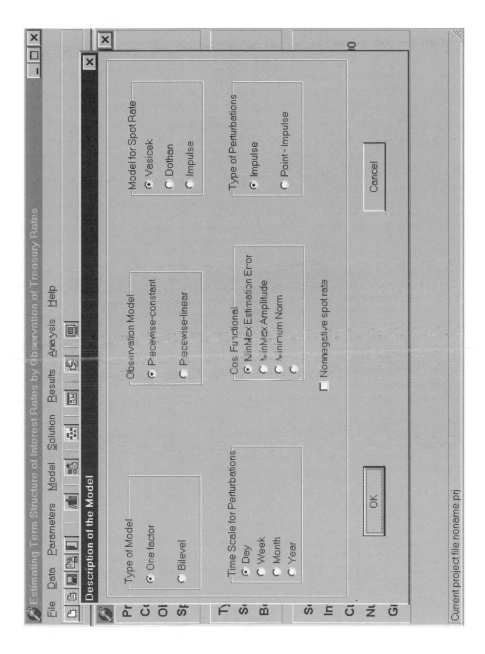

Figure 14.5 Description of the model

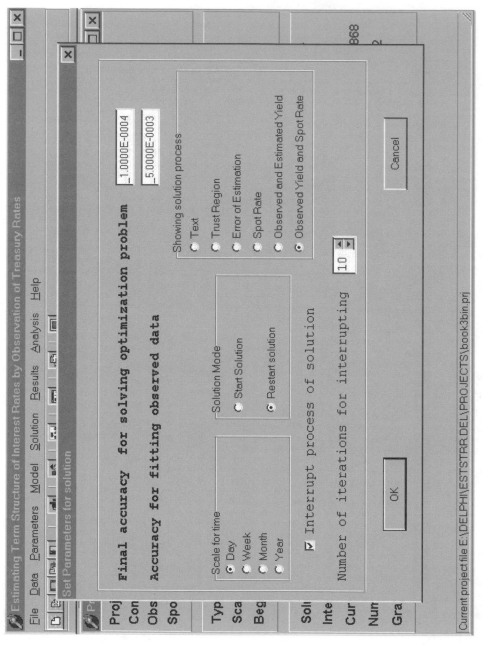

Figure 14.6 Description of the parameters

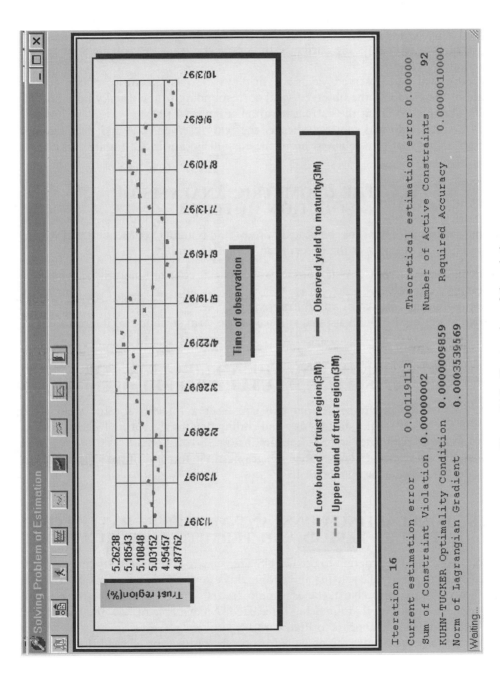

Figure 14.7 Trust region of the solution

has made during the description of parameters phase. The trust region is that data-embracing tube having minimal possible width, which contains all the observations. An example of the geometrical structure is given in Figure 14.7.

The current error of the estimation gives the accuracy of the currently computed estimated trajectory with respect to the observed real data, see Figure 14.8.

The spot rate represents the current estimate of the trajectory of the spot rate as demonstrated in Figure 14.9.

The estimated and observed yields are displays of the trajectories of the current estimate of the yield and the observed yield corresponding to the usually near optimal solution obtained so far at the current iteration, Figure 14.10.

The observed yield and spot rate display the real observed data and the estimated trajectory of the spot rate achieved up to the current iteration, see Figure 14.11.

14.6   THE GEOMETRIC ANALYSIS OF SOLUTION OUTPUTS

The analysis provides further geometrical outputs and is a direct consequence of solving the estimation problem over the observation period accurately.

- Calculating the forecast of the trajectory of a specific constant maturity rate whether partially observable or not.
- Calculating the forecast of an arbitrary yield curve.
- Calculating the three-dimensional surface of the term structure of interest rates.

14.7   FORECASTING THE YIELD CURVE FOR A SELECTED FUTURE PERIOD

In this part of the program the user can construct a forecast for the yield curve according to choices for the starting day and ending day for the future forecast period.

An example of parameter settings appears in Figure 14.12.

If the user selects sheet GRAPH, then the graph of the forecast of the yield curve will appear on the screen as in Figure 14.13.

14.8   FORECASTING CONSTANT MATURITY RATES FOR A FUTURE PERIOD AND TERM TO MATURITY

The user can direct the program to predict US Treasury constant maturity rates. At first it is necessary to specify the starting and ending days for the forecasting period together with the term of maturity. Next, the user indicates the type of bounds for the possible future values of the rates that are being forecasted. An example of how the parameters may be set at this stage appears in Figure 14.14.

Figure 14.15 demonstrates the predicted trajectory of the type of yield that has been selected.

The same forecast but with extremal bounds appears in Figure 14.16.

Finally, the same forecast but with additional curves that we term the *middle* or *median* bounds appears in Figure 14.17.

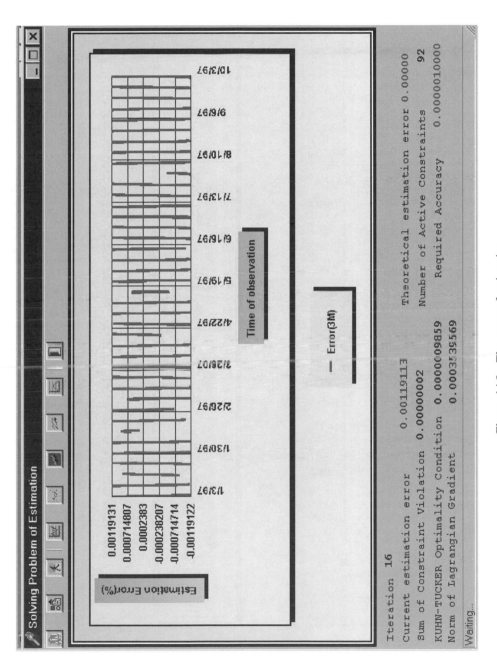

Figure 14.8 The error of estimation

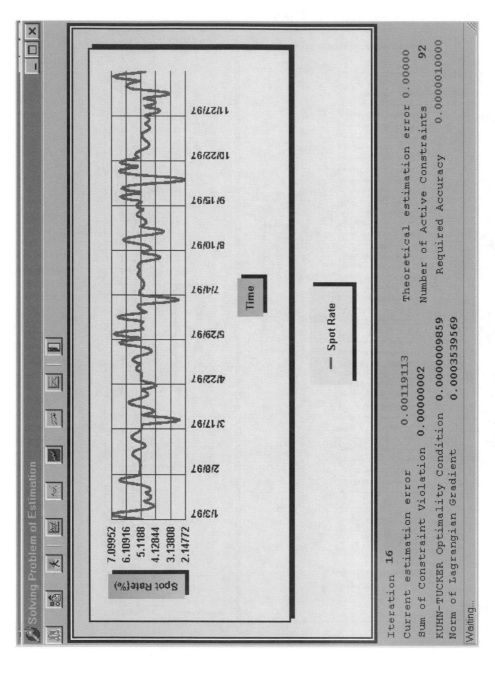

Figure 14.9 Current estimate of the spot rate trajectory

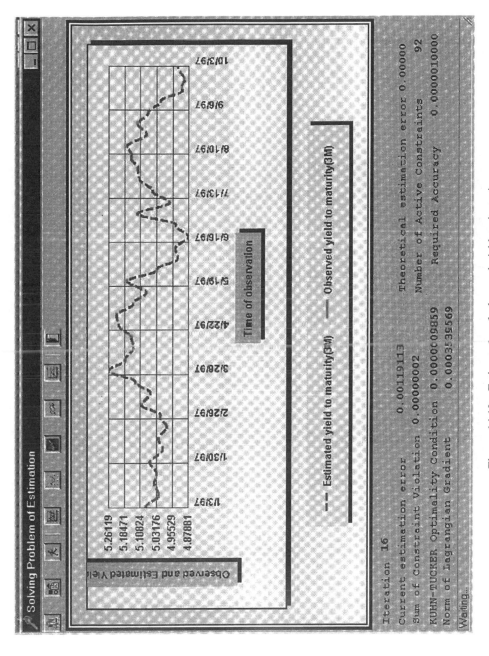

Figure 14.10 Estimated and observed yield trajectories

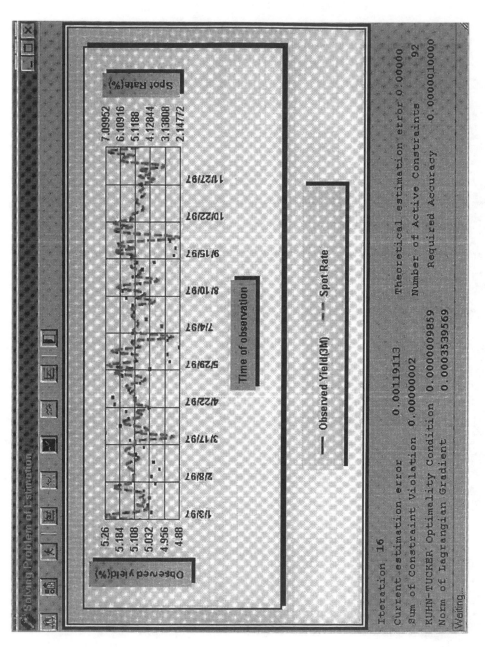

Figure 14.11 Observed yield and spot rate trajectories

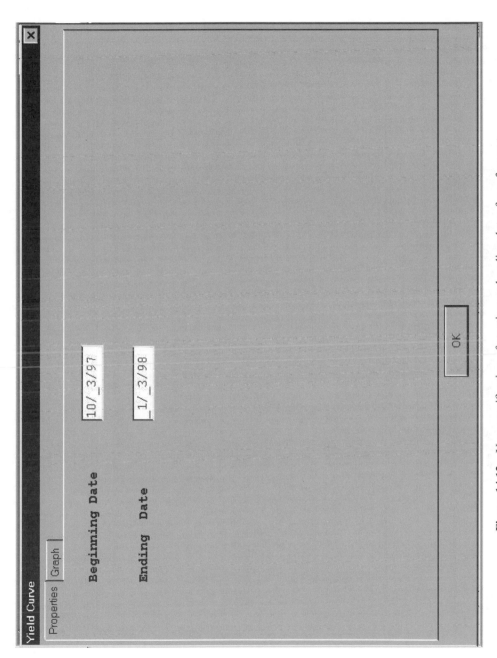

Figure 14.12 User specification of starting and ending dates for a forecast

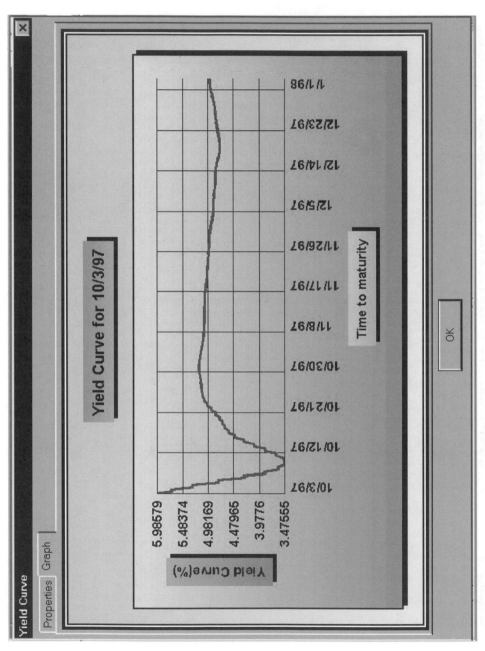

Figure 14.13   Presenting the graph of the forecast

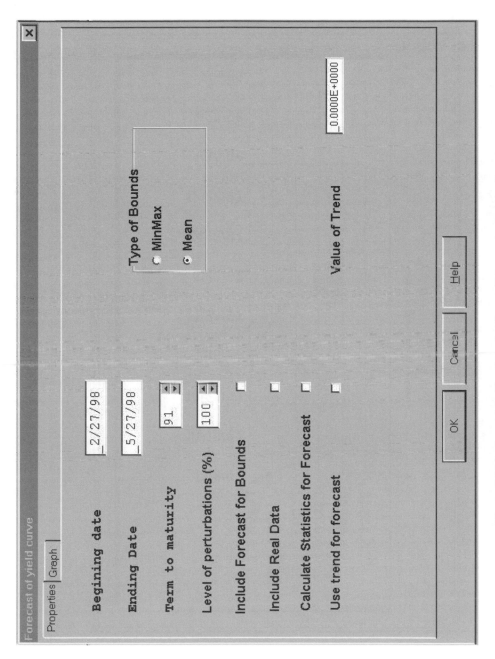

Figure 14.14 Input specifications for forecasting constant maturity rates

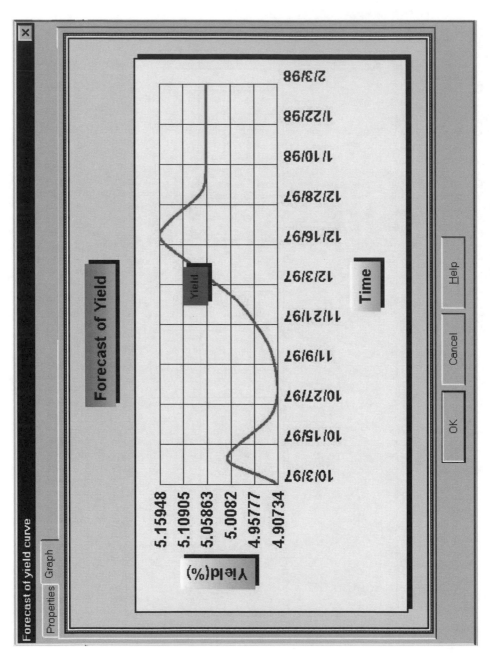

Figure 14.15 Predicted trajectory of the yield

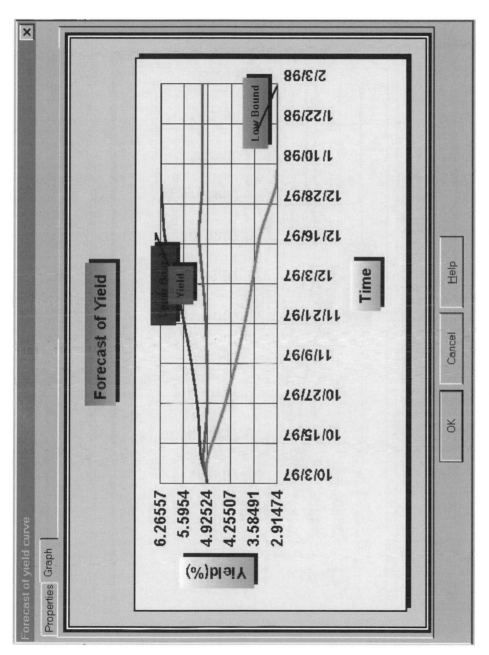

Figure 14.16 Same forecast but with extremal bounds

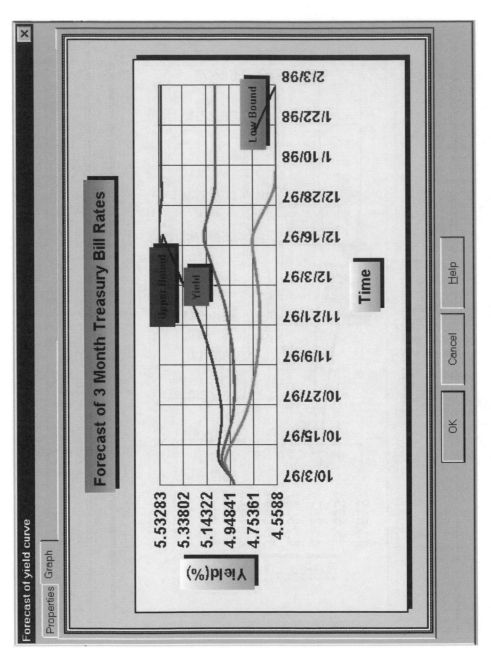

Figure 14.17 Same forecast but with median bounds

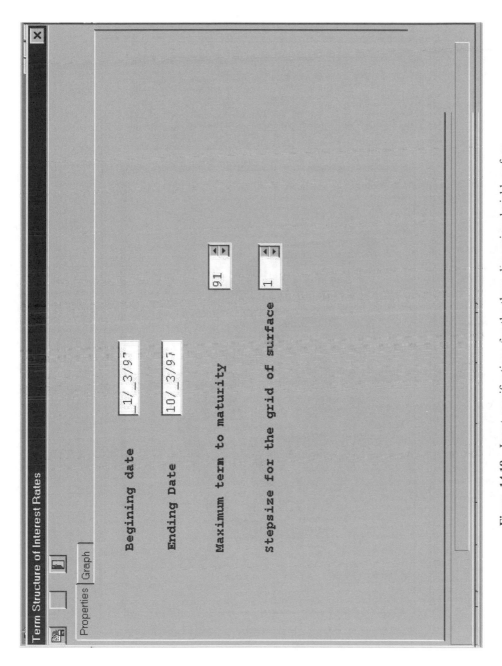

Figure 14.18 Input specifications for the three-dimensional yield surface

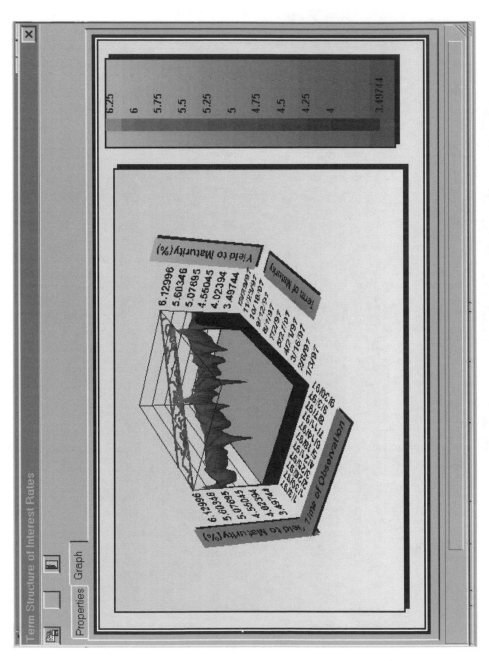

Figure 14.19 The three-dimensional yield surface for the inputs chosen

14.9   THE THREE-DIMENSIONAL TERM STRUCTURE SURFACE RATES FOR A FUTURE PERIOD AND MAXIMUM TIME TO MATURITY

First the user selects the beginning and ending dates of the observation period, the maximum term to maturity and a technical parameter related to the fineness of the three-dimensional graph. An illustration of a particular selection appears in Figure 14.18.

By selecting the sheet GRAPH the user obtains the surface of the term structure of interest rates. The surface corresponding to the above selections appears in Figure 14.19.

The two diagonal boundary curves of the graph have specific financial interpretations. The lower diagonal curve starting from the point 1/3/97 on the 'Term of Maturity' axis is the spot rate curve as the time of observation ranges from 1/3/97 through 9/30/97. The upper diagonal curve corresponding to the starting date 4/4/97 on the 'Term of Maturity' axis is the observed 3-month US Treasury bill rates curve as the time of observation ranges from 1/3/97 through 9/30/97. There are also two other boundary curves. For observation time 1/3/97 we obtain the yield curve as the term to maturity ranges from 1/3/97 to 4/4/97. For observation time 9/30/97 we obtain the yield curve as the term to maturity ranges from 9/30/97 to 12/29/97.

14.10   CHAPTER NOTES

An optimal solution to an optimal observation problem provides estimates of the unknown coefficients of the dynamical system together with the estimates of realized perturbations from the market. The values of the maximal and minimal realized perturbations can be contrasted in a general way with the volatility inputed in the stochastic case. These values are also used for the construction of precision bounds for the forecast as seen for example, in Figures 14.16 and 14.17, which result when the user specifies Figure 14.14. Here are the details.

Upon solving an optimal observation problem values for the optimal perturbations are at hand, e.g. (3.16), (3.37), (3.41), (3.44) and (3.57). For convenience let $\widehat{w}^0(\cdot)$ denote the selected perturbation function built from these and applicable to the future time interval given in (3.18). There are 3 cases we consider and estimates we automatically provide.

1) **Median Path** future perturbations: set $\widehat{w}^0(\cdot) = 0$.
2) **Extremal** future perturbations: set, $\widehat{w}^0_{max} = \max_{t \in [0,\, t_M]} w^0(t)$, and define

$$\widehat{w}^0(t) = \widehat{w}^0_{max}, \text{ for } t \in [t_M, t_Q].$$

$\widehat{w}^0_{min} = \min_{t \in [0,\, t_M]} w^0(t)$, and define

$$\widehat{w}^0(t) = \widehat{w}^0_{min}, \text{ for } t \in [t_M, t_Q].$$

3) **Median–Extremal** future perturbations. Let $n_{max} = \#\{w_i^0 > 0\}$ and $n_{min} = \#\{w_i^0 < 0\}$. Set

$$\widehat{w}_{MedMax}^0 = \frac{1}{n_{max}} \sum_{i=1, w_i^0 > 0}^{M} w_i^0.$$

$$\widehat{w}_{MedMin}^0 = \frac{1}{n_{min}} \sum_{i=1, w_i^0 < 0}^{M} w_i^0.$$

Software Documentation of the
Forward Rate Model

15.1 GETTING STARTED WITH THE PROGRAM *FRateCAD* AND ITS REQUIRED INPUTS

The program *FRateCAD* implements the model of estimating the forward rate and yield curve trajectories by observation of the discrete values of the yields to maturity. The example of the input data could be found in Table 9.2. In this version of the program the problem (9.18) was chosen as the basic model to be specified and solved. By discretization of the constraints of the problem, it has been approximated by a discrete quadratic programming problem with linear constraints. Special rules are applied for constructing the set $\tilde{T}$ used in defining the class of impulse perturbations specified in Chapter 9 via (9.10) and (9.11). The main screen driving the program appears in Figure 15.1. It contains the input data, parameters of the method and results of computation. The input data are described as follows.

The first two columns of Figure 15.1 contain the observed data. The first column corresponds to the date of maturity while the second column describes the corresponding observed yields to maturity. The first four lines of the fourth column contain the parameters needed for solving the optimization problem (9.17). The current time corresponds to the very next day immediately after the date of observation, the so-called 'settlement date'. Beta denotes the parameter β^* used in the model (9.8). The penalty coefficient lets the user specify the penalty parameter θ of the optimization problem (9.18). The bound of perturbation lets the user specify the bounds w_* and w^* for the perturbation function, see (9.11). In the fourth column of Figure 15.1 we have illustrated a particular choice of parameters that has worked well for us in experiments with real Treasury bills yield data provided by the *Wall Street Journal, Interactive Edition*, see Table 9.2. In summary these choices are:

$$\beta^* = -0.1, \quad \theta = 10^6, \quad w_* = -1000, \quad w^* = 1000.$$

15.2 GETTING STARTED, COMMAND BUTTONS: New Project, Open Project, Save As Project, AND Save Project

The command buttons appear at the very top of Figure 15.1 and are used for working with project files and solving optimal observation problems. The first four buttons: *New Project*, *Open Project*, *Save As Project* and *Save Project* serve for manipulation with the project table. The table determined by the first two columns in Figure 15.1 has an Excel format and is stored in the corresponding Excel file. The rightmost button is the *Exit*

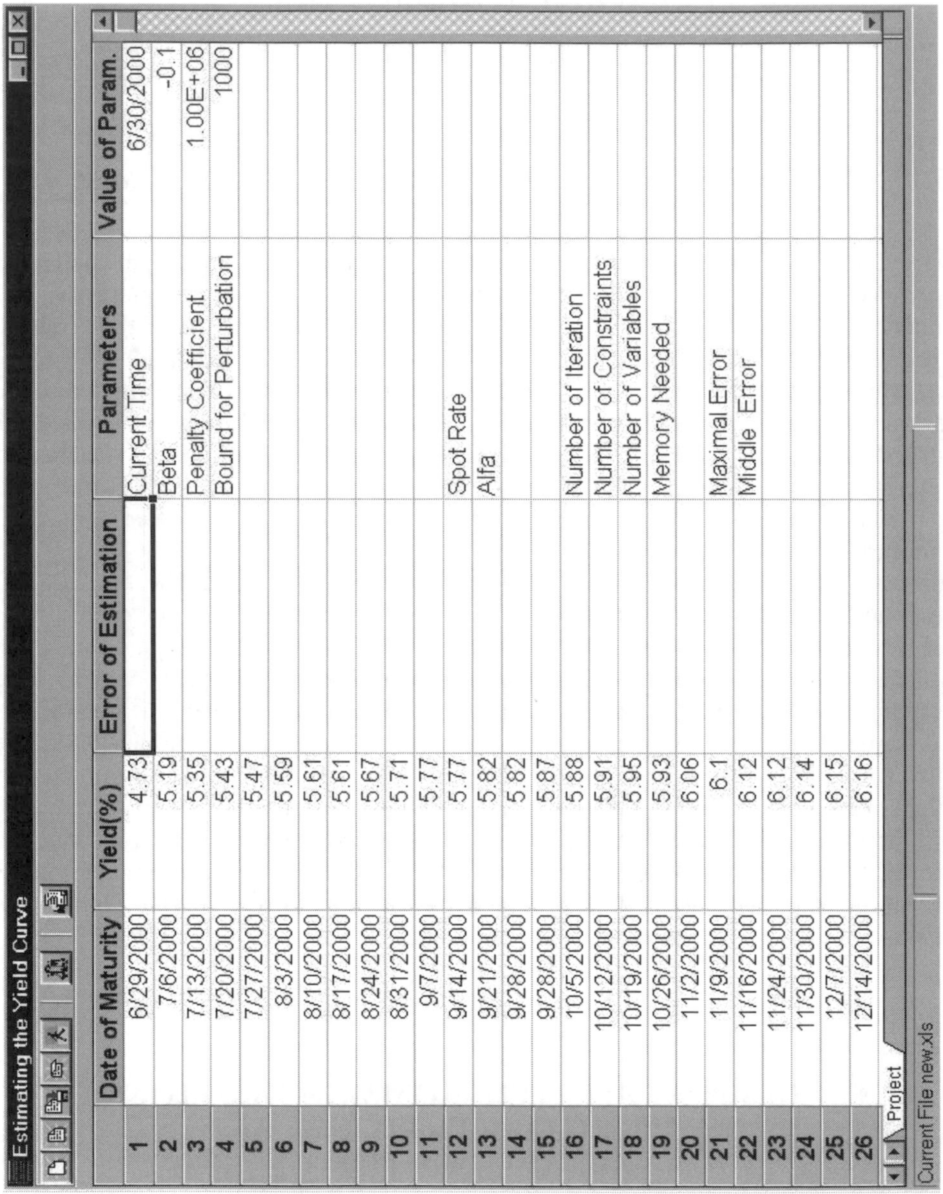

Estimating the Yield Curve

	Date of Maturity	Yield(%)	Error of Estimation	Parameters	Value of Param.
1	6/29/2000	4.73		Current Time	6/30/2000
2	7/6/2000	5.19		Beta	-0.1
3	7/13/2000	5.35		Penalty Coefficient	1.00E+06
4	7/20/2000	5.43		Bound for Perturbation	1000
5	7/27/2000	5.47			
6	8/3/2000	5.59			
7	8/10/2000	5.61			
8	8/17/2000	5.61			
9	8/24/2000	5.67			
10	8/31/2000	5.71			
11	9/7/2000	5.77			
12	9/14/2000	5.77		Spot Rate	
13	9/21/2000	5.82		Alfa	
14	9/28/2000	5.82			
15	9/28/2000	5.87			
16	10/5/2000	5.88		Number of Iteration	
17	10/12/2000	5.91		Number of Constraints	
18	10/19/2000	5.95		Number of Variables	
19	10/26/2000	5.93		Memory Needed	
20	11/2/2000	6.06			
21	11/9/2000	6.1		Maximal Error	
22	11/16/2000	6.12		Middle Error	
23	11/24/2000	6.12			
24	11/30/2000	6.14			
25	12/7/2000	6.15			
26	12/14/2000	6.16			

Project

Current File new.xls

Figure 15.1 Main screen of the forward rate estimation model

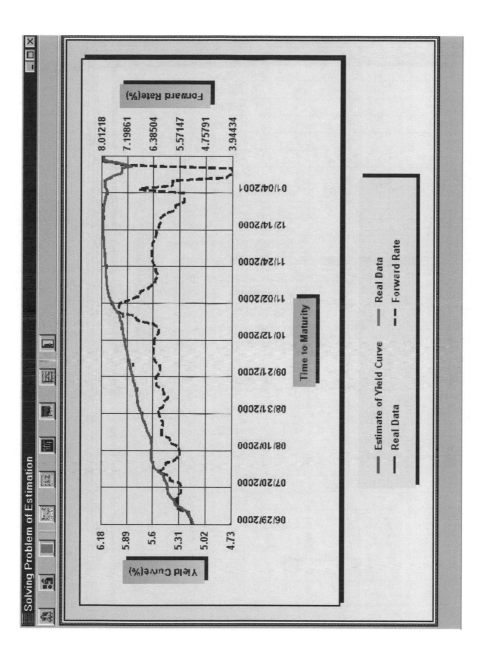

Figure 15.2 Estimated curves together with their command button

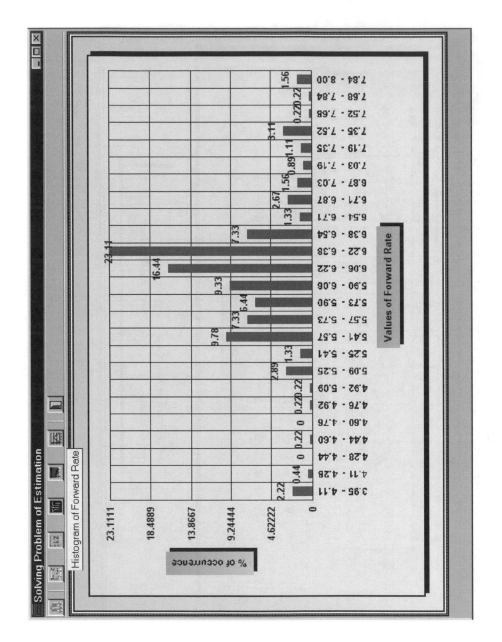

Figure 15.3   Histogram of occurrences of forward rates values

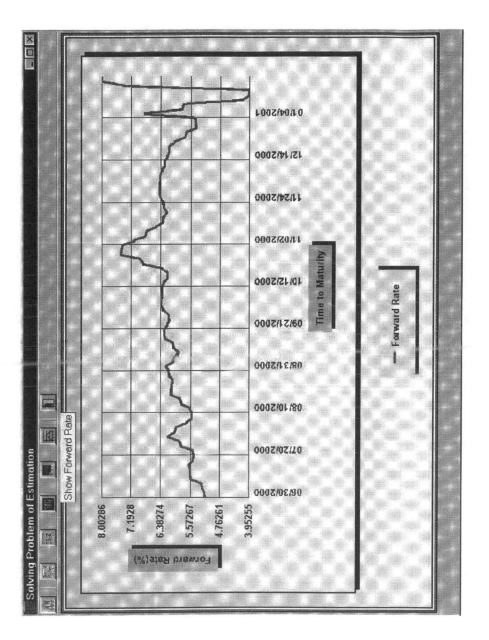

Figure 15.4 Computed forward rate curve

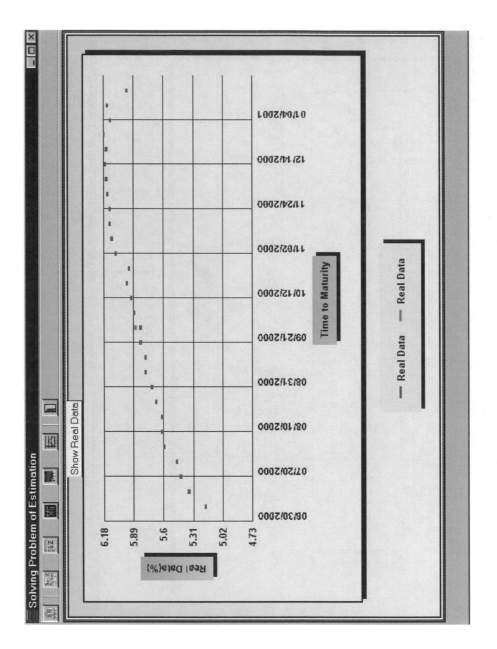

Figure 15.5   Graph developed from actual yield data

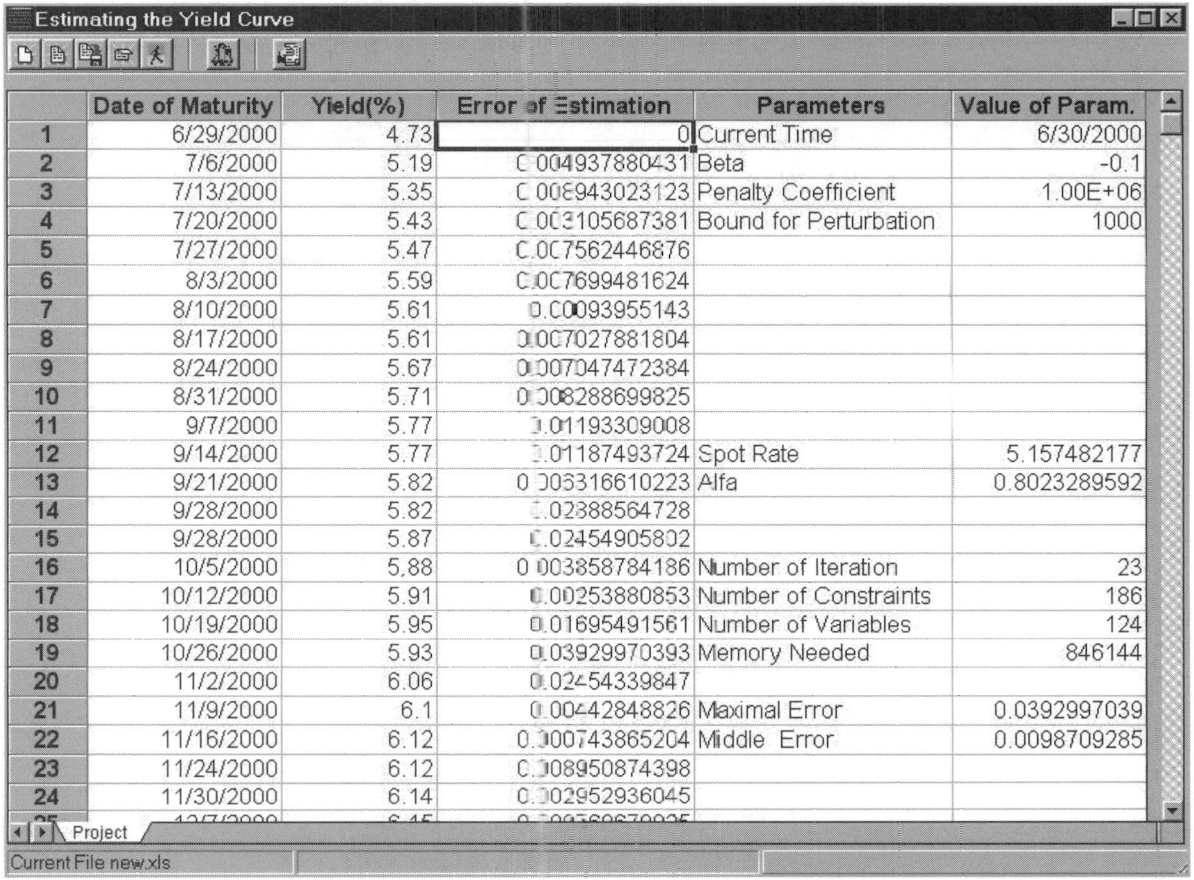

Estimating the Yield Curve

	Date of Maturity	Yield(%)	Error of Estimation	Parameters	Value of Param.
1	6/29/2000	4.73	0	Current Time	6/30/2000
2	7/6/2000	5.19	0.00493788043	Beta	-0.1
3	7/13/2000	5.35	0.00894302312	Penalty Coefficient	1.00E+06
4	7/20/2000	5.43	0.00310568738	Bound for Perturbation	1000
5	7/27/2000	5.47	0.00756244687		
6	8/3/2000	5.59	0.00769948162		
7	8/10/2000	5.61	0.00093955143		
8	8/17/2000	5.61	0.00070278818		
9	8/24/2000	5.67	0.00070747238		
10	8/31/2000	5.71	0.00082886998		
11	9/7/2000	5.77	0.01193309008		
12	9/14/2000	5.77	0.01187493724	Spot Rate	5.157482177
13	9/21/2000	5.82	0.00331661022	Alfa	0.8023289592
14	9/28/2000	5.82	0.02388564728		
15	9/28/2000	5.87	0.02454905802		
16	10/5/2000	5.88	0.00385878418	Number of Iteration	23
17	10/12/2000	5.91	0.00253880853	Number of Constraints	186
18	10/19/2000	5.95	0.01695491561	Number of Variables	124
19	10/26/2000	5.93	0.03929970393	Memory Needed	846144
20	11/2/2000	6.06	0.02454339847		
21	11/9/2000	6.1	0.00442848826	Maximal Error	0.0392997039
22	11/16/2000	6.12	0.00074386520	Middle Error	0.0098709285
23	11/24/2000	6.12	0.00895087439		
24	11/30/2000	6.14	0.00295293604		

Project

Current File new.xls

Figure 15.6 Excel file for detail of the solution results

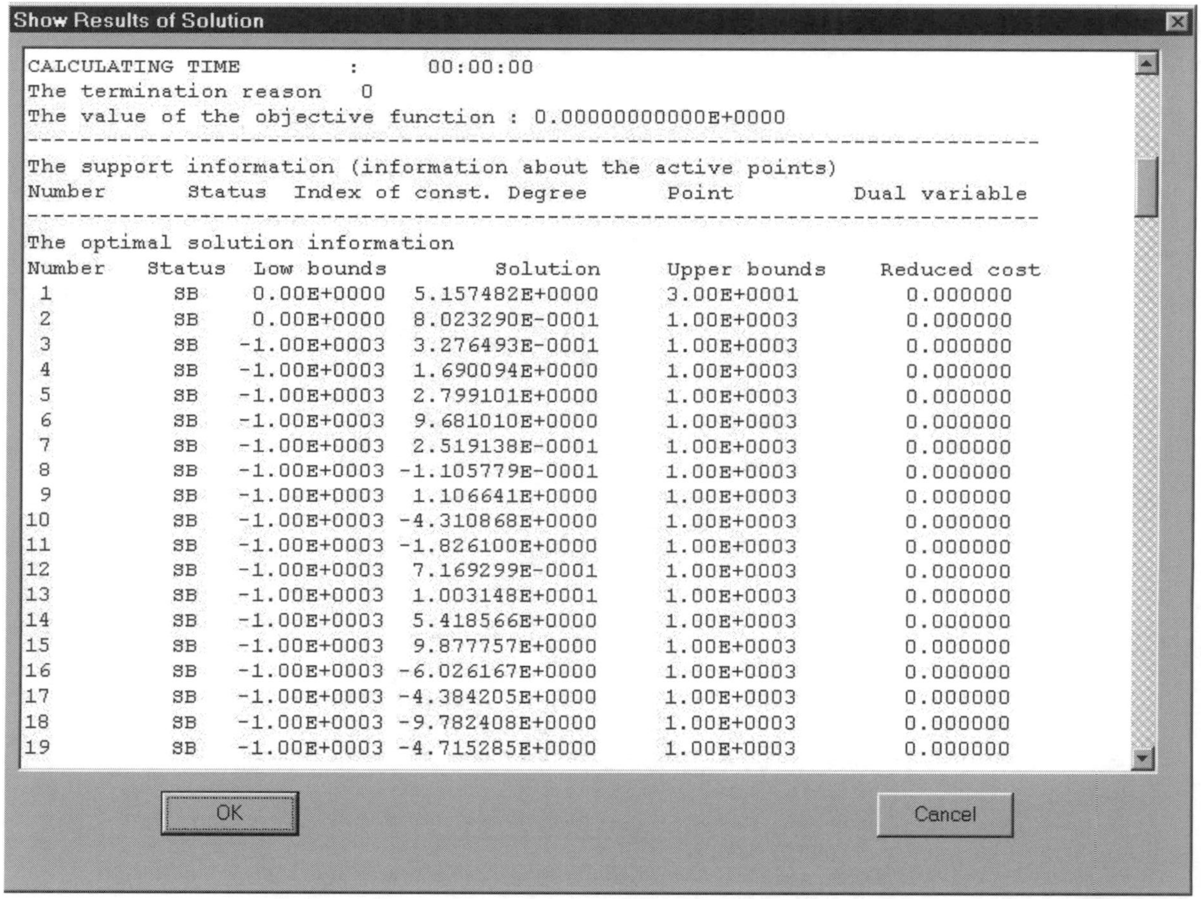
Show Results of Solution
CALCULATING TIME : 00:00:00
The termination reason 0
The value of the objective function : 0.0000000000E+0000
The support information (information about the active points)
Number Status Index of const. Degree Point Dual variable
The optimal solution information
Number Status Low bounds Solution Upper bounds Reduced cost
1 SB 0.00E+0000 5.157482E+0000 3.00E+0001 0.000000
2 SB 0.00E+0000 8.023290E-0001 1.00E+0003 0.000000
3 SB -1.00E+0003 3.276493E-0001 1.00E+0003 0.000000
4 SB -1.00E+0003 1.690094E+0000 1.00E+0003 0.000000
5 SB -1.00E+0003 2.799101E+0000 1.00E+0003 0.000000
6 SB -1.00E+0003 9.681010E+0000 1.00E+0003 0.000000
7 SB -1.00E+0003 2.519138E-0001 1.00E+0003 0.000000
8 SB -1.00E+0003 -1.105779E-0001 1.00E+0003 0.000000
9 SB -1.00E+0003 1.106641E+0000 1.00E+0003 0.000000
10 SB -1.00E+0003 -4.310868E+0000 1.00E+0003 0.000000
11 SB -1.00E+0003 -1.826100E+0000 1.00E+0003 0.000000
12 SB -1.00E+0003 7.169299E-0001 1.00E+0003 0.000000
13 SB -1.00E+0003 1.003148E+0001 1.00E+0003 0.000000
14 SB -1.00E+0003 5.418566E+0000 1.00E+0003 0.000000
15 SB -1.00E+0003 9.877757E+0000 1.00E+0003 0.000000
16 SB -1.00E+0003 -6.026167E+0000 1.00E+0003 0.000000
17 SB -1.00E+0003 -4.384205E+0000 1.00E+0003 0.000000
18 SB -1.00E+0003 -9.782408E+0000 1.00E+0003 0.000000
19 SB -1.00E+0003 -4.715285E+0000 1.00E+0003 0.000000
OK
Cancel

Figure 15.7 Detailed information about the computed optimal solution

button, and is used for leaving the program. The remaining two buttons are used for solving the optimization problem and displaying solution information.

15.3   COMMAND BUTTONS WITHIN THE SOLVING-THE-ESTIMATION-PROBLEM WINDOW

The solving-the-estimation-problem window is used for solving problem (9.18). Figure 15.2 is an example of the screen. The screen consists of a chart corresponding to the problem to be solved and command buttons. The first button starts the solution of the problem. The last is used for returning to the main window. Other buttons are used for displaying different types of graphs. Four types of graphs are implemented in the program. The graph in Figure 15.2 represents observed data and estimates of the forward rate and yield curve.

The histogram graph in Figure 15.3 gives the percentage occurrence of interval values of computed forward rates.

The forward rate graph in Figure 15.4 represents the estimate of the trajectory of the forward rate.

The real data graph in Figure 15.5 displays the observed yields to maturity depending on the time to maturity.

After solving the observation problem, the solution is stored in the table of the main window, see Figure 15.6. The third column of the table gives information about the error of the estimation (the fifth column displays the estimate of spot rate, the parameter α of the problem and the maximal and median errors of estimation (9.24)).

15.3.1   A Standard Volatility Measure

Let R_i denote the forward rates appearing in Figure 15.3 of which there are 23 in this illustration. Let f_i denote the frequency of occurrence of R_i. Then the standard statistics for this figure are the following:

$$\text{Mean} \qquad \bar{R} = \sum_{i-1}^{23} R_i p_i = 6.09175,$$

$$\text{Variance} \qquad \text{var} = \sum_{i=1}^{23} (R_i - \bar{R})^2 p_i = 0.40157, \qquad (15.1)$$

$$\text{Standard deviation} = \sqrt{\text{var}} = 0.63370.$$

15.4   THE MATHEMATICAL PROGRAMMING SOLUTION RESULTS WINDOW

The results window is used for displaying the information about parameters of the problem (9.18) and also gives a detailed description of its solution. An example of such a dialog is shown in Figure 15.7.

References

[1] E. J. Anderson and P. Nash (eds.), *Linear Programming in Infinite Dimensional Spaces*, Wiley, New York, 1987.

[2] K. Back, Yield curve models: a mathematical review. In J. Ledermann, R. Klein and I. Nelkin (eds.), *Option Embedded Bonds*, Irwin, New York, 1996, Chapter 1.

[3] P. P. Boyle, Recent models of the term structure of interest rates with actuarial applications. *Transactions of the 21st International Congress*, **4**: 95–104, 1980.

[4] R. H. Brown and S. M. Schaefer, Interest rate volatility and the shape of the term structure. *Philosophical Transactions of the Royal Society London, Series A*, **347**: 563–576, 1994.

[5] G. D. Burghardt, T. M. Belton, M. Lane and R. McVey, *Eurodollar Futures and Options: Controlling Money Market Risk*, Irwin Professional, Chicago, 1991 (an Institutional Investor Publication).

[6] G. D. Burghardt, T. M. Belton, M. Lane and J. Papa, *The Treasury Bond Basis: An In-Depth Analysis for Hedgers, Speculators, and Arbitrageurs*, McGraw-Hill, New York, 1994 (Revised Edition).

[7] J. Y. Campbell, A. W. Lo and A. C. MacKinlay, *The Econometrics of Financial Markets*, Princeton University Press, Princeton, NJ, 1997.

[8] K. C. Chan, G. A. Karolyi, F. A. Longstaff and A. B. Sanders, An empirical comparison of alternative models of the short-term interest rate. *Journal of Finance*, **47**: 1209–1227, 1992.

[9] F. L. Chernousko, *The Estimating of State for Dynamic Systems*, Nauka, Moscow, 1989 (in Russian).

[10] A. R. Conn and N. I. M. Gould, An exact penalty function for semi-infinite programming. *Mathematical Programming*, **37**: 19–40, 1987.

[11] I. D. Coope and G. A. Watson, A projected Lagrangian algorithm for semi-infinite problems. *Mathematical Programming*, **32**: 337–356, 1985.

[12] G. B. Dantzig, *Linear Programming and Extensions*, Princeton University Press, Princeton, NJ, 1963.

[13] H. M. Deitel, P. J. Deitel and T. R. Nieto, *Visual Basic 6: How to Program*, Prentice Hall, Upper Saddle River, NJ, 1999.

[14] P. Dennis and R. J. Rendleman Jr., An LP approach to synthesis option replication with transaction costs and multiple security selection. *Advances in Futures and Options Research*, **8**: 53–84, 1995.

[15] E. Epstein and P. Wilmott. A new model for interest rates. *International Journal of Theoretical and Applied Finance*, **1**: 195–226, 1998.

[16] F. J. Fabozzi, *Bond Markets, Analysis and Strategies*, Prentice Hall, Upper Saddle River, NJ, 1996 (Third Edition).

[17] F. J. Fabozzi (ed.), *The Handbook of Fixed Income Securities*, Irwin Professional, Chicago, 1997 (Fifth Edition).

[18] A. V. Fiacco and K. O. Kortanek (eds.), *Semi-Infinite Programming and Applications*. Lecture Notes in Economics and Mathematical Systems No. 215, Springer-Verlag, New York, 1983.

[19] R. Gabasov, F. M. Kirillova and O. I. Kostyukova, A method for the optimal control of the motion of a dynamic system in the presence of constantly operating perturbations. *Journal of Applied Mathematics and Mechanics*, **56**: 755–764, 1992.

[20] R. Gabasov, F. M. Kirillova and O. I. Kostyukova, Optimization of a linear control system under real-time conditions. *Journal of Computing Systems Sciences*, **31**: 1–14, 1992.

[21] R. Gabasov, F. M. Kirillova and S. Prischepova, *Optimal Feedback Control*. Lecture Notes in Economics and Information Systems No. 207, Springer-Verlag, Berlin, 1995.

[22] H. U. Gerber and E. S. W. Shiu, Option pricing by Esscher transforms. *Transactions of the Society of Actuaries*, **46**: 99–140, 1994.

[23] K. Glashoff and S.-Å. Gustafson, *Linear Optimization and Approximation*. Applied Mathematical Sciences No. 45, Springer-Verlag, New York, 1983 (original edition in German, 1978).

[24] M. A. Goberna and M. A. López, *Linear Semi-Infinite Optimization*. Wiley Series in Mathematical Methods in Practice, Wiley, Chichester, 1998.

[25] S.-Å. Gustafson and K. O. Kortanek, Semi-infinite programming and applications. In B. Korte, A. Bachem and M. Grotschel (eds.), *Mathematical Programming the State of the Art Bonn 1982*, Springer-Verlag, Berlin, 1983, pp. 132–157.

[26] S.-Å. Gustafson, K. O. Kortanek and W. O. Rom, Non-Chebyshevian moment problems. *SIAM Journal of Numerical Analysis*, **7**: 335–342, 1970.

[27] D. Heath, R. Jarrow and A. Morton, Bond pricing and the term structure of interest rates; a new methodology. *Econometrica*, **60**: 77–105, 1992.

[28] R. Hettich, An implementation of a discretization method for semi-infinite programming. *Mathematical Programming*, **34**: 354–361, 1986.

[29] R. Hettich and K. O. Kortanek, Semi-infinite programming: theory, methods, and applications. *SIAM Review*, **35**: 380–429, 1993.

[30] R. Hettich (ed.), *Semi-Infinite Programming*. Lecture Notes in Control and Information Systems No. 15, Springer-Verlag, Berlin, 1979.

[31] J. C. Hull, *Options, Futures, and Other Derivative Securities*, Prentice Hall, Englewood Cliffs, NJ, 1993 (Third Edition).

[32] K. Ito, Multiple Wiener integral. *Journal of the Mathematical Society of Japan*, **3**: 157–169, 1951.

[33] K. Ito, On a formula concerning stochastic differentials. *Nagoya Mathematical Journal*, **3**: 55–65, 1951.

[34] R. N. Kahn. In F. J. Fabozzi (ed.), *Estimating the U.S. Treasury Term Structure of Interest Rates: Instrumental Strategies and Analysis*, Probus, Chicago, 1990, Chapter 9.

[35] R. E. Kalman, A new approach to linear filtering and prediction problems. *Journal of Basic Engineering*, **82I**: 34–45, 1960.

[36] R. W. Kolb, *Futures, Options, and Swaps*, Blackwell, Malden, MA, 2000 (Third Edition).

[37] V. Kolmanovskii and A. Myshkis, *Applied Theory of Functional Differential Equations*. Mathematics and Its Application, Soviet Series, Kluwer Academic, Dordrecht, 1992.

[38] K. O. Kortanek, Perfect duality in generalized linear programming. In A. Prekopa (ed.), *Proceedings IX International Symposium on Mathematical Programming*, North-Holland/Publishing House of the Hungarian Academy of Sciences, 1976, pp. 43–58.

[39] K. O. Kortanek and V. G. Medvedev, Models for estimating the structure of interest rates from observations of yield curves. In M. Avellaneda (ed.), *Quantitative Analysis in Financial Markets*, World Scientific, Singapore, 1999, pp. 53–120.

[40] K. O. Kortanek and H. No, A central cutting plane algorithm for convex semi-infinite programming problems. *SIAM Journal of Optimization*, **3**: 901–918, 1993.

[41] O. I. Kostyukova, Investigation of the linear extremal problem with continuum constraints. Technical Report Preprint 26 (336), Institute of Mathematics, Academy of Sciences of BSSR, 1988 (in Russian).

[42] O. I. Kostyukova, Superbasic plan of linear extremal problem with continuum of constraints. *Doklady Akademii Nauk BSSR*, **33**: 687–689, 1989.

[43] N. N. Krasovsky, *Theory of Control with Movement*, Nauka, Moscow, 1976 (in Russian).

[44] A. B. Kurzansky, *Control and Observation in Indefiniteness Conditions*, Nauka, Moscow, 1977 (in Russian).

[45] Alexander Levin. Linear systems theory in stochastic pricing models. In *Yield Curve Dynamics*, pages 123–146. Glenlake Publishing Company, Ltd., Chicago-London-New Delhi, 1997. Editor Ronald J. Ryan.

[46] Alexander Levin and D. James Daras. A methodology for market rate analysis and forecasting. In *Yield Curve Dynamics*, pages 57–73. Glenlake Publishing Company, Ltd., Chicago-London-New Delhi, 1997. Editor Ronald J. Ryan.

[47] T. A. Marsh, Term structure of interest rates and the pricing of fixed income claims and bonds. Technical Report, UC Berkeley, Walter A. Haas School of Business, Berkeley, CA, 1997.

[48] G. Medvedev and S. H. Cox, The market price of risk for affine interest rate term structures. In *Proceedings of the 6th International AFIR-Colloquium Nuremberg Vol. 1*, VVW Karlsruhe, Germany, 1996, pp. 913–924. (Aktuarielle Ansätze für Finanz-Risken AFIR 1996).

[49] V. G. Medvedev, Algorithm for solving the optimal observation problem with nonconvex a priori distribution of initial state. *Automatic Remote Control*, **10**: 121–130, 1993.

[50] V. G. Medvedev, Optimal observations of initial state and input disturbances for dynamic systems. *SAMS*, **14**: 275–288, 1994.

[51] V. G. Medvedev, Positional algorithm for optimal observations of linear dynamical systems. *SAMS*, **16**: 93–111, 1994.

[52] V. G. Medvedev, The method of construction of approximate solutions of linear optimal control problems with state constraints. Technical Report, Department of Optimal Control Methods, Byelorussian State University, Minsk, 1995 (appeared in Proceedings of XII International Conference, Wroclaw, Poland, 12–15 September 1995).

[53] M. Musiela and M. Rutkowski, *Martingale Methods in Financial Modeling: Theory and Applications*, Springer-Verlag, Berlin, 1997.

[54] H. H. Panjer (ed.), *Financial Economics with Applications to Investments, Insurance, and Pensions*, Wiley, Schaumburg, IL, 1998 (The Actuarial Foundation).

[55] S. R. Pliska, *An Introduction to Mathematical Finance Discrete Time Models*, Blackwell, Malden, MA, 1998.

[56] R. Rebonato, *Interest-Rate Option Models*. Financial Engineering Series, Wiley, Chichester, 1998 (Second Edition).

[57] R. Reemtsen and J.-J. Rückmann (eds.), *Semi-Infinite Programming*. Nonconvex Optimization and Its Applications Vol. 25, Kluwer Academic, Boston, 1998.

[58] S. F. Richard, An arbitrage model of the term structure of interest rates. *Journal of Financial Economics*, **6**: 33–57, 1978.

[59] S. M. Ross, *An Introduction to Mathematical Finance Options and Other Topics*, Cambridge University Press, Cambridge, 1999.

[60] T. Schittkowski, NLPQL: a FORTRAN subroutine solving constrained nonlinear programming problems. *Annals of Operations Research*, **5**: 485–500, 1986.

[61] M. Sole Staffa, *Un approccio dinamico per il moto dello Spot Rate in base ad osservazoni sulla Curva dei Rendimenti: il caso del mercato italiano*. Ph.D. thesis, Universiatá degli Studi di Roma — La Sapienza, Dipartimento di Scienze Attuariali e Finanziarie, 1999.

[62] Y. Tanaka, M. Fukushima and T. Ibaraki, A globally convergent SQP method for semi-infinite nonlinear optimization. *Journal of Computational and Applied Mathematics*, **23**: 141–153, 1988.

[63] O. Vasicek, An equilibrium characterization of the term structure. *Journal of Financial Economics*, **5**: 177–188, 1977.

[64] K. R. Vetzal, A survey of stochastic continuous time models of the term structure of interest rates. *Insurance: Mathematics and Economics*, **14**: 139–161, 1994.

[65] N. Wiener, *The Extrapolation, Interpolation, and Smoothing of Stationary Time Series with Engineering Applications*, The Technology Press/Wiley, New York, 1949.

[66] P. Wilmott, S. Howson and J. Dewyne, *The Mathematics of Financial Derivatives, A Student Introduction*, Cambridge University Press, Cambridge, 1997.

[67] P. Wilmott, *Paul Wilmott on Quantitative Finance*, Vols. 1 and 2, Wiley, Chichester, 2000.

Index

3-Month Treasury Bill Rates, 110
3M Treasury Bill Rate Auction Average, 90, 95

Adaptive spot rate estimator, 56
Admissible Spot Rate Functions, 32
Affine stochastic models, 90
Analog of the HJM model, 136
Arbitrage, 4, 144, 149, 150
Ask yield, 143
Asset price trajectories, 25
Asset prices, 19
Average rate of growth, 20

Bid yield, 143
Bid-ask optimal observation problem, 121
Bilevel model with differing maturities, 77
Bilevel model perturbations, 63, 69
Bilevel spot rate model, 63
Bond call option, 160
Bonds having Common maturity, 33
Bonds with differing maturities, 57
Bond yields, 9, 10
Bonds at par, 9, 10
Bootstrapping method, 16
Borel measures and integrals, 166
Bounding functions on uncertain price changes, 20
Brownian motion, 20, 31

Cauchy Formula, 21, 26, 27, 36, 41, 46, 50, 54, 117
Classes of perturbation functions, 89
Continuous interest rate compounding, 6
Continuous piecewise linear asset prices, 24
Control problems, 26
Conventional multi-period long term rate, 8, 11
Conventional multi-period loan, 7
Courtadon-type Model with Impulse Perturbations, 53

Currency exchange, 1

Day count convention, 4
Days to maturity, 5, 25, 144, 146
Delta functions, 24
Differential equation under uncertainty, 21
Discount bond price, 15, 33
Discount bond price forecast, 35
Discrete uncertainty walk, 21
Distribution of unknown parameters, 32, 85
Dothan Model with Impulse Perturbations, 52, 77
Dynamical system under uncertainty, 26, 116
Dynamical systems selection criteria, 116

Effective coupon rate, 9
Efficient market hypothesis, 19
Error of estimation, 25, 43, 46, 184, 185
Estimated nonarbitrage future price interval, 145
Estimating arbitrage opportunities, 144, 148, 150
Estimating the term structure software, 176
External input perturbations, 22

Face Value of a Bond, 9
Fair estimated forward offered rate, 144, 145, 149
Family of one period rates, 3
Forecasting constant maturity rates software, 184
Forecasting bounds on yields, 184, 191, 193, 194, 198
Forward rate curve, 14, 18, 113, 117, 203

Forward rate differential system, 117, 136
Forward rate estimation input data, 199
Forward rate forecast function, 65, 117
Forward rate formula, 6
Forward rate graph, 201, 203, 207

Forward rate trajectories, 189, 199
Forward rate-spot rate dynamical system, 136
Forward rates, 11, 12, 135
Forward rates dynamical system, 117
Forward rates, discrete, 13, 14, 18
Forward rates, instantaneous, 14, 65
Forward rates, non-negative, 65
Forward term structure, 11

Generalized finite sequences, 166
Guaranteed amplitude bounds, 92

Hedging analysis, 154
Heterogeneous type data, 113
Histogram of forward rates, 202
Histogram volatility, 207
History of the perturbations, 26
Homogeneous type data, 113

Implied maturity rates, 11
Impulse perturbations, 23, 24, 32, 37, 80, 89, 117, 175
Impulse perturbations of prices, 137
Impulse representation of the spot rate, 139
Incomplete information, 28
Infinite linear program, 28, 31
Input perturbations, 22
Interest rate tree, 152
International Swap Dealers Association, Inc., 5
Intertemporal exchange, 1, 2

Jensen's inequality, 66

Linear differential systems analog, 31
Linear differential systems model, 33, 50
Linear dynamical system with no perturbations, 40
Linear dynamical systems under uncertainty, 26
Linear programming ask problem, 156
Linear programming bid problem, 156
London Interbank Offered Rate, 5
Long term interest rates, 1, 3, 9, 11

Market price of risk, 84
Market price of risk estimation, 85
Market price of risk, stochastic processes case, 87
Markov property, 20, 25
Martingale filtrations, 161
Martingale (risk neutral) probabilities, 157, 160, 161
Maximum absolute value of the forecast error, 110
Mean absolute percentage error, 110

Mean absolute value of the forecast error, 110
Mean drift function, 89
Mean path solutions to dynamical systems, 90
Mean rate of return, 20
Mean reversion, 83, 90, 92, 175
Measurement error, 28
Minimax amplitude, 92
Minimax estimation problem, 25, 28, 31, 34, 40, 57
Model selection for term structure estimation, 136, 176
Multiperiod annuity, 9
Multiple day–period loan, 5
Multiple maturity-based spot rate estimate, 57

Nonrandom stock price, 20
Nonstochastic observation models, 26
Nonarbitrage necessary condition, 82
Nonarbitrage sufficient condition, 84
Nondifferential equation, continuous time Model, 54

Observation models, 22, 23, 24, 33, 43, 71, 72, 80, 113
Observation period, 25, 175
Optimal hedging portfolios, 156
Optimal observation problems, 27, 43, 56, 61, 84, 89, 92, 116, 119, 120, 121, 122, 176
Observation surface-model, 60
Observed daily prices, 22
Observed yield to maturity, 43, 55, 66, 70, 75, 76, 182, 197
One factor spot rate model, 27, 31, 70

Parameter Space, 32
Parameter-admissible yield, 34
Parameters for term structure estimation, 41, 176
Perturbation choice criteria, 92
Piecewise linear representation of the spot rate, 140
Point-impulse perturbations, 23, 24, 32, 80, 89, 175
Position of a real time system, 55
Precision of forecasts, 97
Premium Factor of a bond, 9
Price based optimal observation problem, 120, 121
Probability distributions, 19, 22
Program Problem model, 26

Range of forecasts, 97
Real time observations and estimates, 55
Relative maximum absolute values of the forecast error, 110
Reliability of Forecasts, 95

Semi-infinite programming dual pair, 165, 166
Semi–infinite programming algorithms, 26, 167
Short term average daily rate, 3
Short term interest rate, 1
Slater interiority optimization condition, 167
Smoothness of the estimation and accuracy, 122
Solving the estimation problem, 207
Spline approximations, 48, 55
Spot rate differential equation under uncertainty, 31, 40
Spot rate estimation problem, 37, 47, 55, 56, 64
Spot rate forecast function, 34, 37, 46, 50, 54, 57
Spot rate representations, 32, 139, 140
Spot rate trajectories, 69, 90, 186, 188
St. Louis Federal Reserve Bank data, 90, 97, 112
Stochastic differential equations, 26, 31, 84
Stochastic processes, 19, 20, 89
Support problems optimization method, 167, 174
Supports problems numerical method, extended, 169

Term structure for a fixed maturity, 138
Term structure software input data, 175

Term structure of interest rates, 9, 12, 32, 63, 136, 136
Term structure surface, 13, 175, 196, 198
Terms of trade, 2
Time-to-maturity, 33, 55
Trust region, 63, 181

Unbiased expectations hypothesis, 15
Uncertain change in asset price, 20
Unit conventional bond, 9
Universal backtesting data period, 95

Vasicek-type basic linear dynamical system, 35, 141
Vasicek-type model with impulse perturbations, 37, 71, 77
Vasicek-type model with point-impulse perturbations, 47, 77
Volatility, 31, 89

Yield curve forecasted trajectories, 184, 187, 190, 192, 199, 200, 201
Yield of an asset, 9
Yield structure approximations, 11
Yield to maturity, 13, 55, 154
Yield to maturity, instantaneous, 13, 15, 80
Yield surface, estimated, 77, 195, 196
Yields, piecewise constant, 15